focus on IRELAND

◆ *inspiring places, beautiful spaces* ◆

This is a Parragon Publishing Book
First published in 2006

Parragon Publishing
Queen Street House
4 Queen Street
Bath, BA1 1HE, U.K.

Produced by AA Publishing

Unjacketed ISBN-13: 978-1-4054-8750-4
Jacketed ISBN-13: 978-1-4054-8769-6

Colour reproduction by Modern Age
Printed in China by CT Printing Ltd

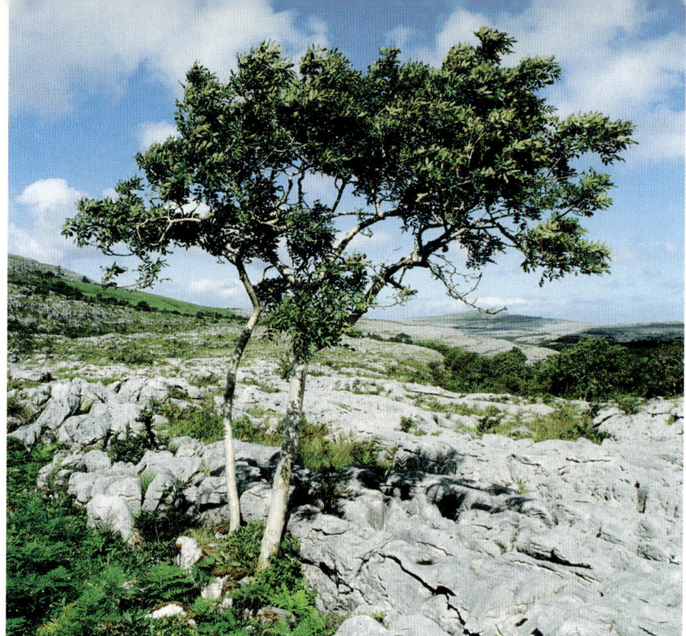

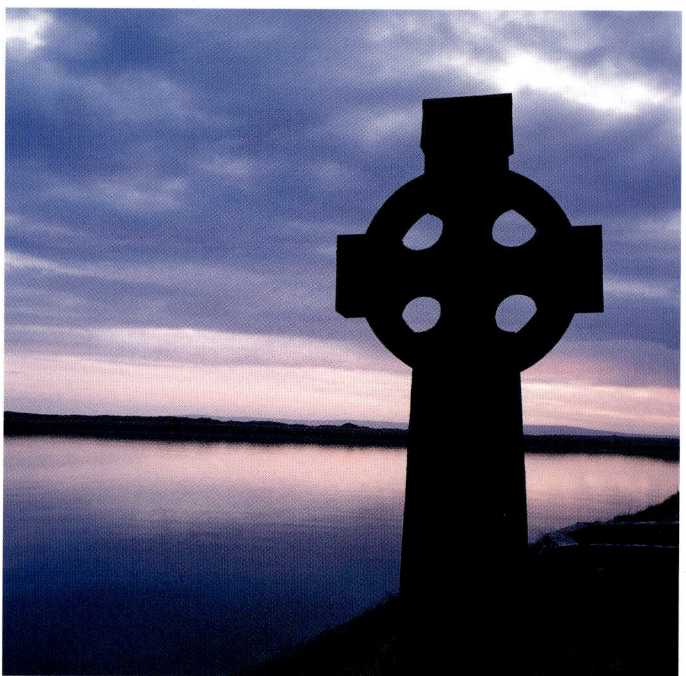

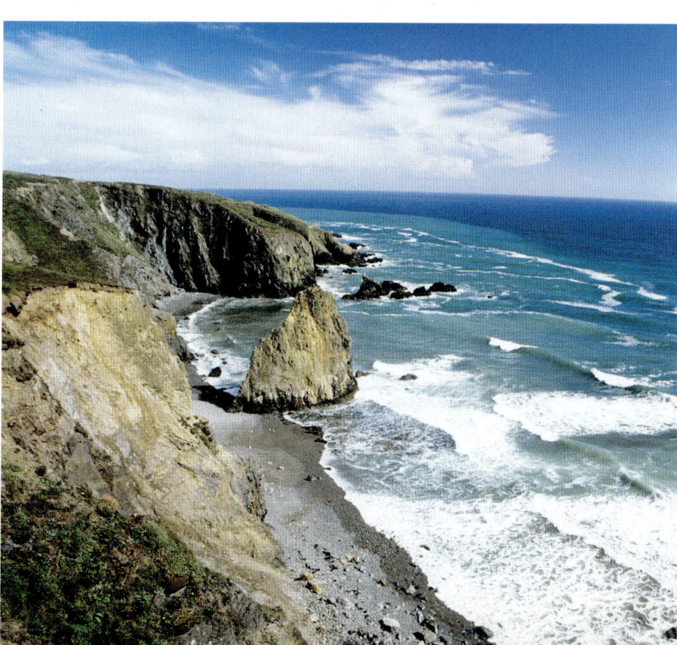

PICTURES FROM TOP TO BOTTOM:
Trees and flowers force their way between limestone ridges on the rocky upland wilderness of the Burren.

Celtic crosses on Inishmore, one of the Aran Islands, commemorate islanders who died overseas or at sea.

Surf crashes against the rocks along the rugged Tramore coastline in the southern county of Waterford.

PAGE 3: The Wicklow Mountains provide a backdrop to the tree-covered hills near Sally Gap.

PAGE 4: A ride in a jaunting car is a fine way to see the Muckross Estate in County Kerry.

focus on IRELAND

◆ inspiring places, beautiful spaces ◆

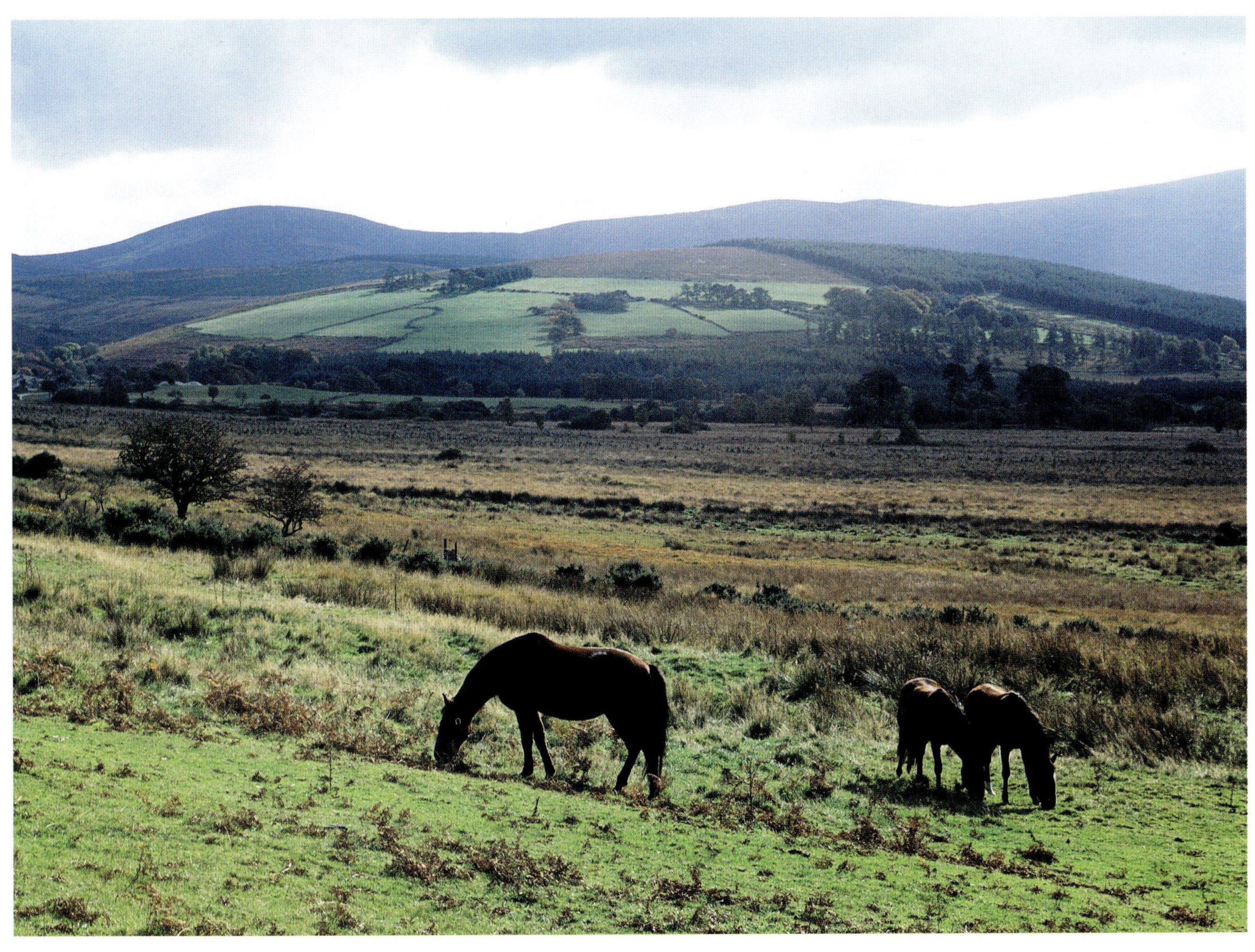

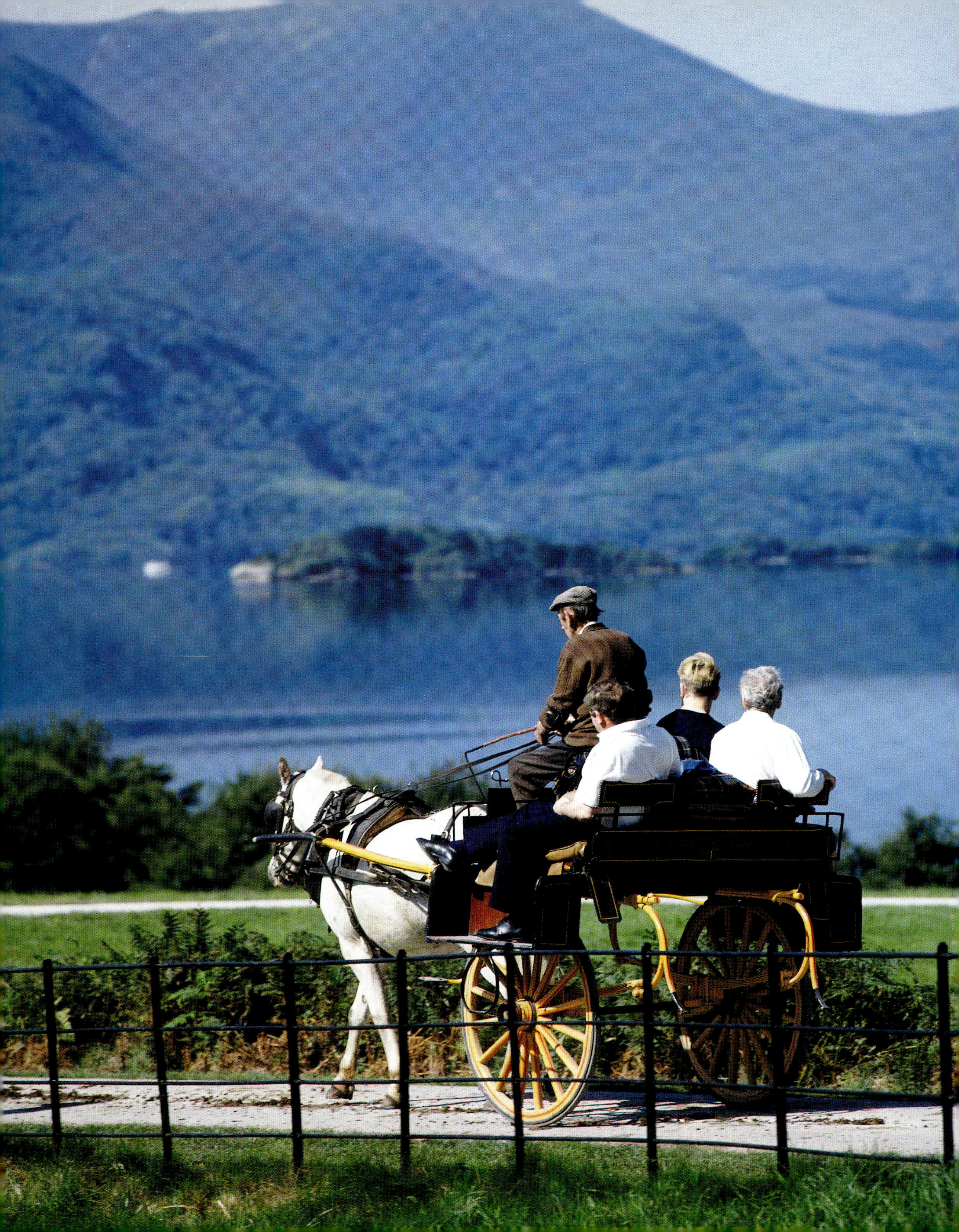

INTRODUCTION

Ireland (Éire) is Europe's third largest island, lying between the Irish Sea and the Atlantic Ocean about 50 miles off the western shores of Britain. Politically, it is divided into the Republic of Ireland, which covers the south, east, west and northwest, and Northern Ireland, the northeast part of the island, which is a state within the United Kingdom. Dublin and Belfast are their respective capitals.

Not for nothing is Ireland known as the 'Emerald Isle'. Its mild, maritime climate and all-too-frequent gentle rainfall (heaviest in the west) produce lush green vegetation all over the island. Within the mountains that girdle much of the coastline lie low, central plains, bisected from north to south by the great River Shannon and its tributaries that form a huge network of navigable inland waterways.

Countless loughs (the Irish equivalent of English lakes or Scottish lochs) – hauntingly beautiful and an angler's dream – and huge tracts of peat bogland are characteristic features of the landscape. So too are patchwork fields and rolling hills, winding country roads, scattered farmsteads, tiny hamlets, whitewashed thatched cottages and traditional fishing villages. Irish beaches, especially in the southwest corner, are second to none.

Natural wonders and must-sees for any visitor to Ireland include the Giant's Causeway – a platform of interlocking hexagonal basalt columns that march into the sea – and the Mountains of Mourne, both in Northern Ireland; the Burren, in the west, a special area of limestone where alpine and Mediterranean plants grow alongside each other; and the Cliffs of Moher, which drop vertically into the sea at the edge of County Clare.

Evidence of Ireland's history can be seen wherever you go. Prehistoric megalithic tombs, stone circles, ring forts and cairns are scattered across the country, many of which are closely associated with Celtic legend and mythology. The Hill of Tara in County Meath was the seat of the High Kings of Ireland, while Newgrange, also in County Meath, was said to be a fairy mound, home of Oenghus, the god of love.

As a result of St Patrick's arrival in the 5th century the island became known as the cradle of Roman Catholic Christianity. Consequently, the island has a rich heritage of monastic architecture ranging from carved high crosses to the ruins of great monasteries and the distinctive, pencil-shaped round towers – found only in Ireland – such as those at Glendalough in County Wicklow or Clonmacnoise in County Offaly. Many fine churches and cathedrals were built at this time too, such as St Mary's Cathedral in Limerick.

Norman and Anglo-Irish castles and fortified tower houses dating mostly from the late 12th to early 16th centuries characterize the west and southwest. One of these, Blarney Castle in County Cork, has gained fame through the Blarney Stone, believed to have special powers. Anyone who kisses the stone is said to acquire the gift of the gab (a way with words) – one of the most charming aspects of so many Irish people.

In the early 18th century Palladian architecture took Ireland by storm, putting its stamp on practically every building of any size. As the century progressed, the style evolved into the elegant Georgian houses, squares and streets for which Dublin is renowned; it is also exemplified in stately homes such as Mount Stewart in County Derry and its magnificent gardens.

The trick of a visit to Ireland is to take things slowly: enjoy what turns up – or doesn't – besides, it's almost a sacrilege to hurry. Explore the country lanes; take time for a chat about nothing in particular; go with the flow. Pervading everyday life is the craic (pronounced crack) – that peculiarly Irish tradition of fun, good conversation and laughter.

Then of course there's Irish music, the lifeblood of the people and the backbone of their culture, celebrated throughout the country in festivals but also in every pub across the country. No matter where you go you'll find musicians, singers and storytellers sharing their talents and enthusiasm with anyone who has the time and inclination to listen. Ireland is a country in which no one is a stranger for long.

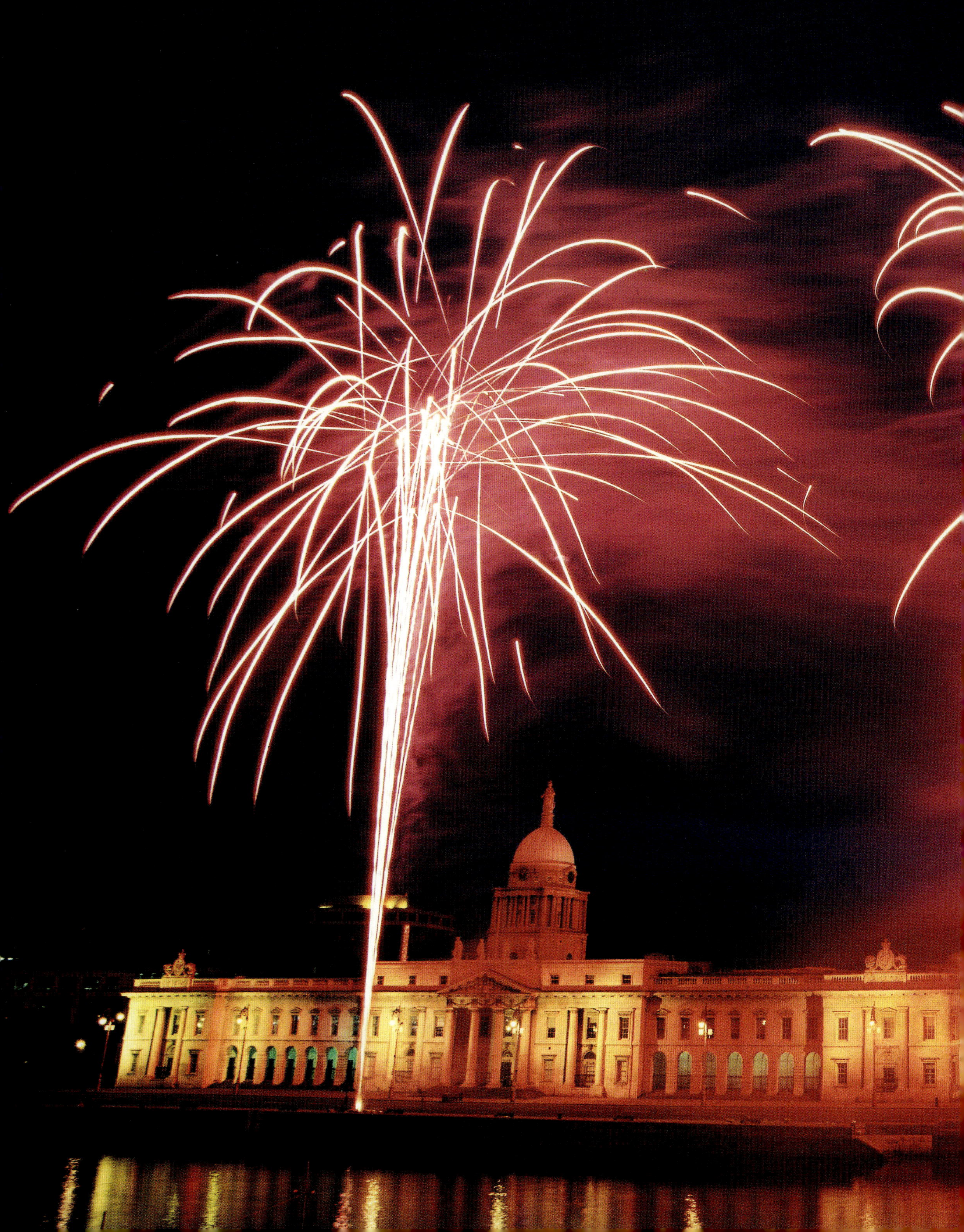

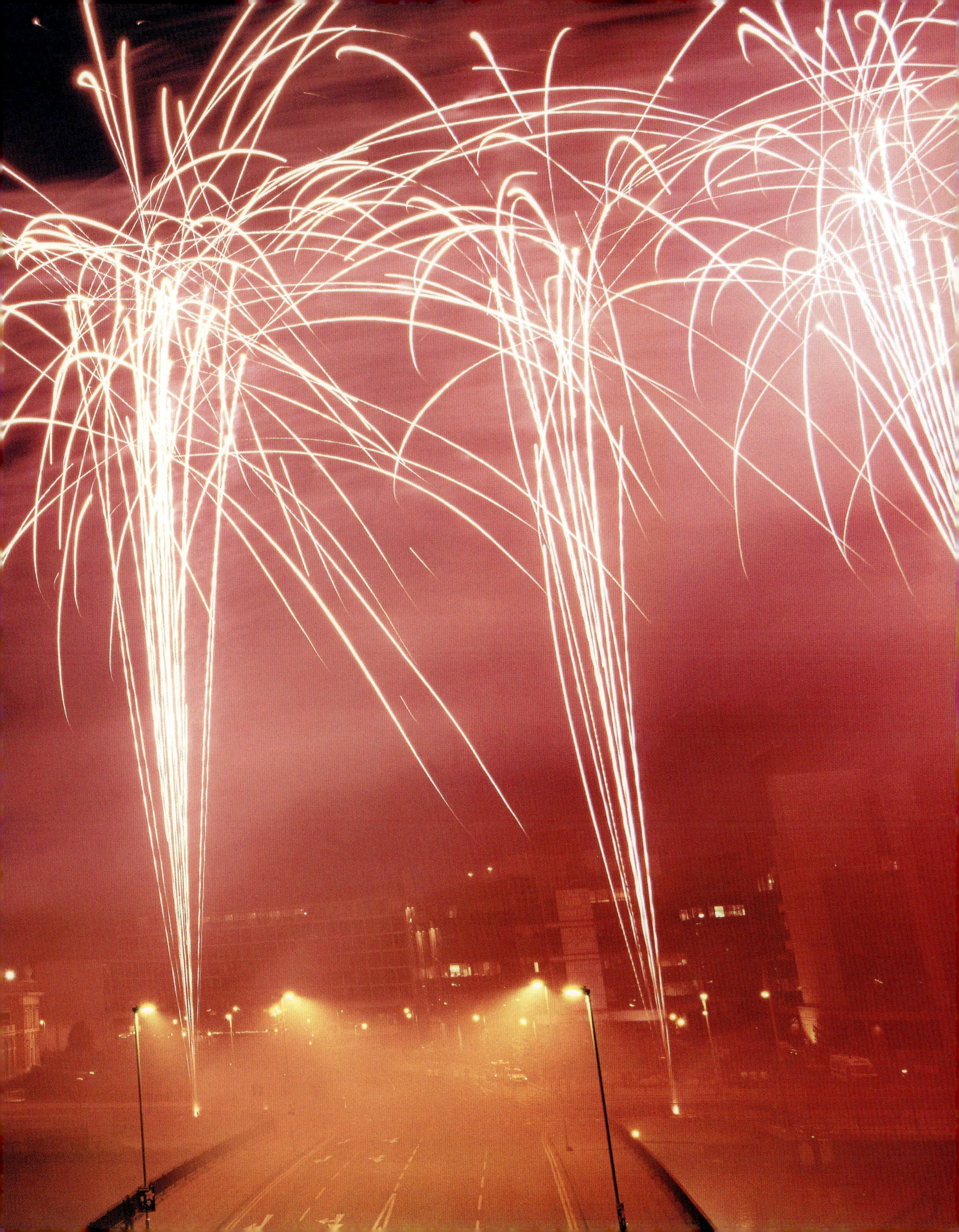

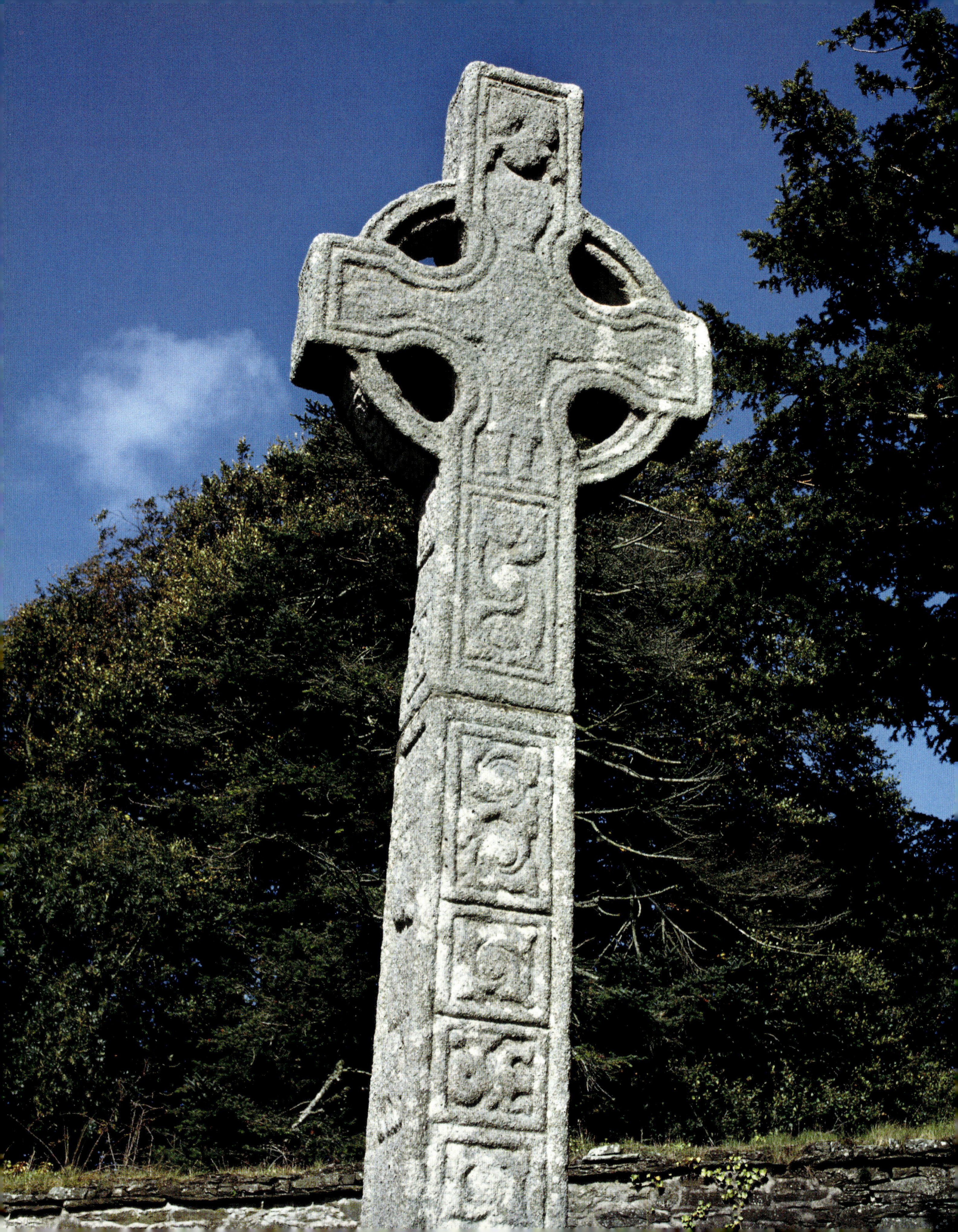

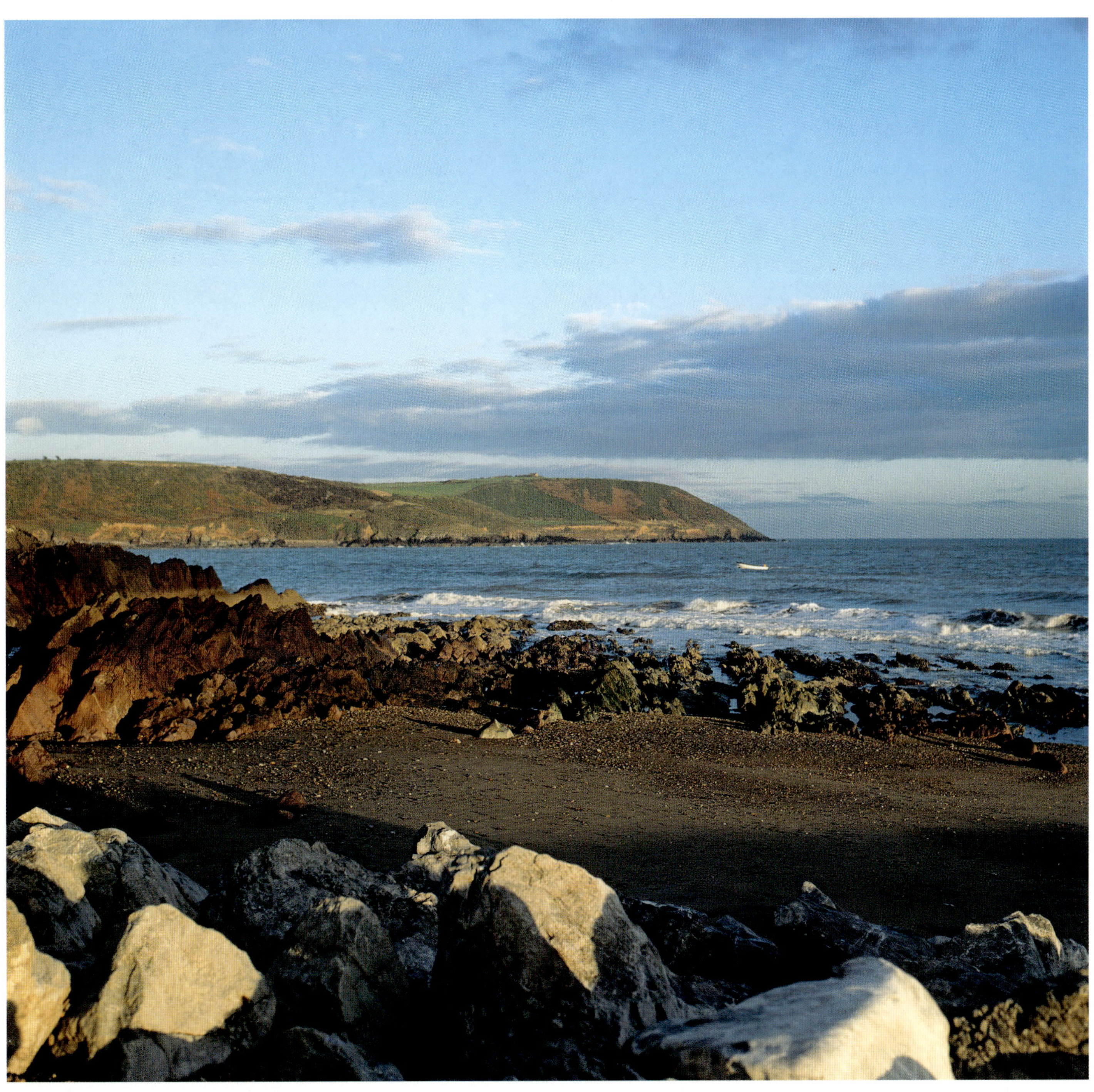

The evening sun casts long shadows over Blackball Head, at Youghal. This resort in the southeast of County Cork has long been one of Ireland's most popular vacation destinations.
Opposite: the 9th-century stone high cross just outside Moone, in County Kildare. The name Moone comes from the Gaelic words Maen Colmcille, which means 'Colmcille's property'.
Pages 7–8: St Patrick's Day is celebrated with fireworks in Dublin. Here the 18th-century Custom House can be seen beside the River Liffey.

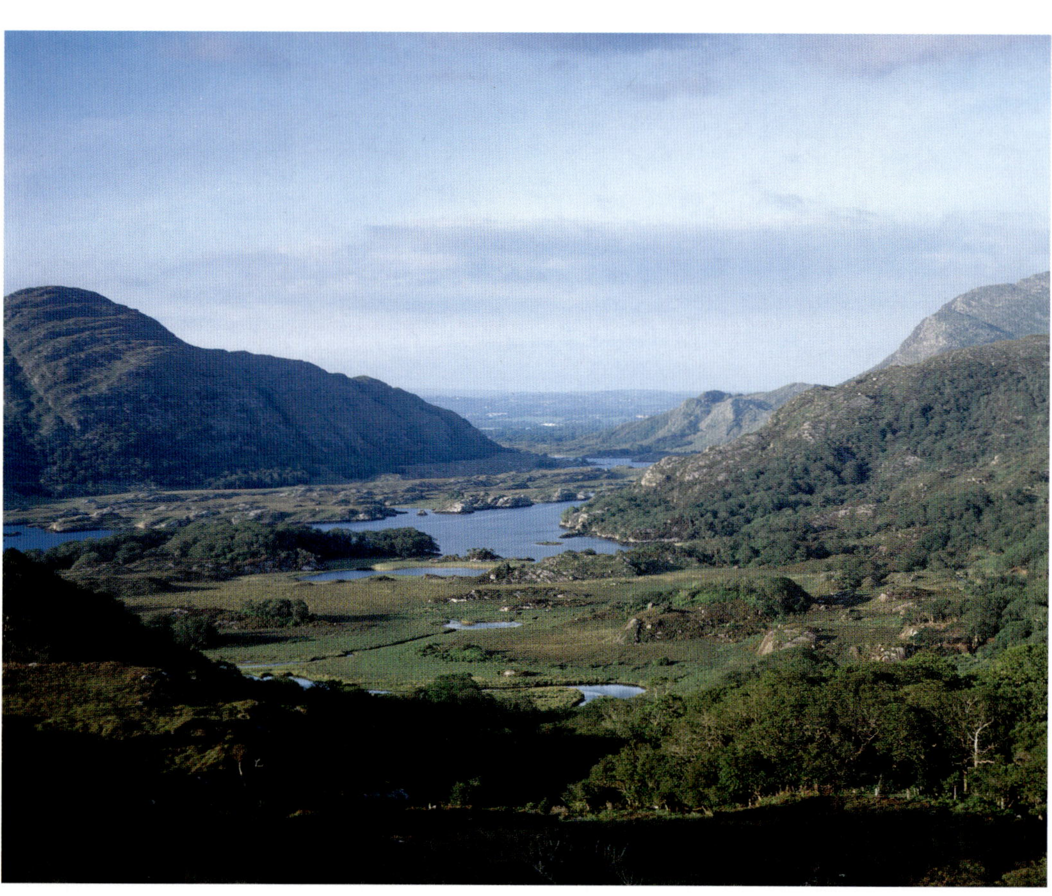

The Killarney mountains and lakes as seen from Ladies' View (a viewpoint named after Queen Victoria's ladies-in-waiting) on the Ring of Kerry in Killarney National Park. Lough Leane is the largest of the lakes, with Muckross Lake and the Upper Lake upstream of it.

Opposite: the tide goes out at Coumeenole Beach at the end of the Dingle Peninsula, the most northerly of the mountainous headlands of County Kerry and the most westerly point of the Republic of Ireland.

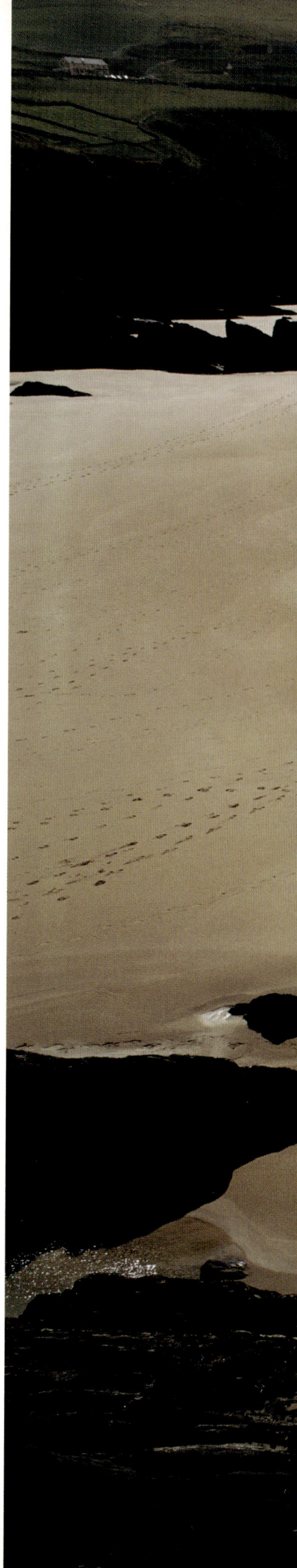

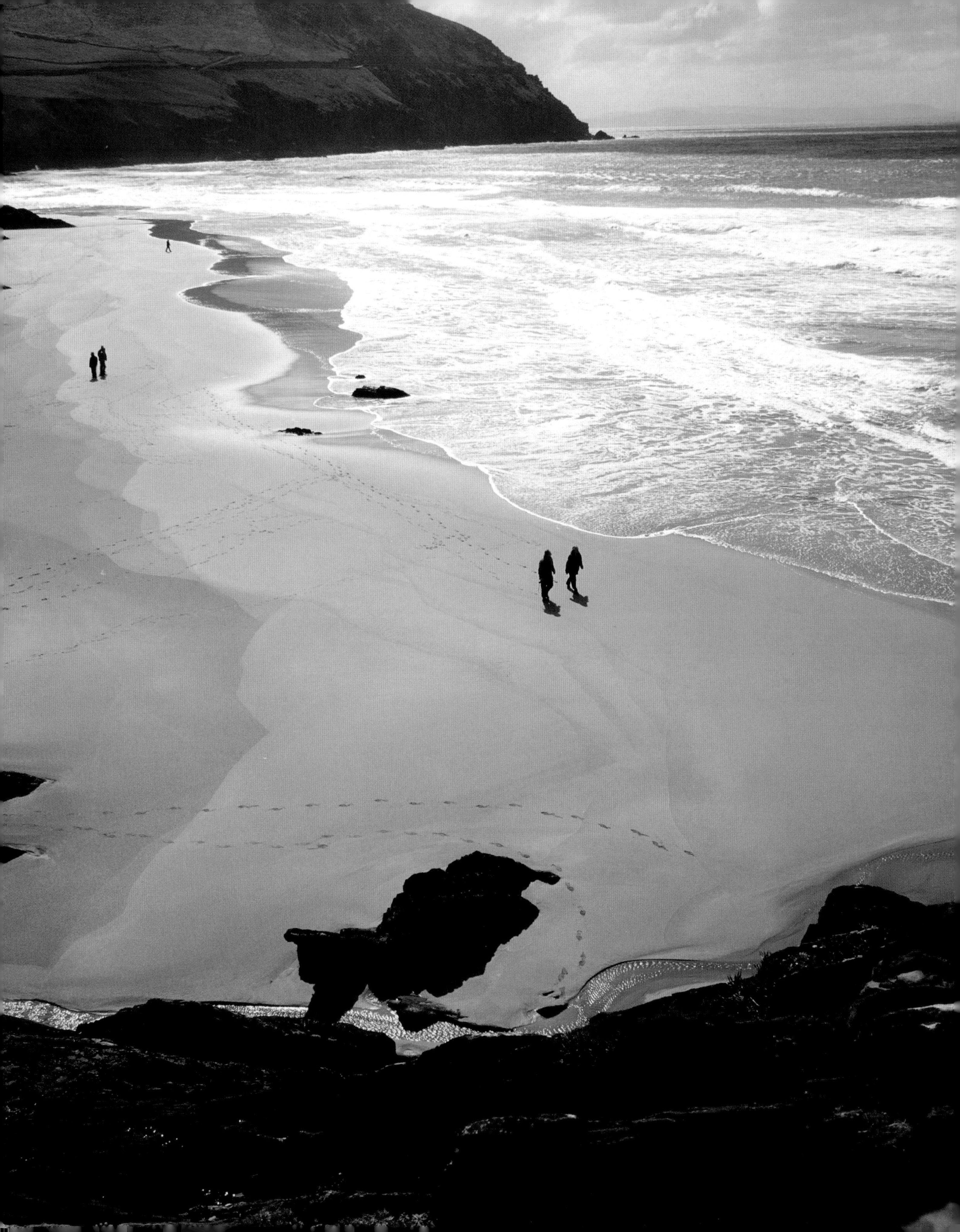

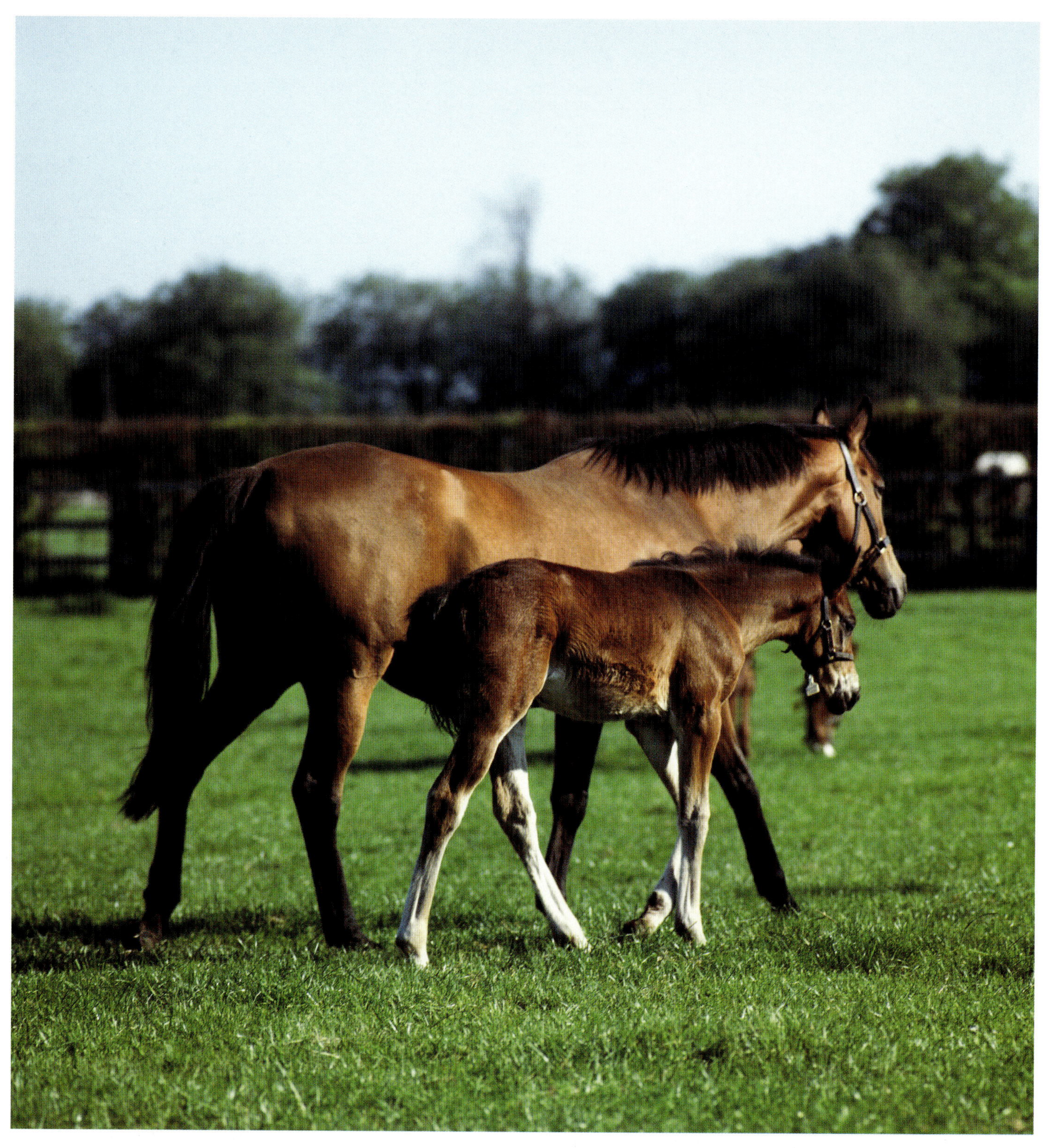

A mare with her foal at the Irish National Stud near Kildare. Established in 1946, the stud develops and promotes Irish bloodstock as well as being among Ireland's major tourist attractions.
Opposite: Gougane Barra Forest Park in County Cork. The chapel stands on the site of a hermitage founded by Finbarr, the patron saint of Cork, in the 6th century.

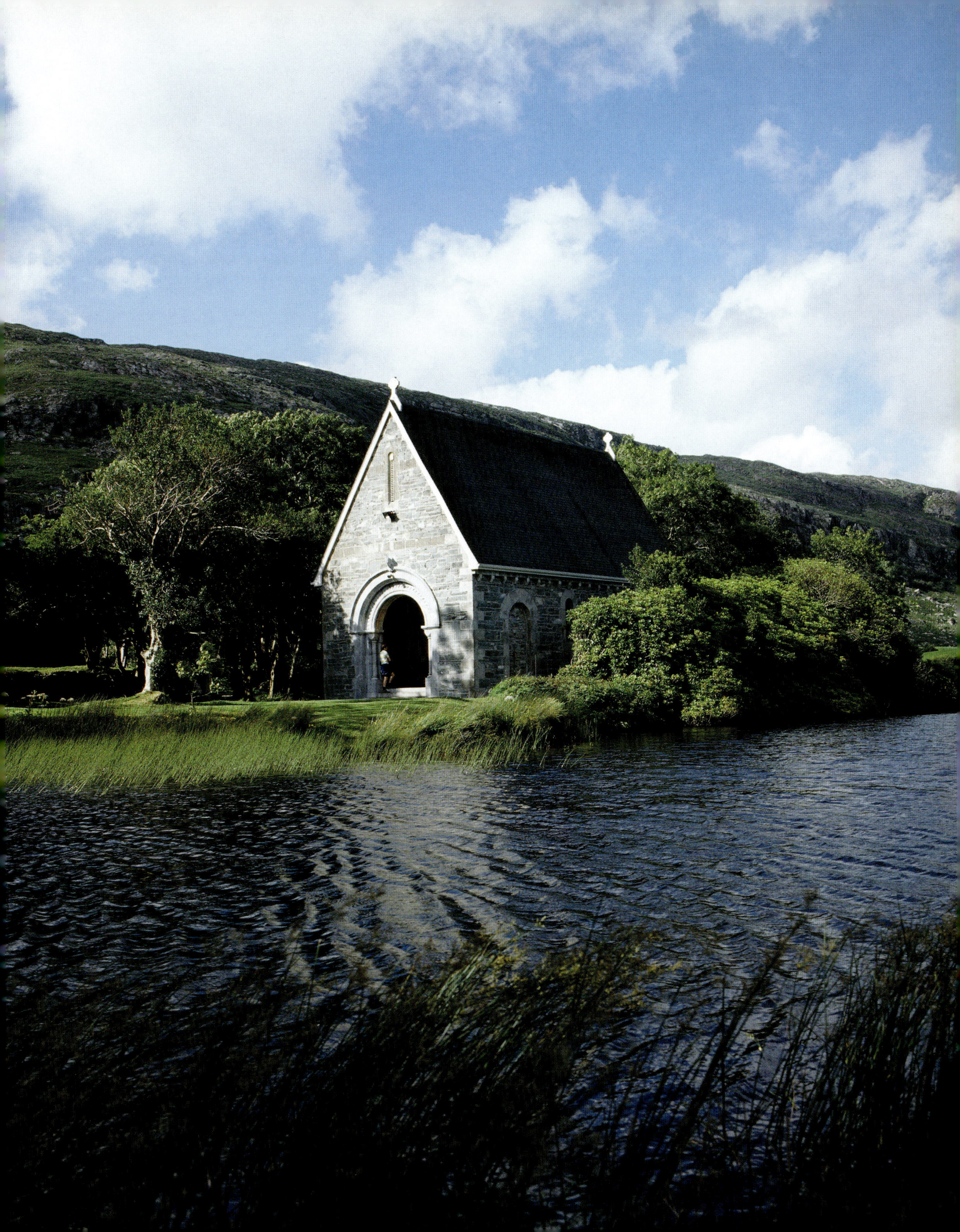

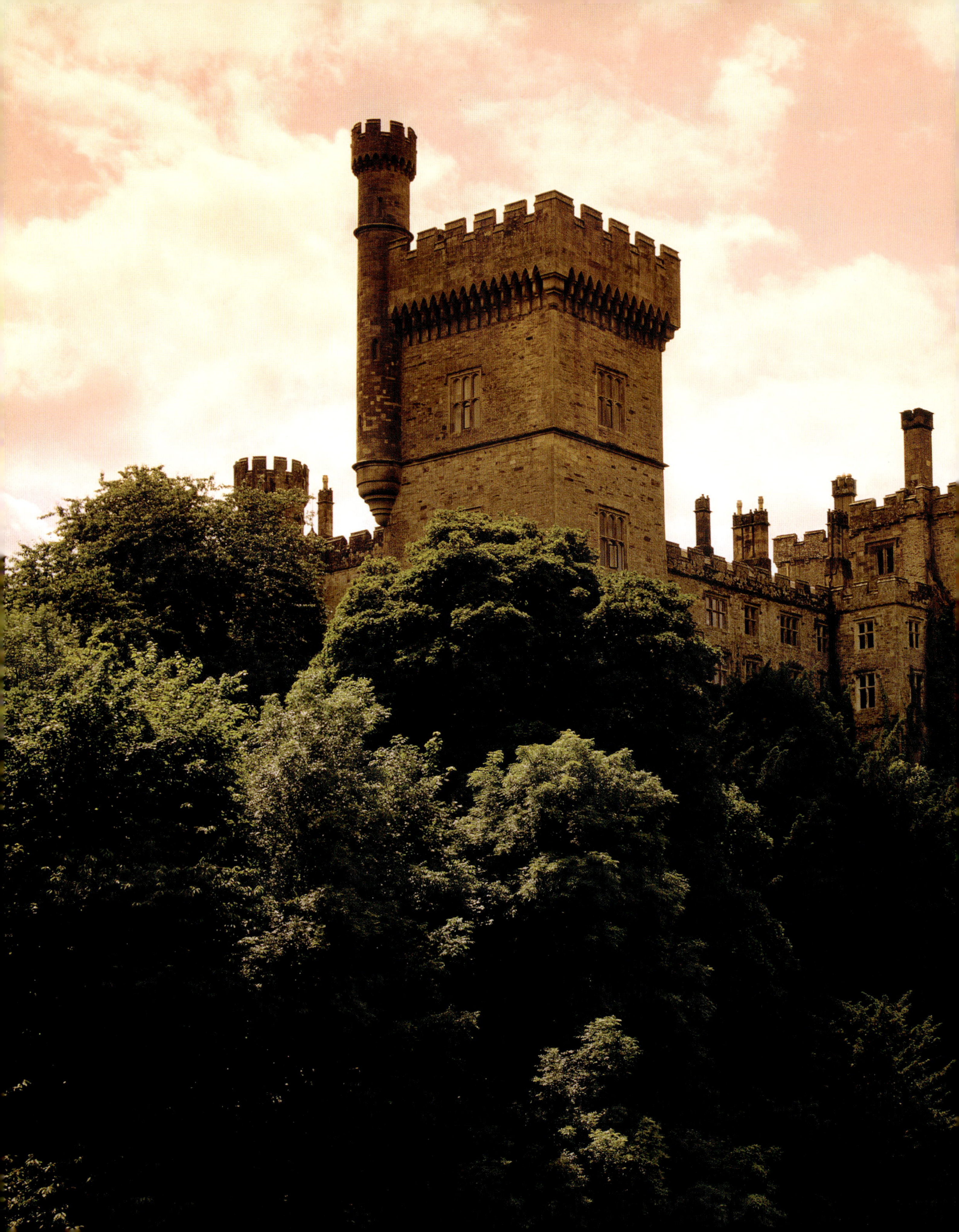

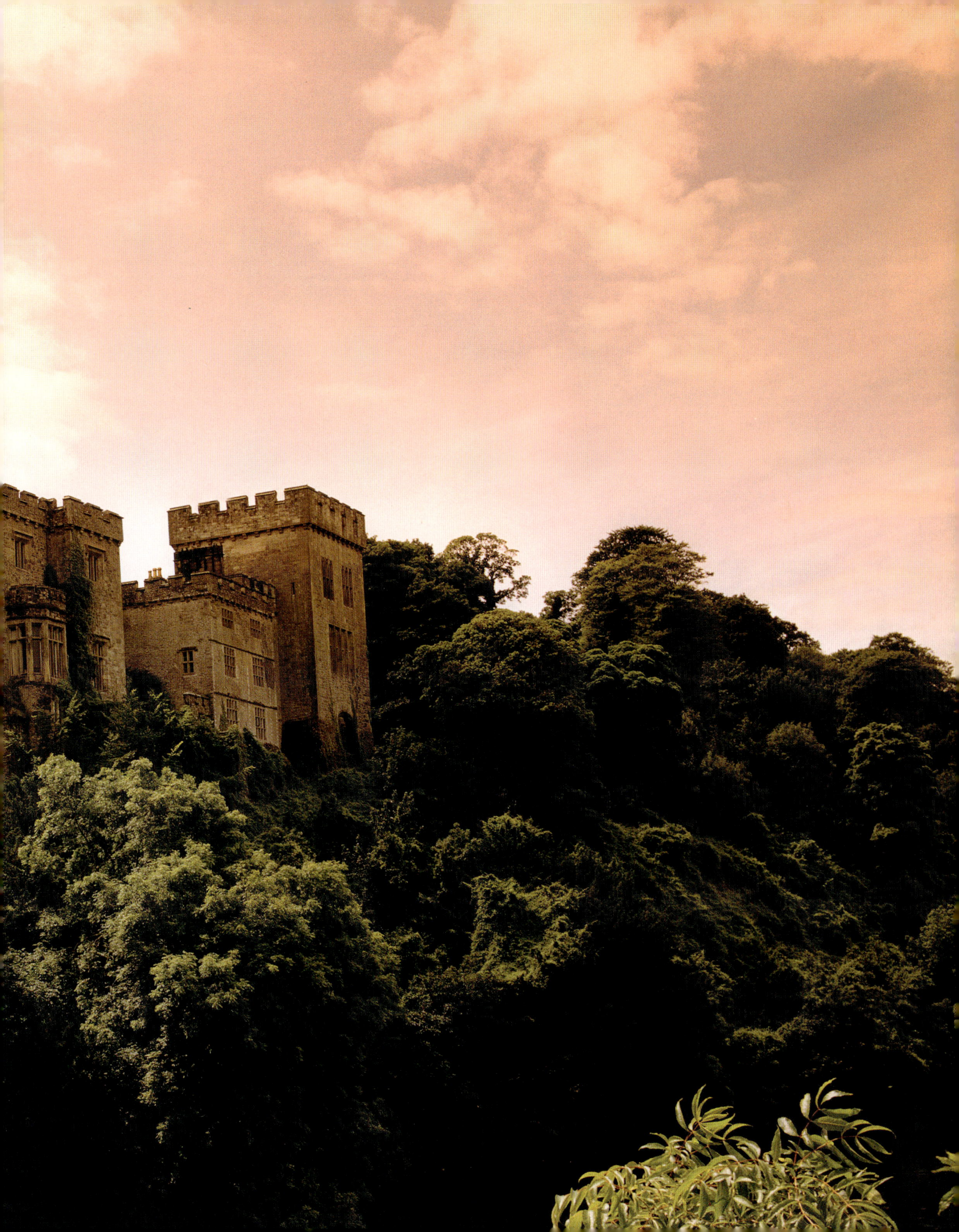

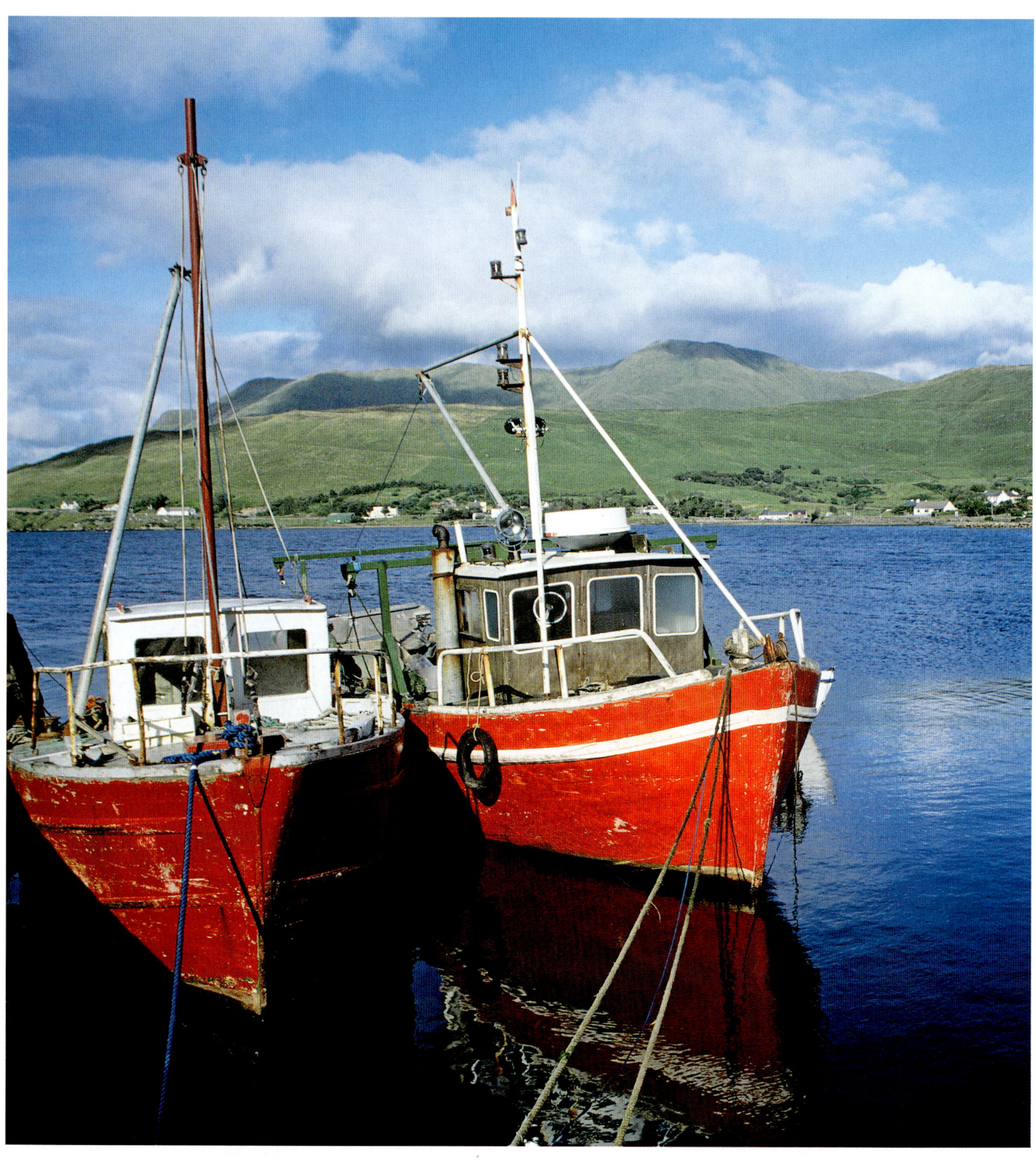

Leenane's fishing harbor is at the head of the natural inlet of Killary Harbour in Connemara.
Previous page: Lismore Castle in County Waterford has been the home of the Dukes of Devonshire since 1753.

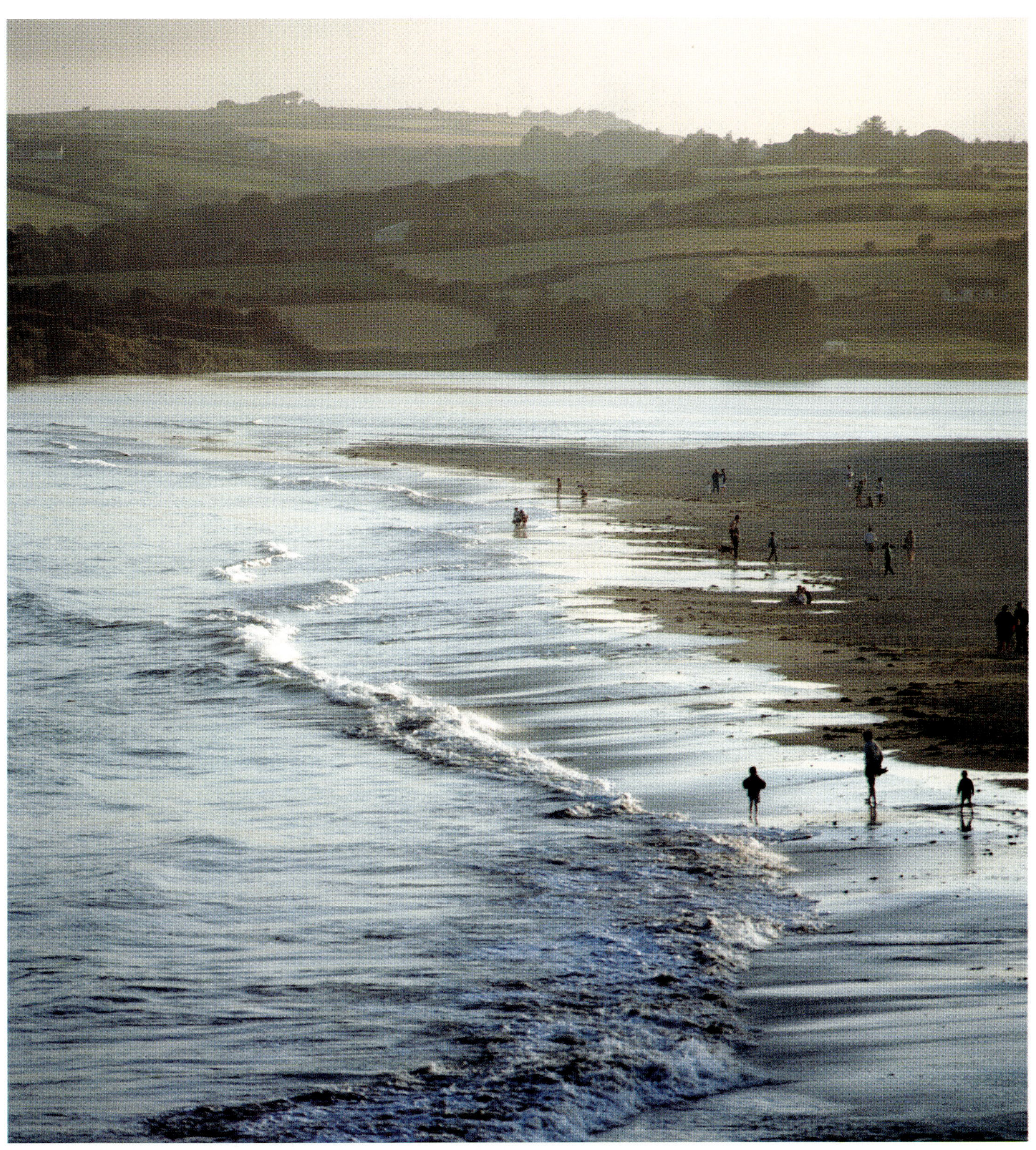

Wonderful sandy beaches characterize Inchydoney Island, 3 miles south of the town of Clonakilty (Cloich na Coillte) in County Cork. The island is linked to the mainland by a causeway.

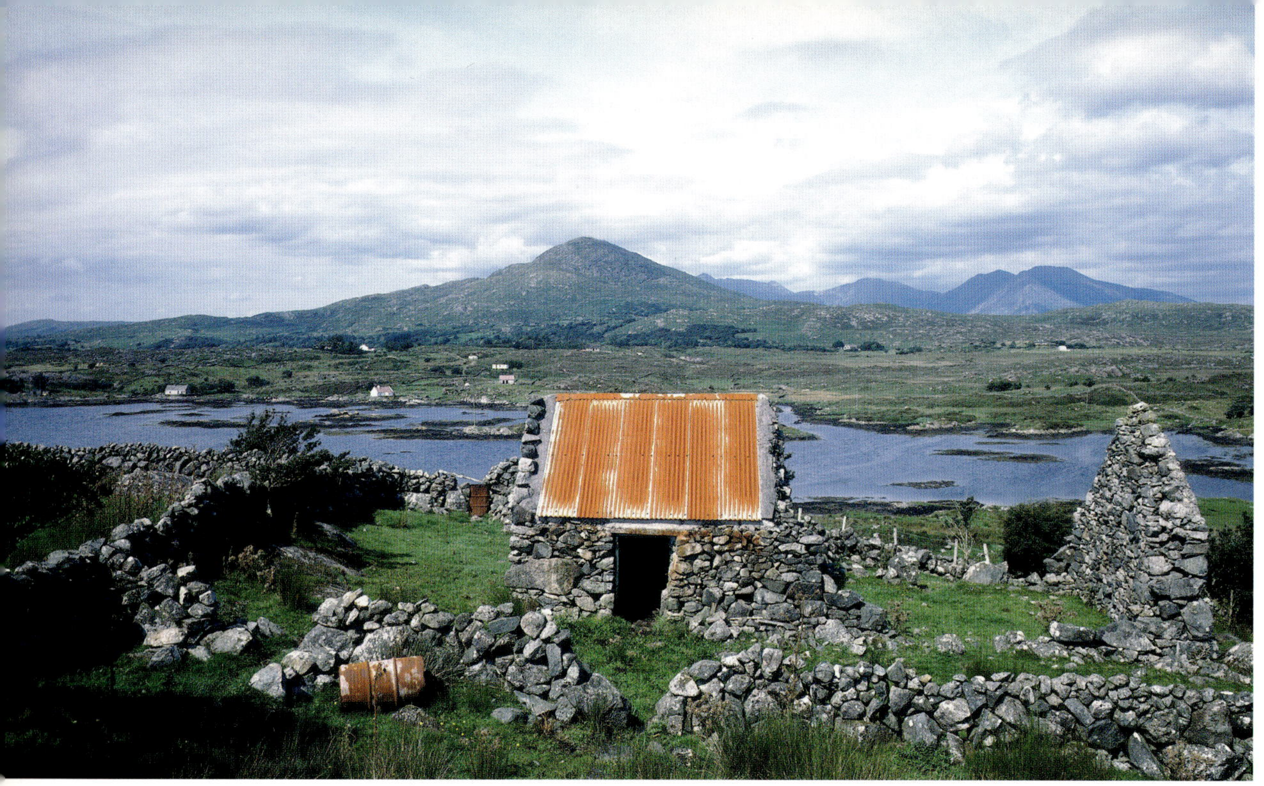

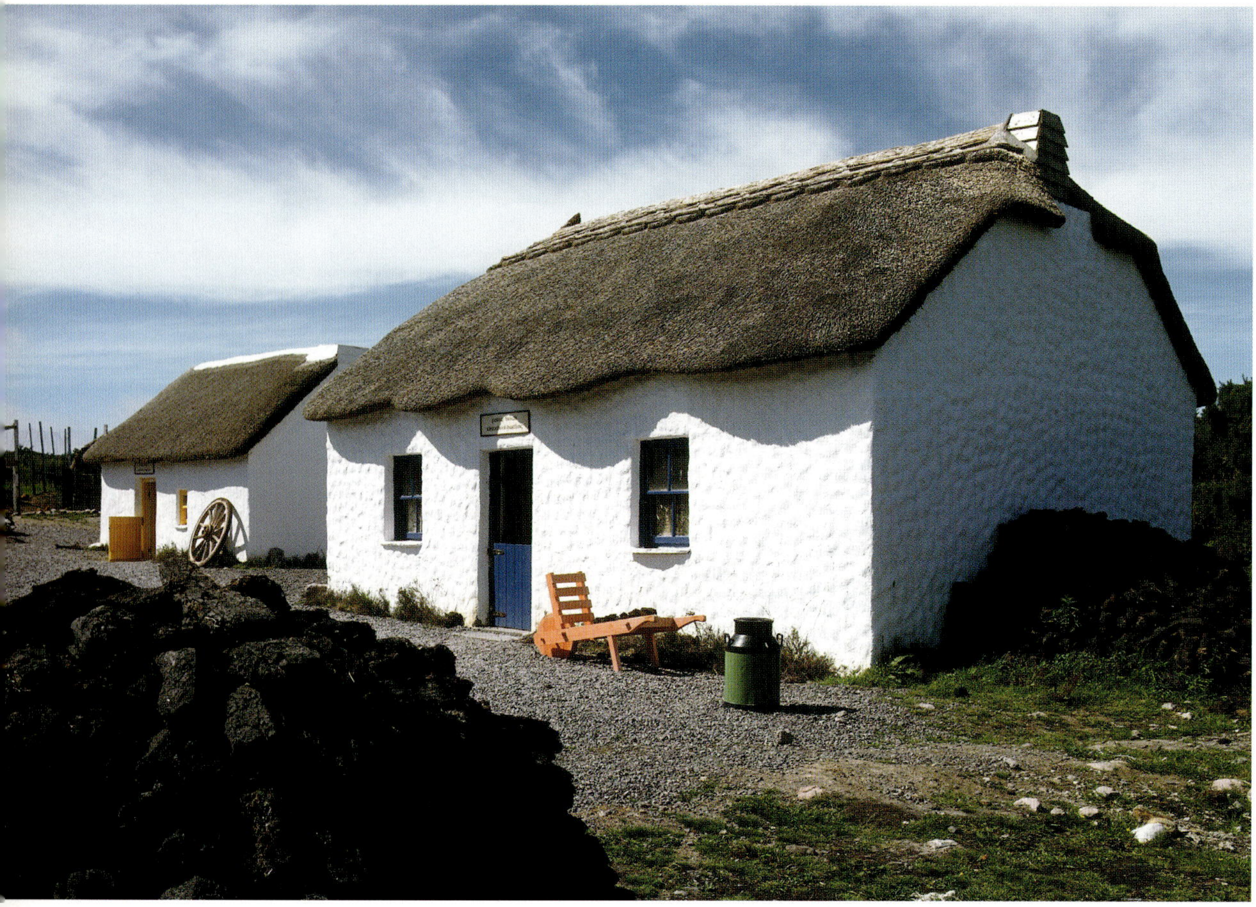

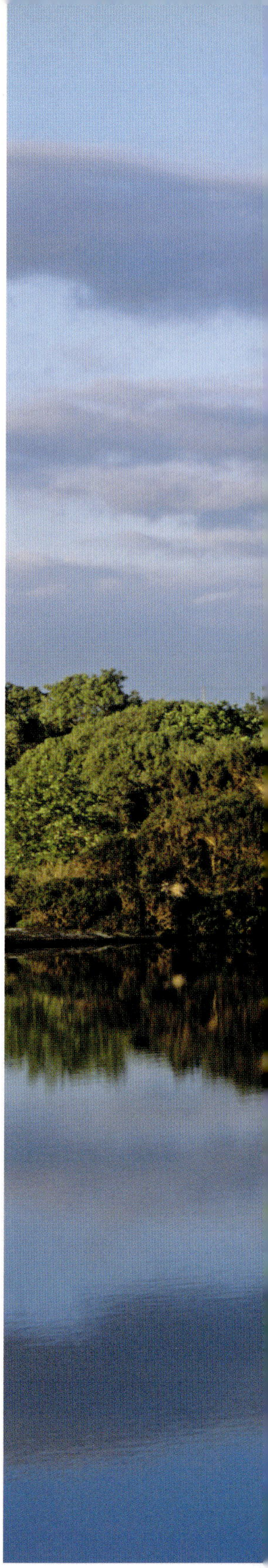

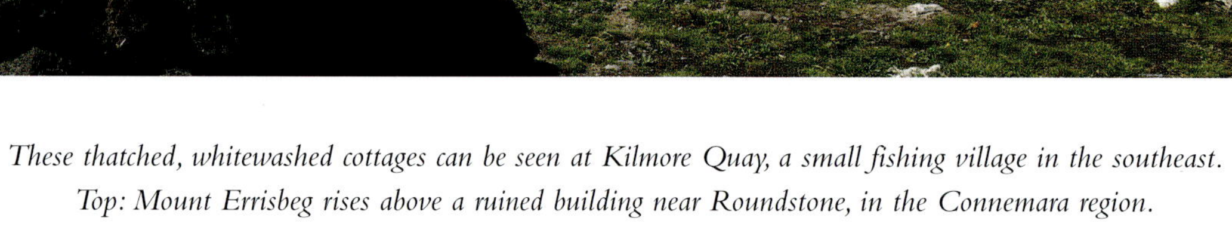

These thatched, whitewashed cottages can be seen at Kilmore Quay, a small fishing village in the southeast.
Top: Mount Errisbeg rises above a ruined building near Roundstone, in the Connemara region.

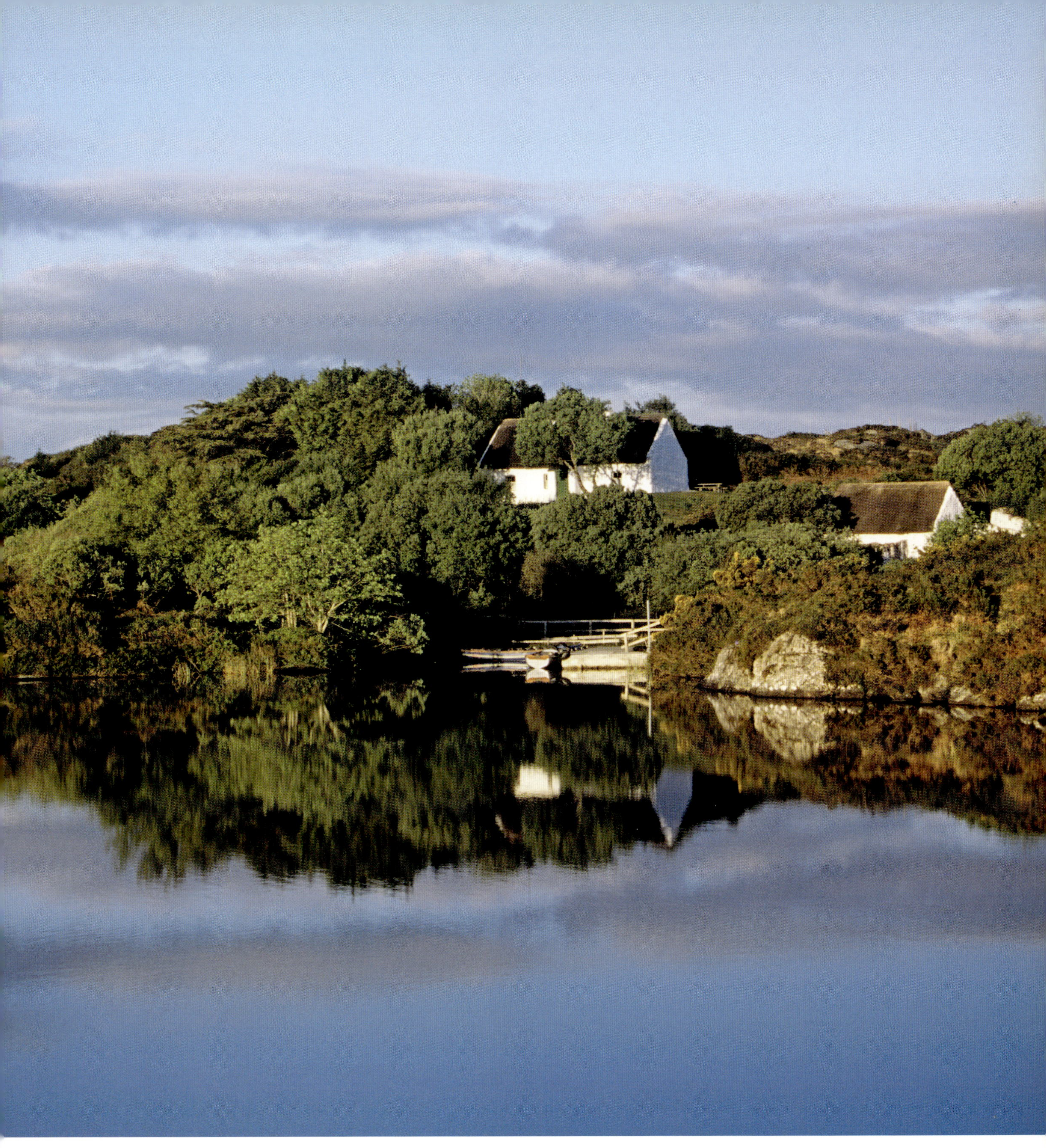

Pádraic Henry Pearse, poet and leader of the 1916 Easter uprising, made this cottage in Connemara near Ros Muc his summer home. It is now a National Monument/Heritage Site and is open to the public.

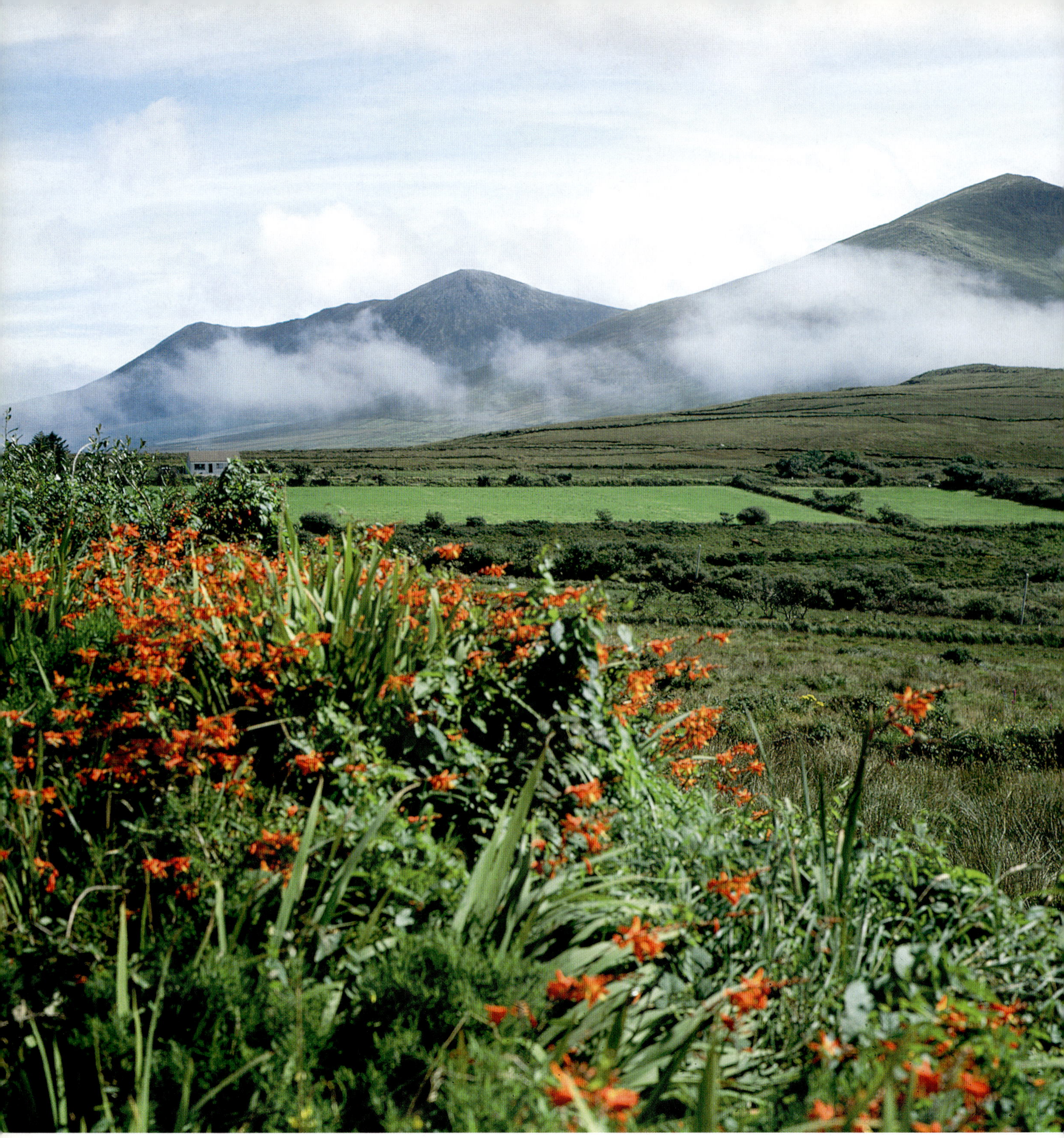

These mountains and green patchwork fields lie on the Ring of Kerry, a circular route covering more than 100 miles in County Kerry. It starts from the town of Killarney and heads around the Iveragh Peninsula.

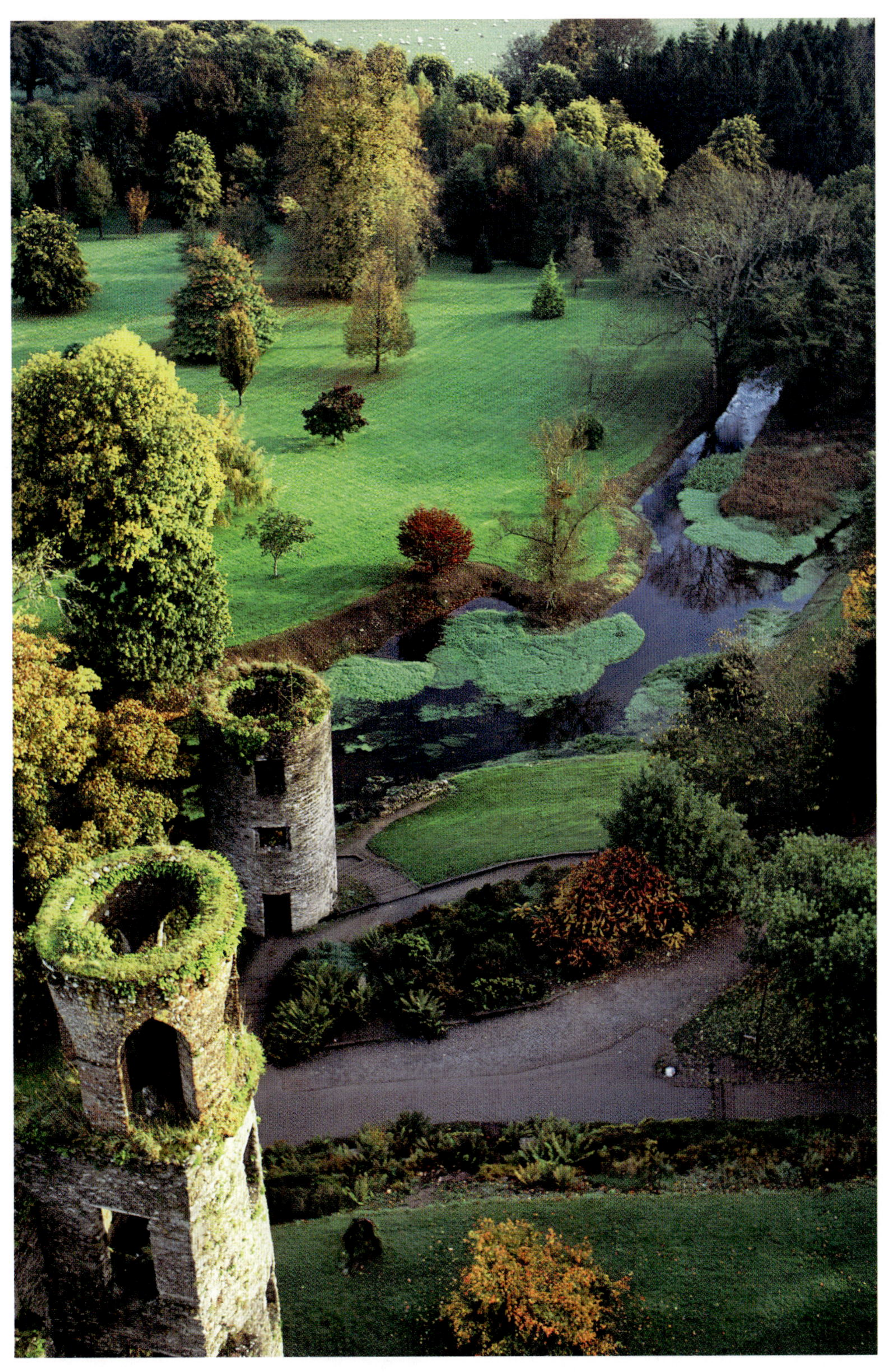

Extensive gardens and ancient parkland surround Blarney Castle and nearby Blarney House, built in the 19th century. The stone castle is the third to stand on this site in County Cork.

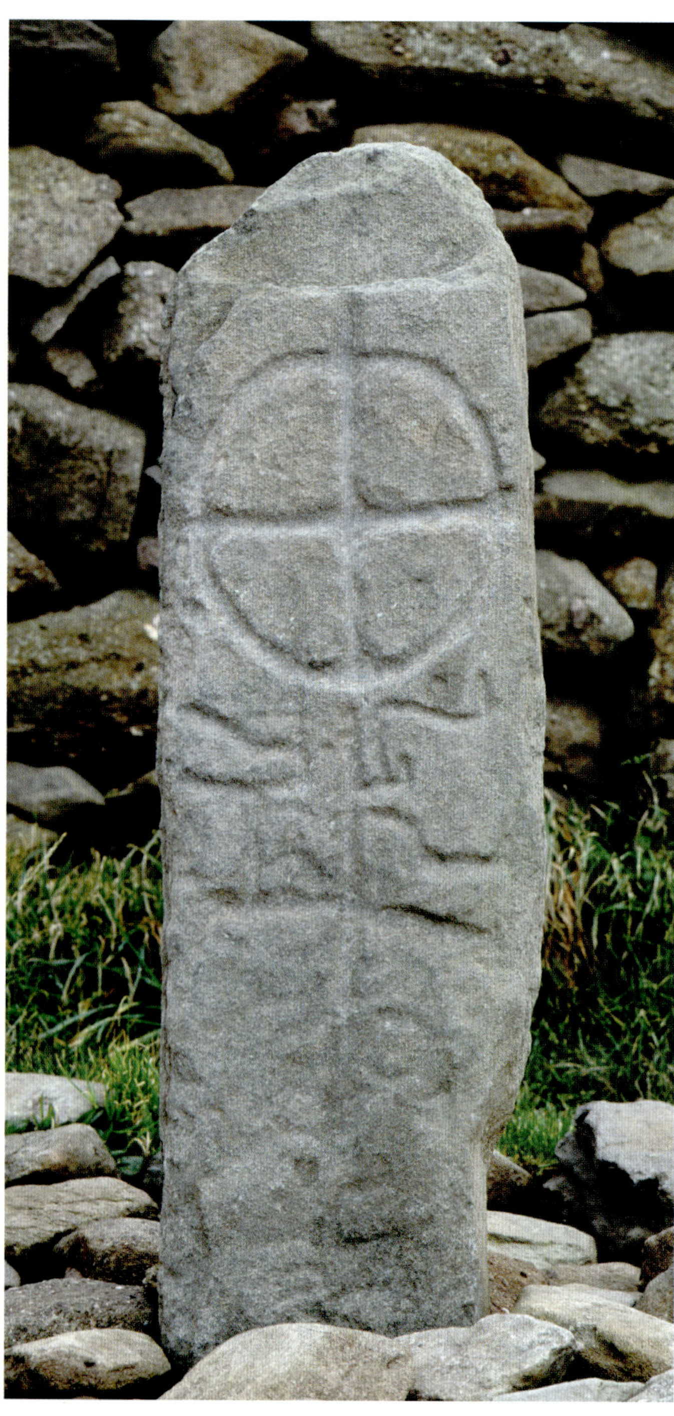

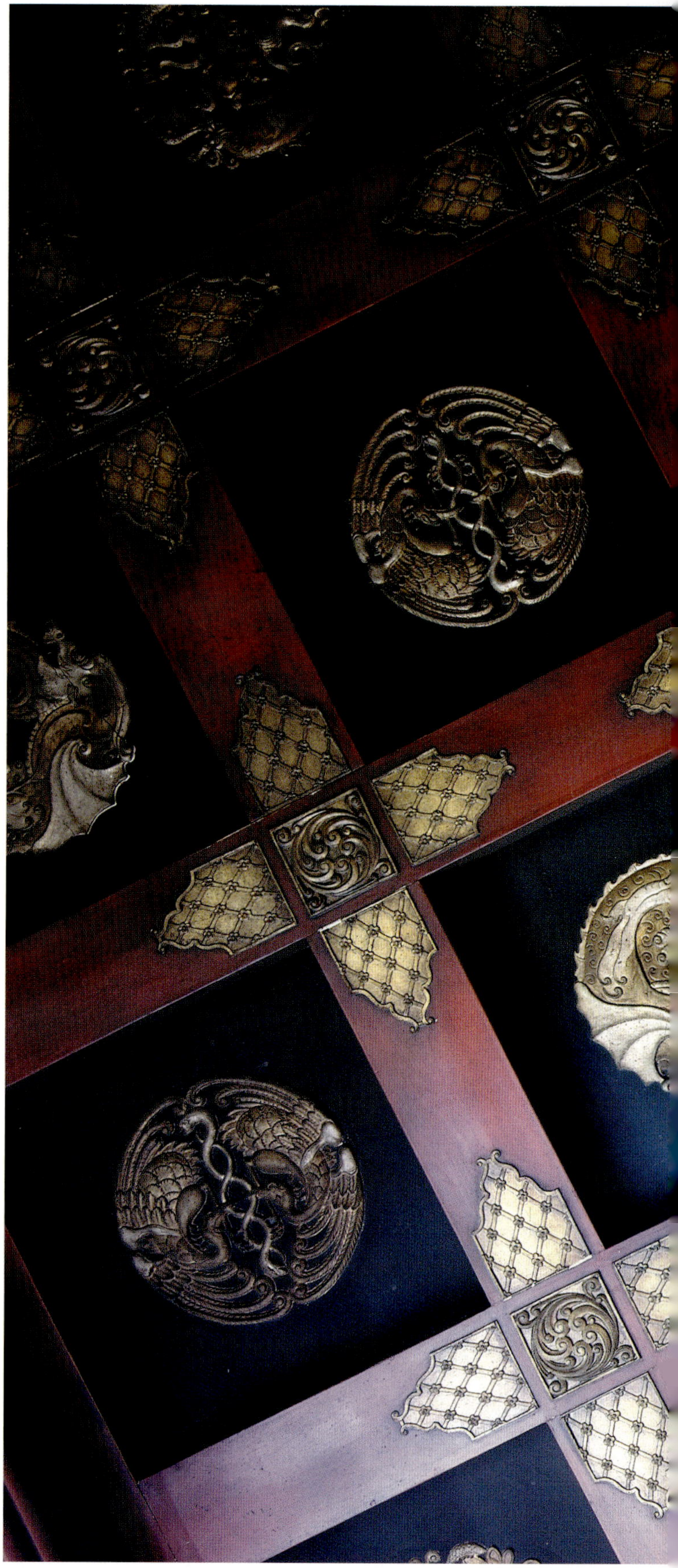

Inside the Gallarus Oratory on the Dingle Peninsula is the Alphabet Stone, a standing pillar carved with Roman and ogham characters. Opposite: this ceiling detail is from the Chester Beatty Library housed in Dublin Castle. The collection comprises artifacts from oriental and western religions, as well as secular items.

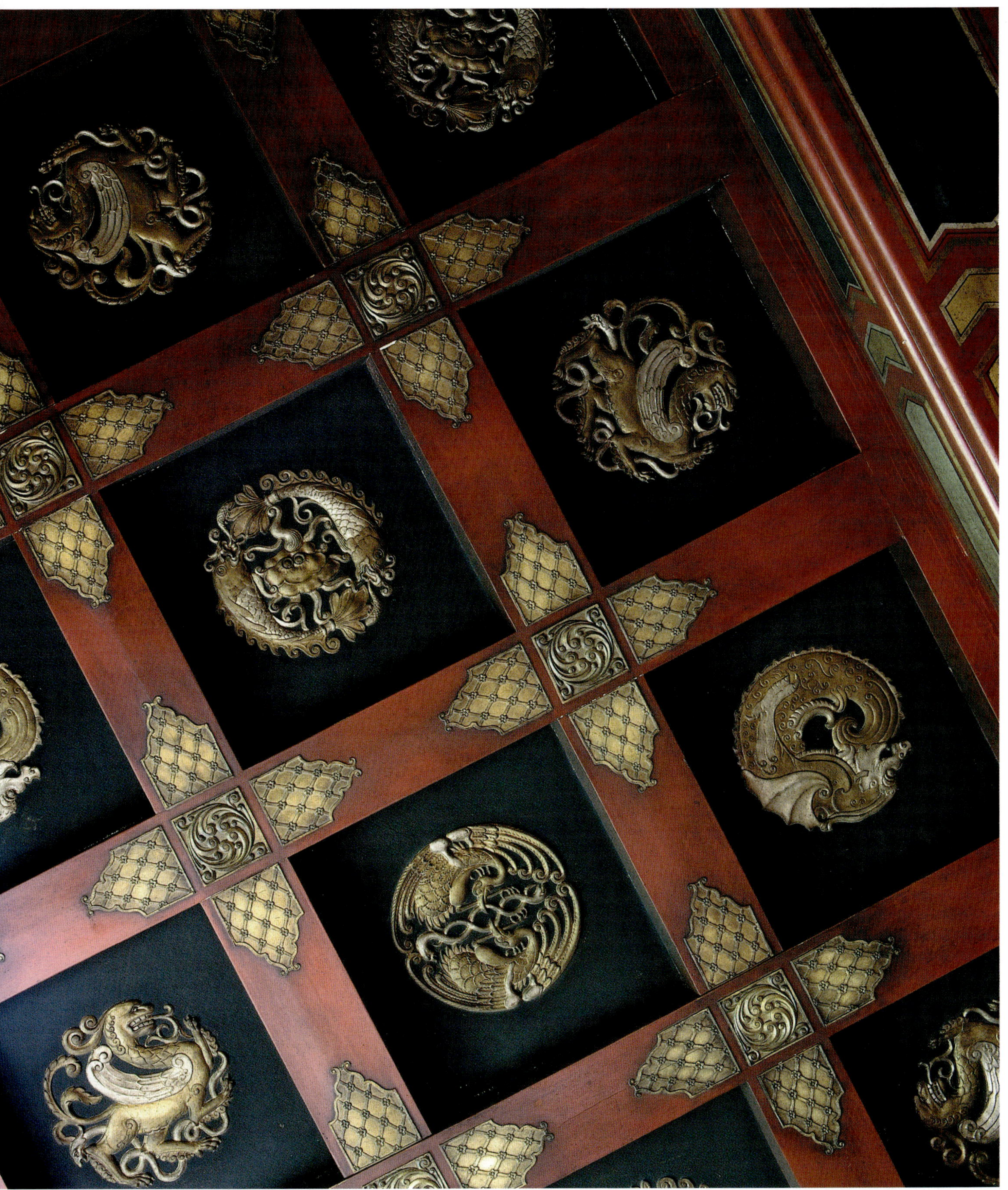

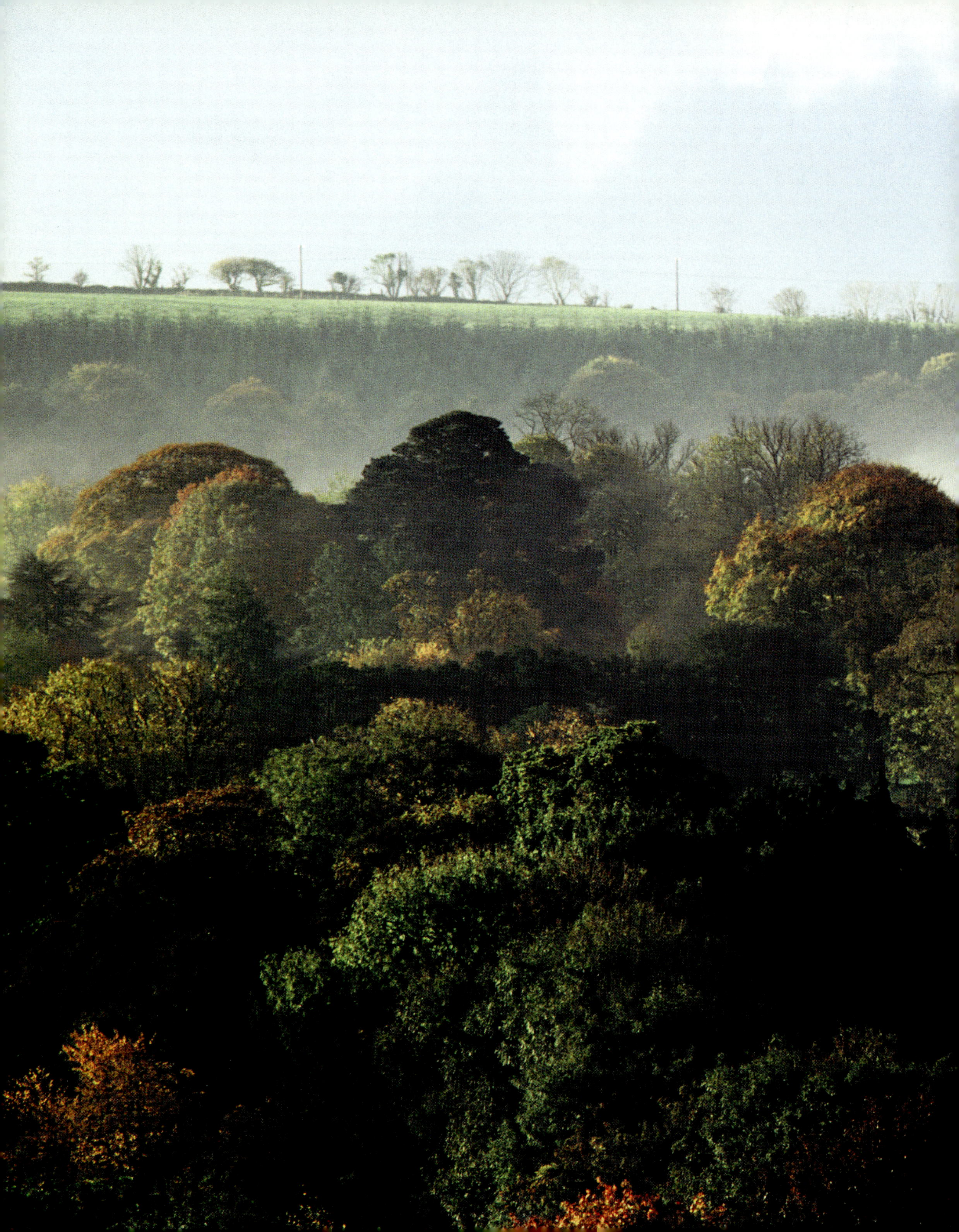

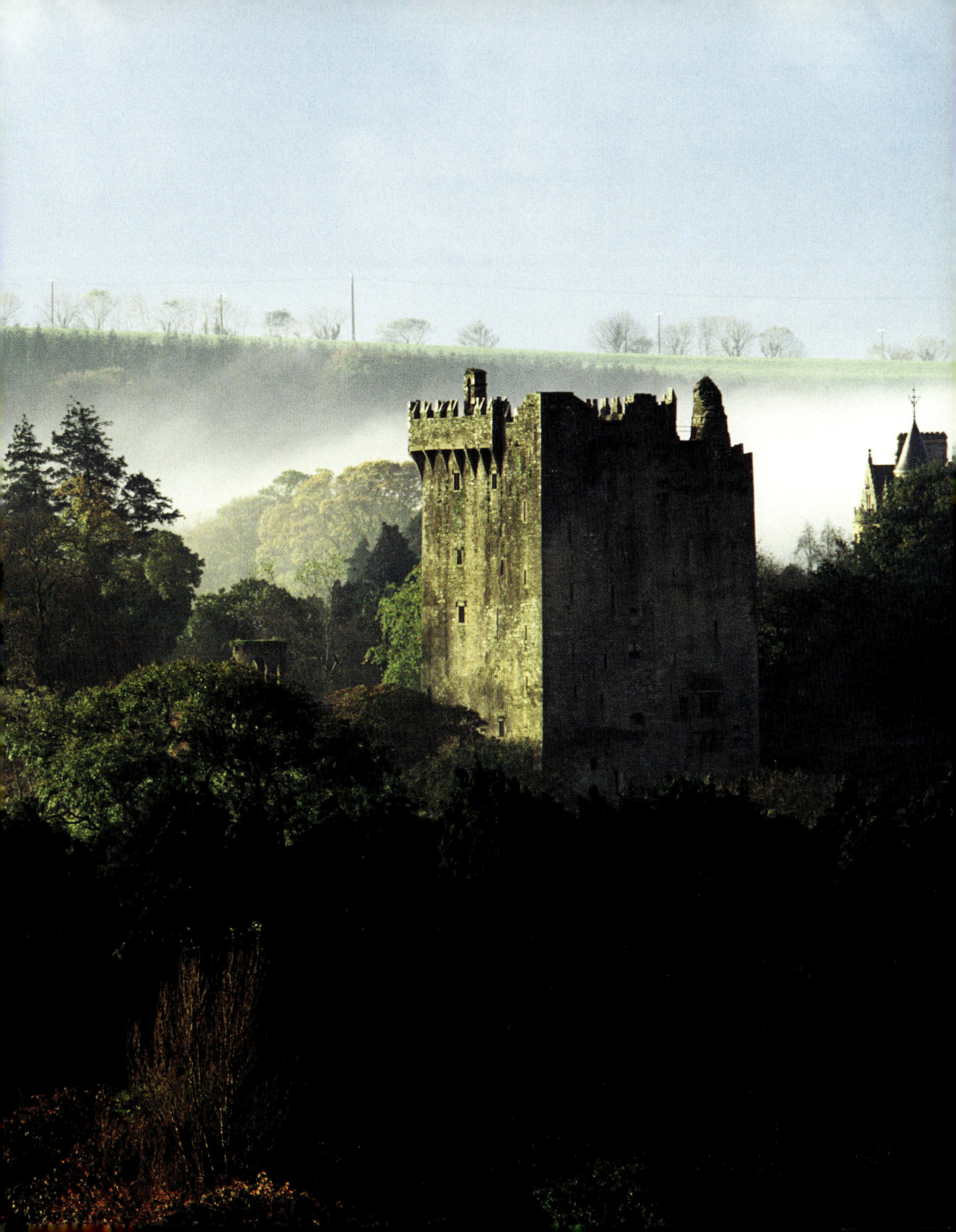

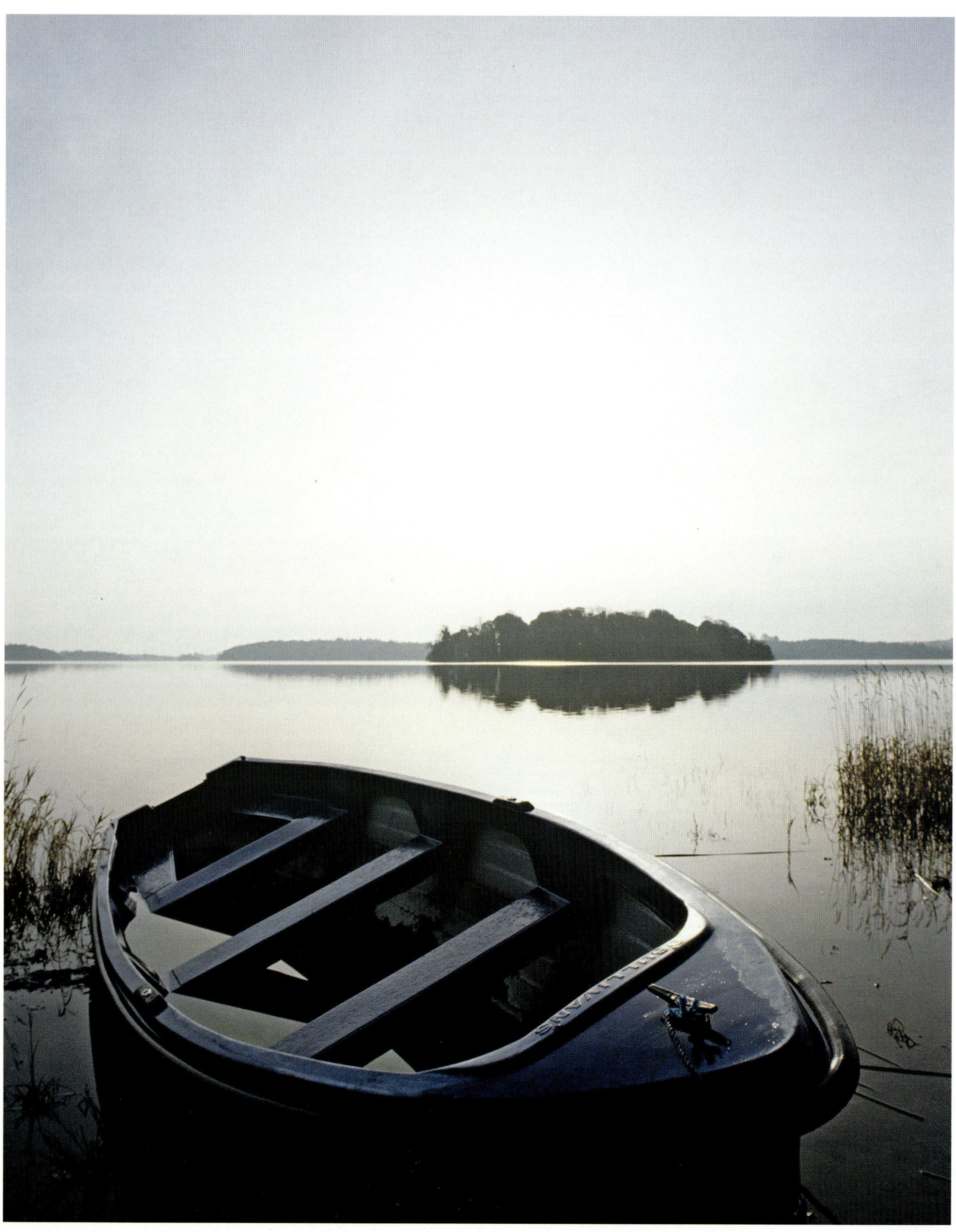

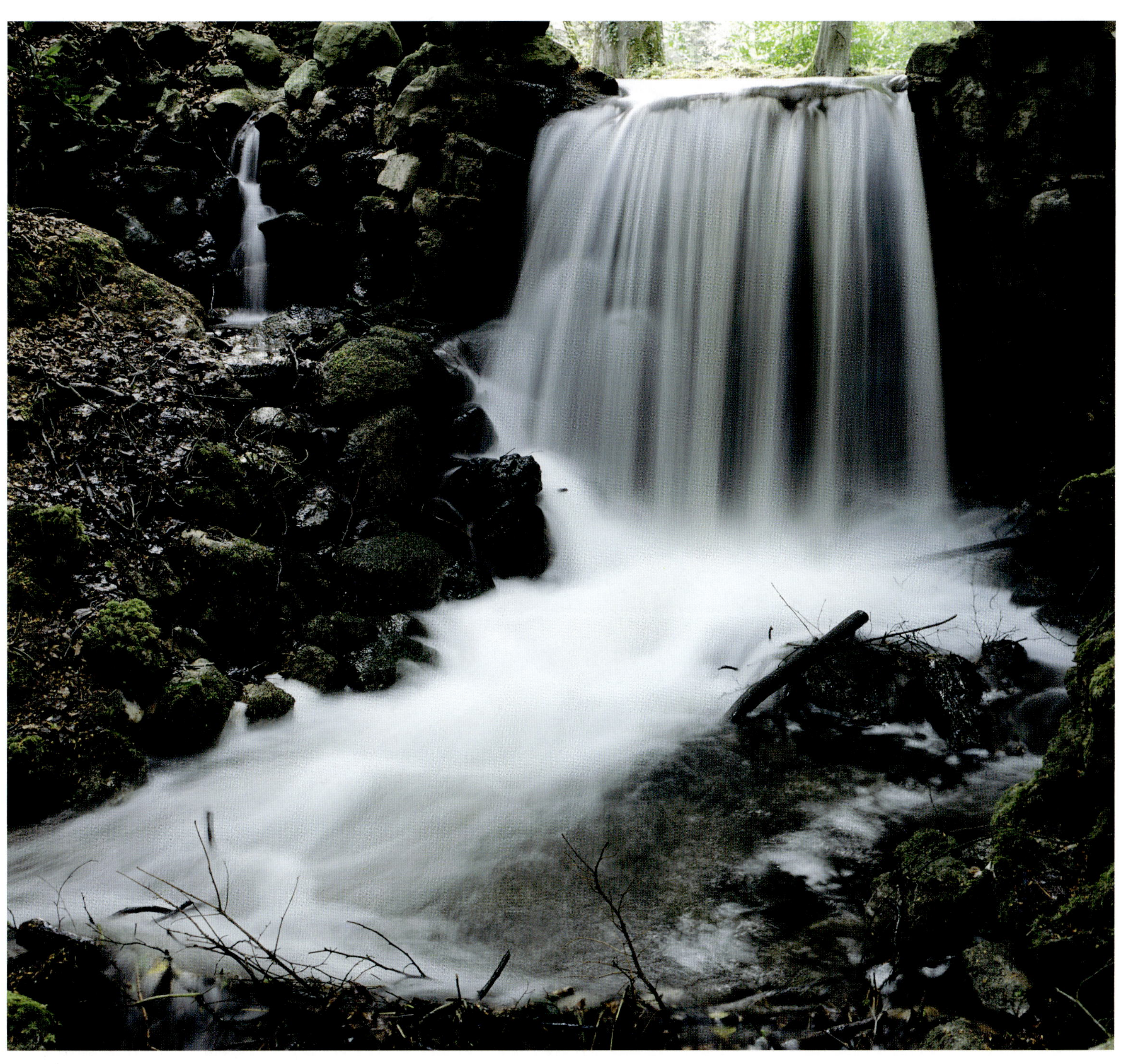

A waterfall in the grounds of Birr Castle, private home of the Parsons family and renowned for its exotic trees and plants, rivers and lake, formal gardens, terraces, and wildflower meadows. Opposite: Lough Key in County Roscommon is part of an 800-acre forest park. Legend says that the fairy king, Tuatha de Danann, drowned when the waters of the lake sprang from the earth. Pages 24–25: a view towards Blarney Castle, with the house just visible to the right.

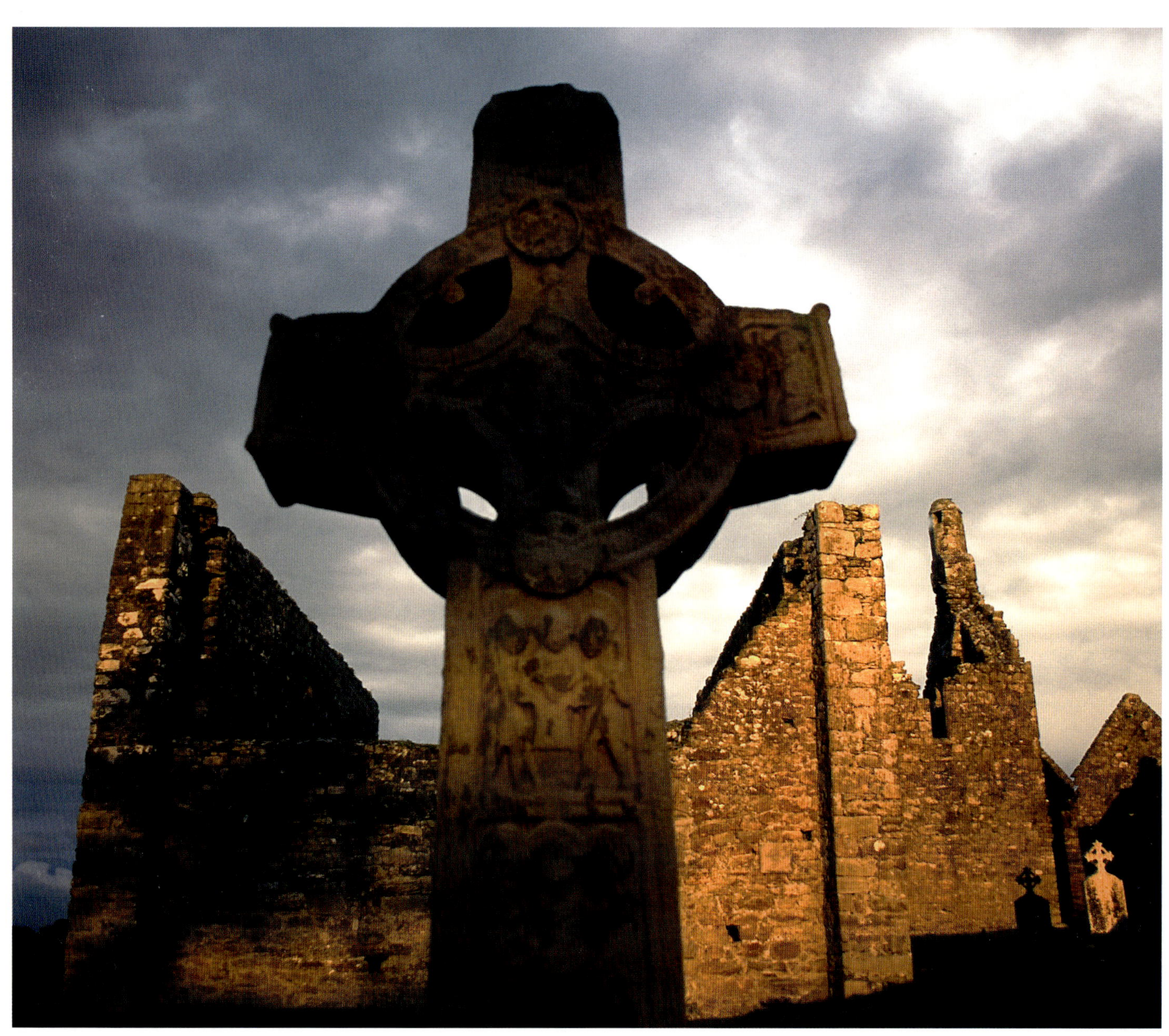

Crosses stand among the ruined buildings of Clonmacnoise in County Offaly. St Ciaran founded the monastery in the 6th century and is believed to be buried in a tiny church on the site.
Opposite: the sun sets over Youghal beach, a 5-mile stretch of sand in the southeast of County Cork. The town is an historic walled seaport at the mouth of the estuary of the River Blackwater.

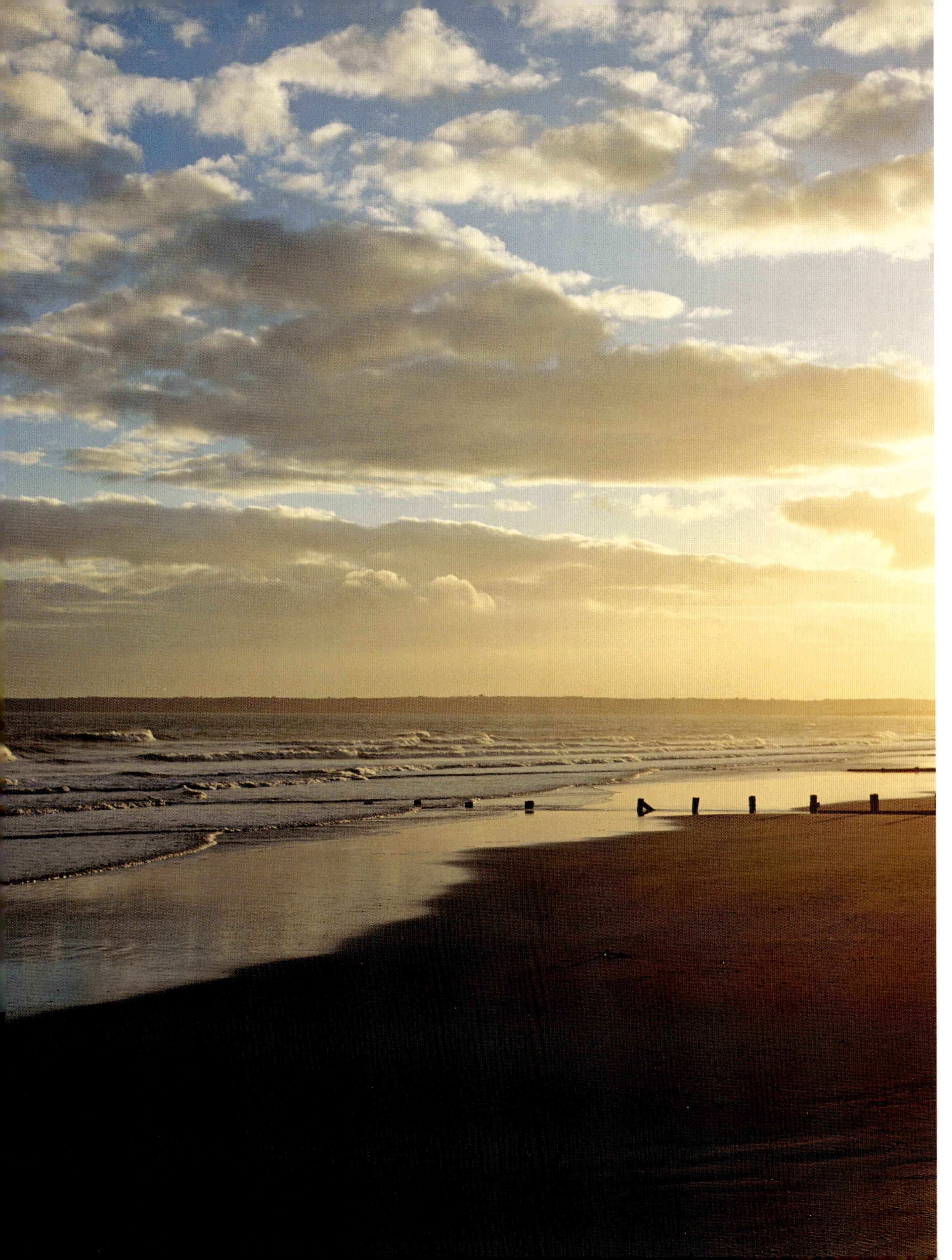

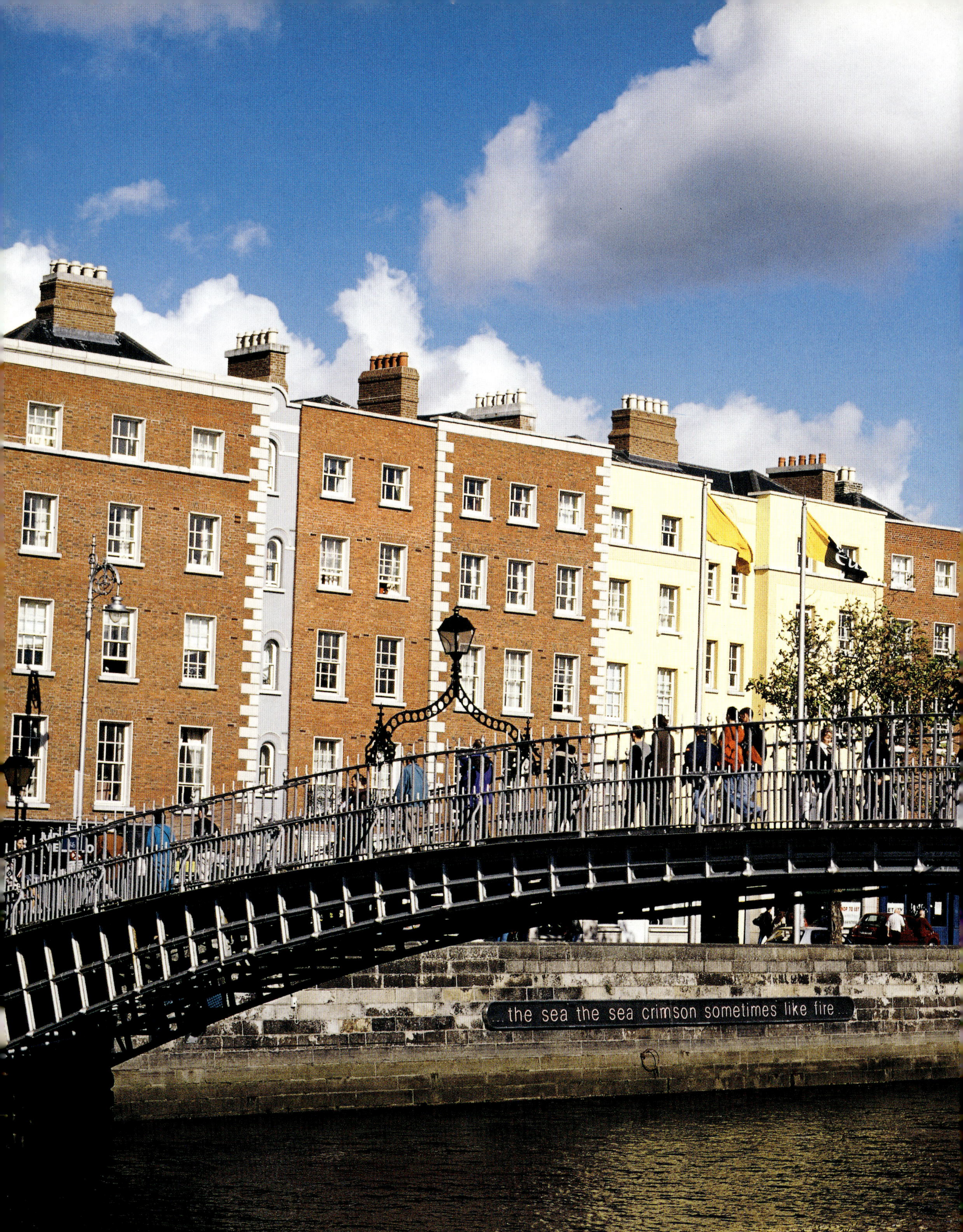
... the sea the sea crimson sometimes like fire ...

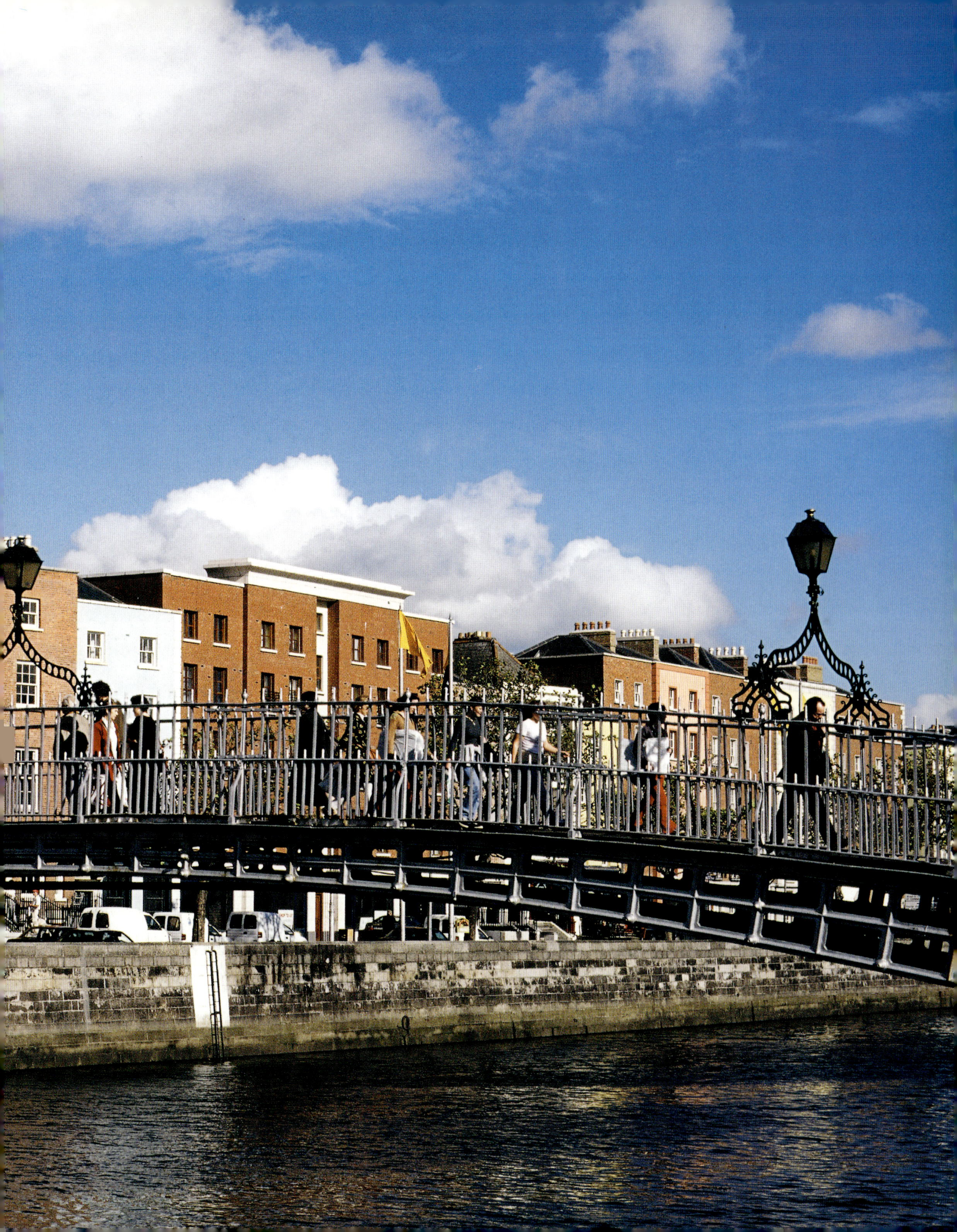

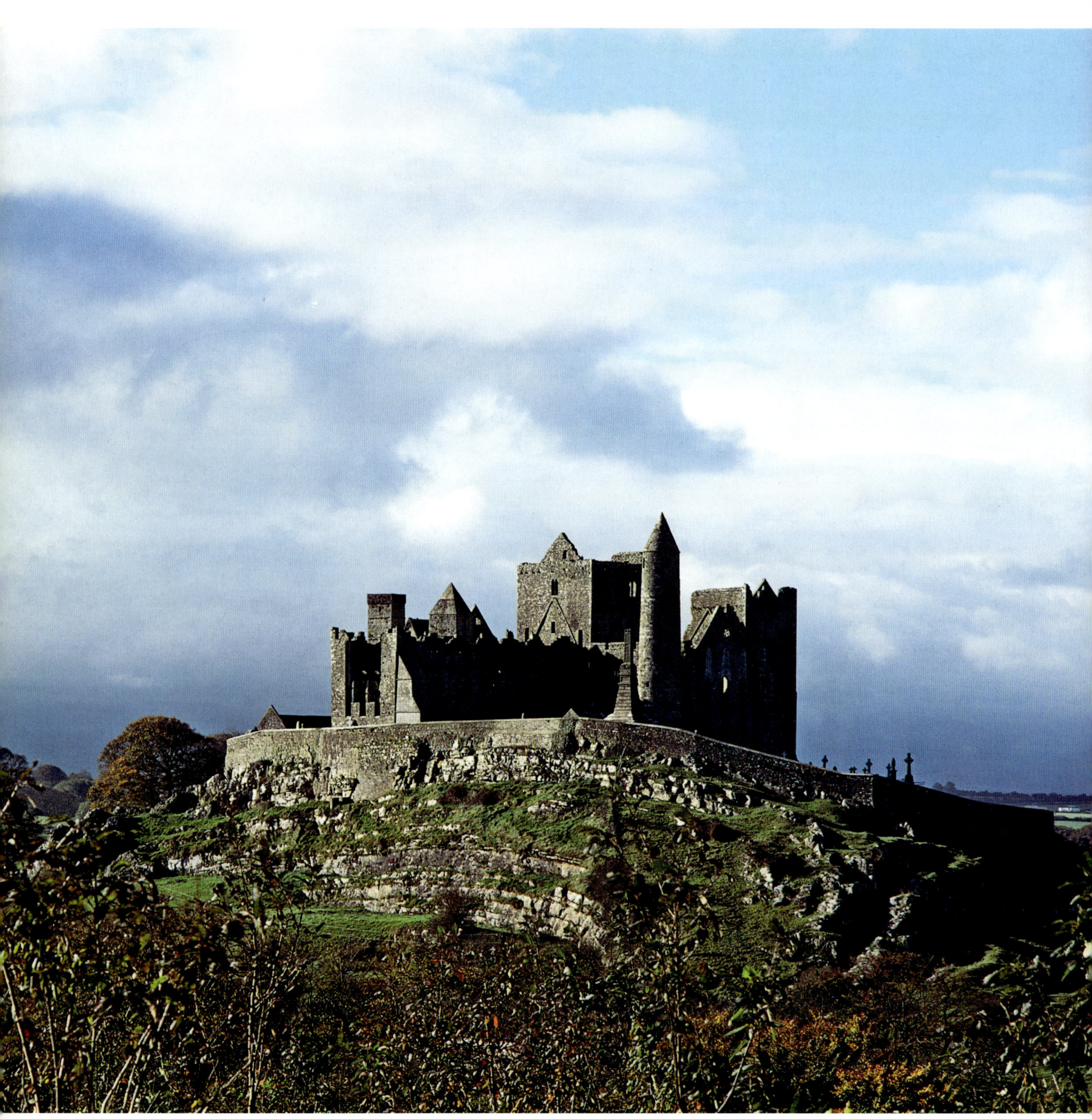

The Rock of Cashel ruins high up on the rock that overshadows the town from the west.
Pages 30–31: Ha'Penny Bridge over the River Liffey in Dublin. Its official name is Wellington Bridge, after the Duke of Wellington. The nickname was given because of the halfpenny toll.

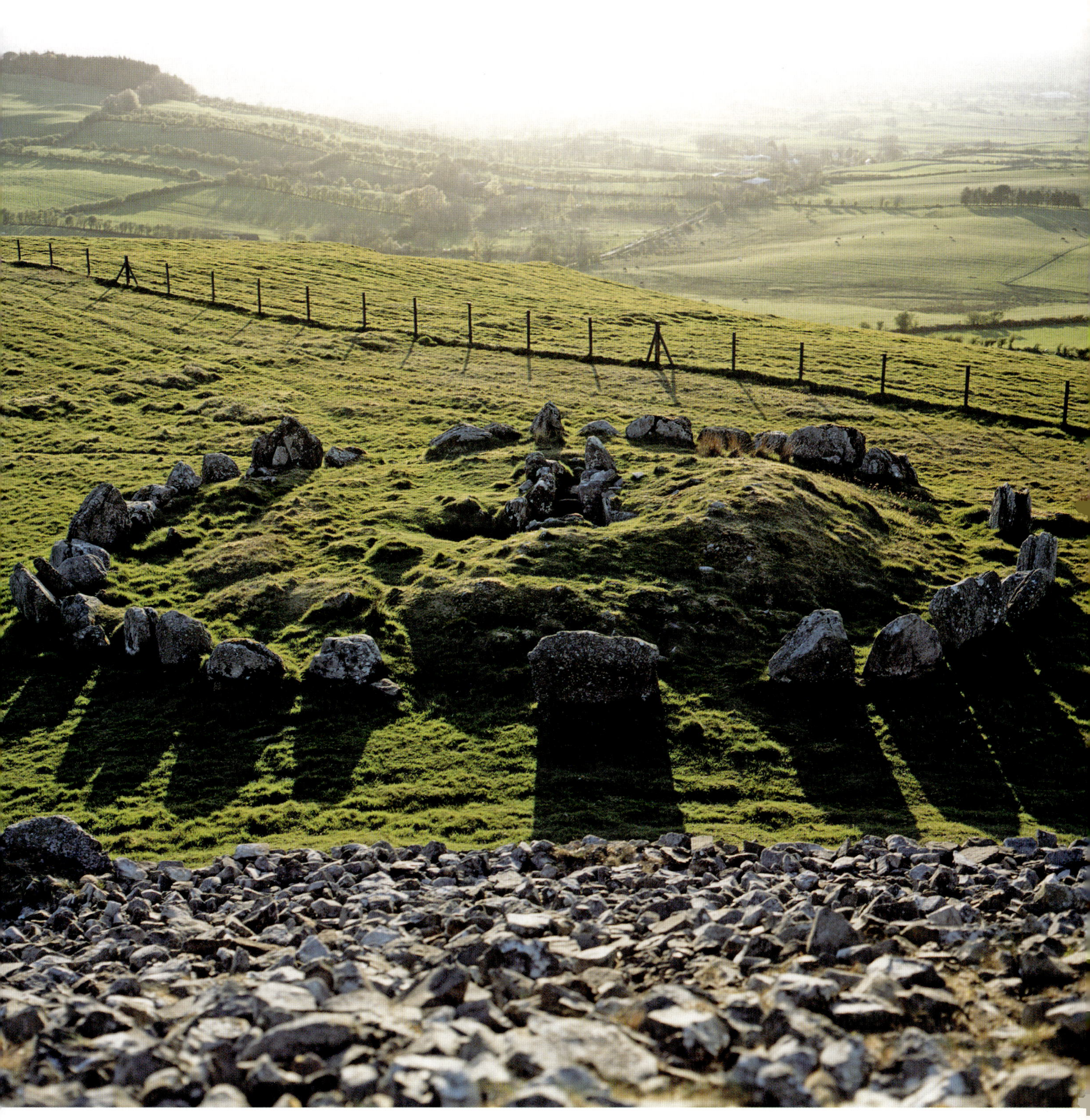

Loughcrew, or the Mountains of the Witch, lies west of Kells in west County Meath. Stretching in a chain over four peaks, the area is scattered with ancient monuments. The sites are dedicated to a witch said to have dropped the stones from her apron as she hopped across the hill.

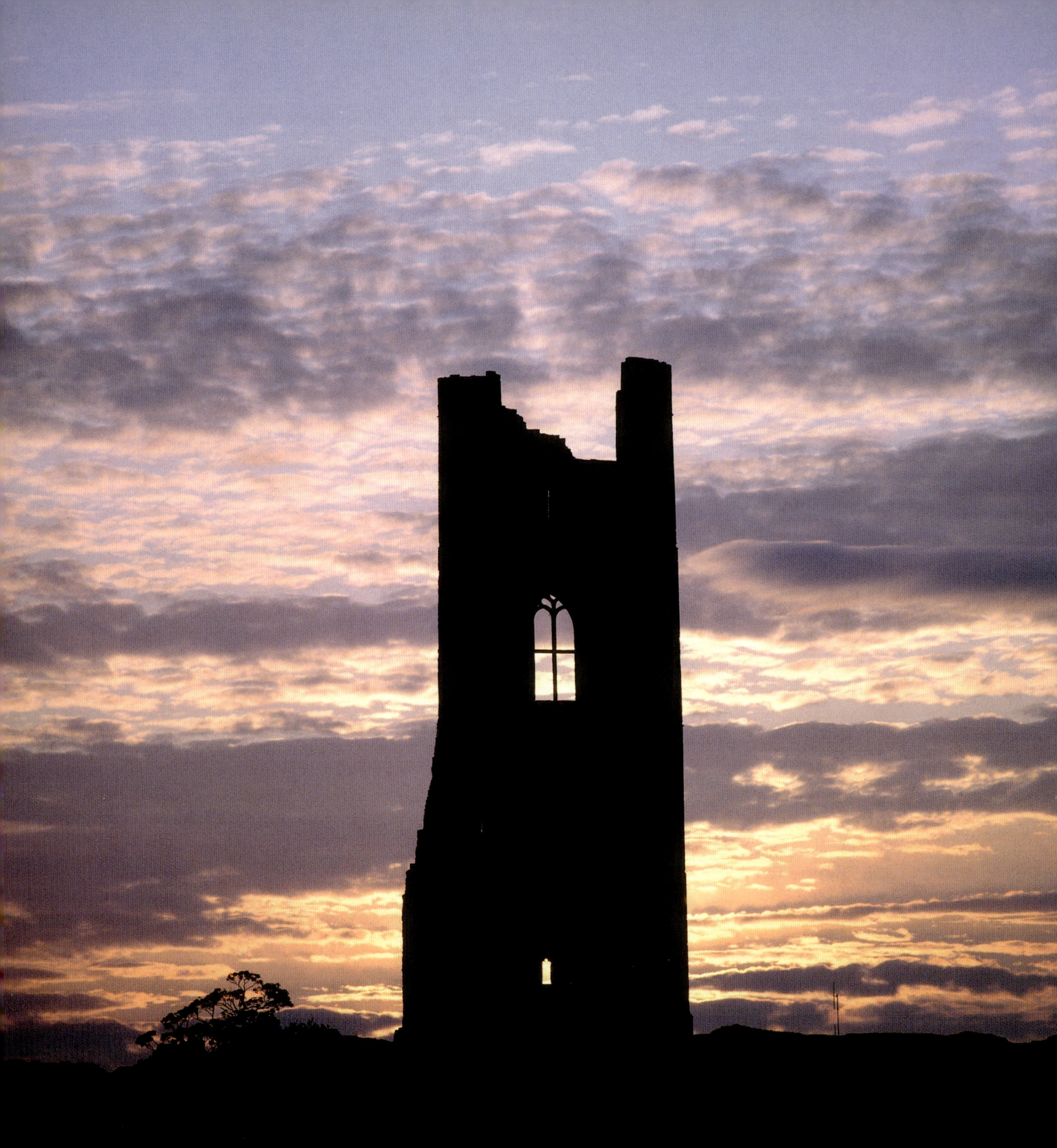

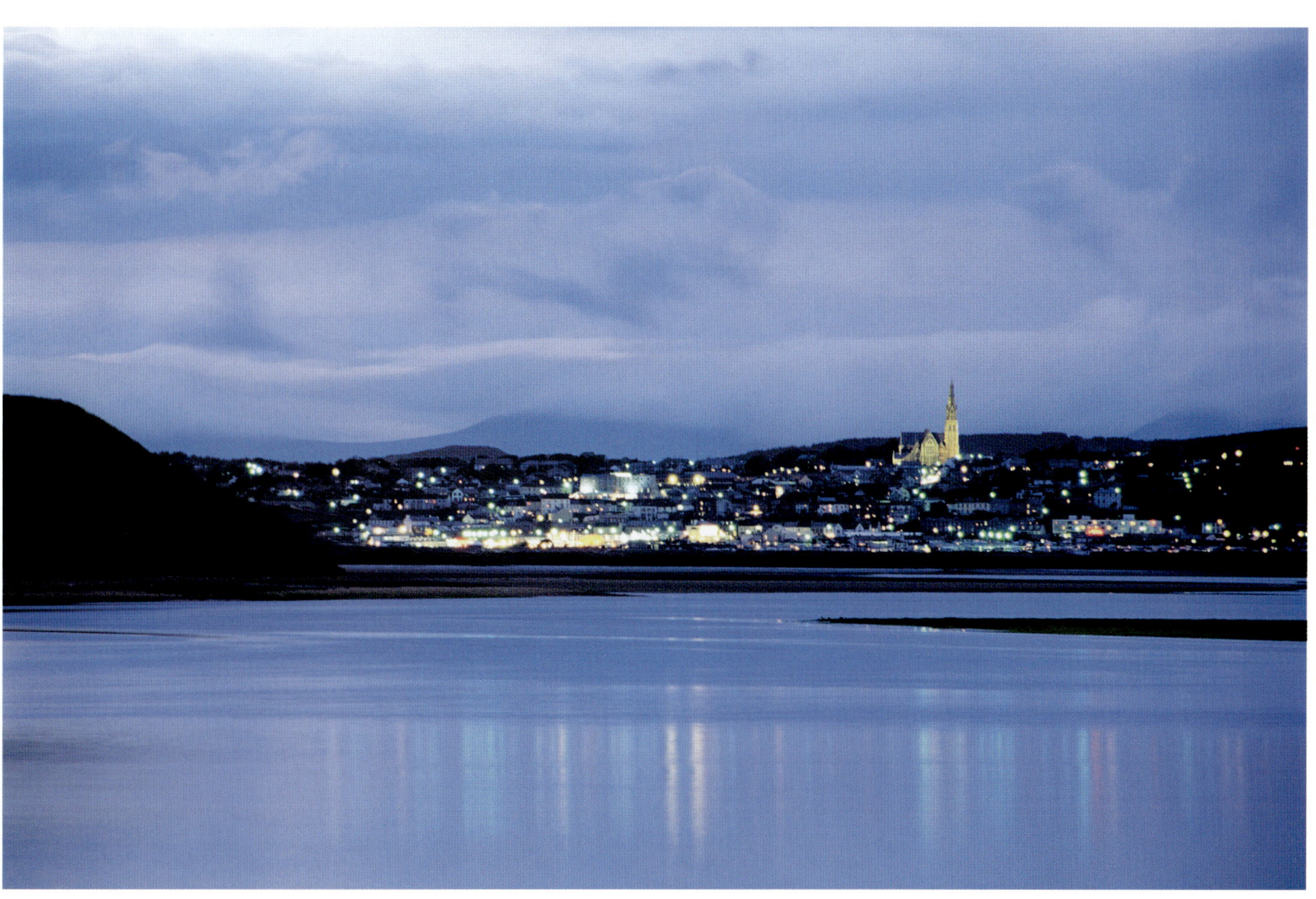

The resort of Tramore sits on a hillside overlooking Tramore Bay in County Waterford. It has a fine promenade and a 3-mile stretch of beach with high sand dunes. Water-based sports on the beach include surfing, windsurfing, and kitesurfing, and there is an amusement park on the sands.
Opposite: a ruined tower known as the Yellow Steeple is all that remains of the 13th-century Augustinian St Mary's Abbey in Trim, County Meath. It overlooks the town from a ridge opposite Trim Castle.

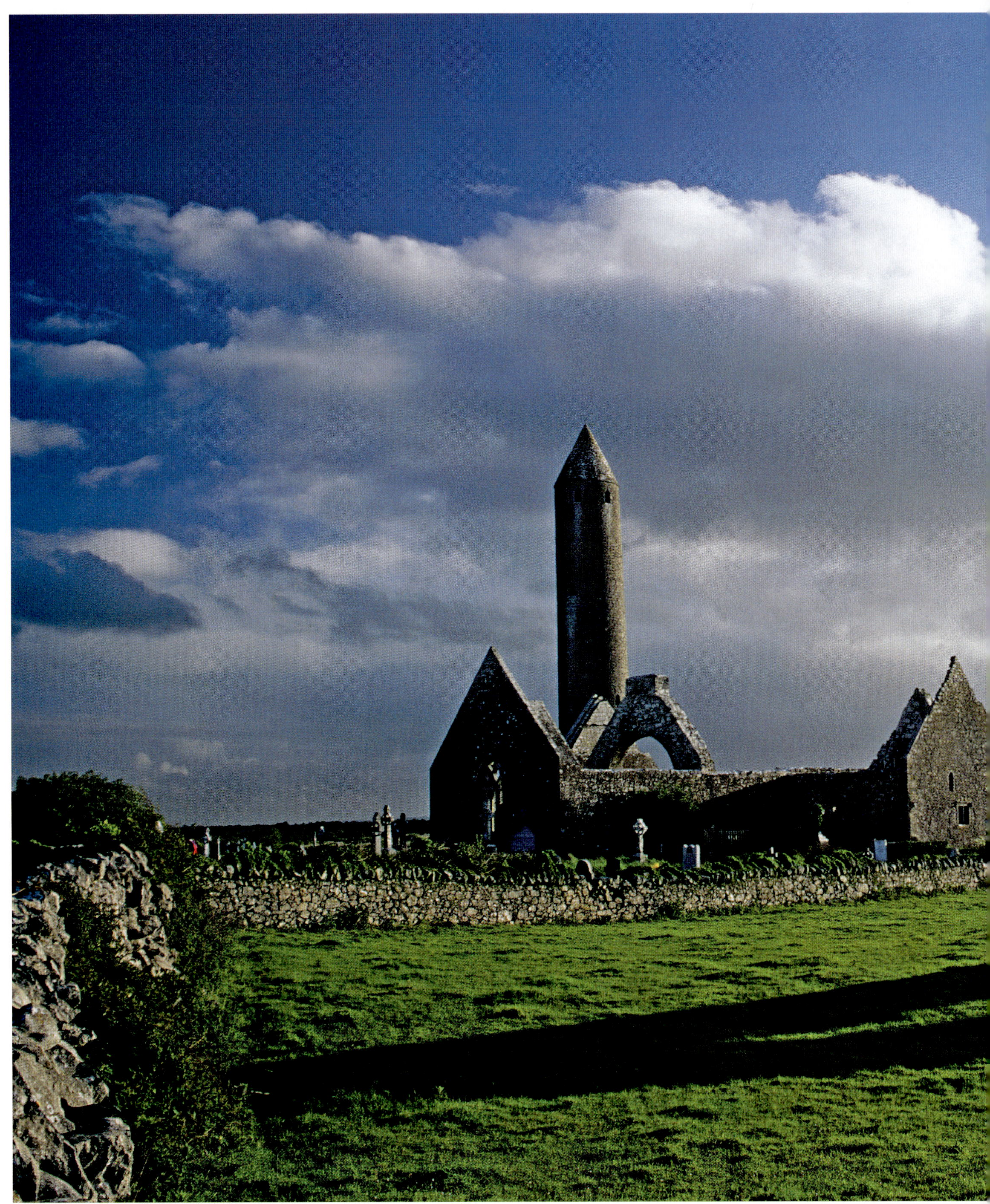

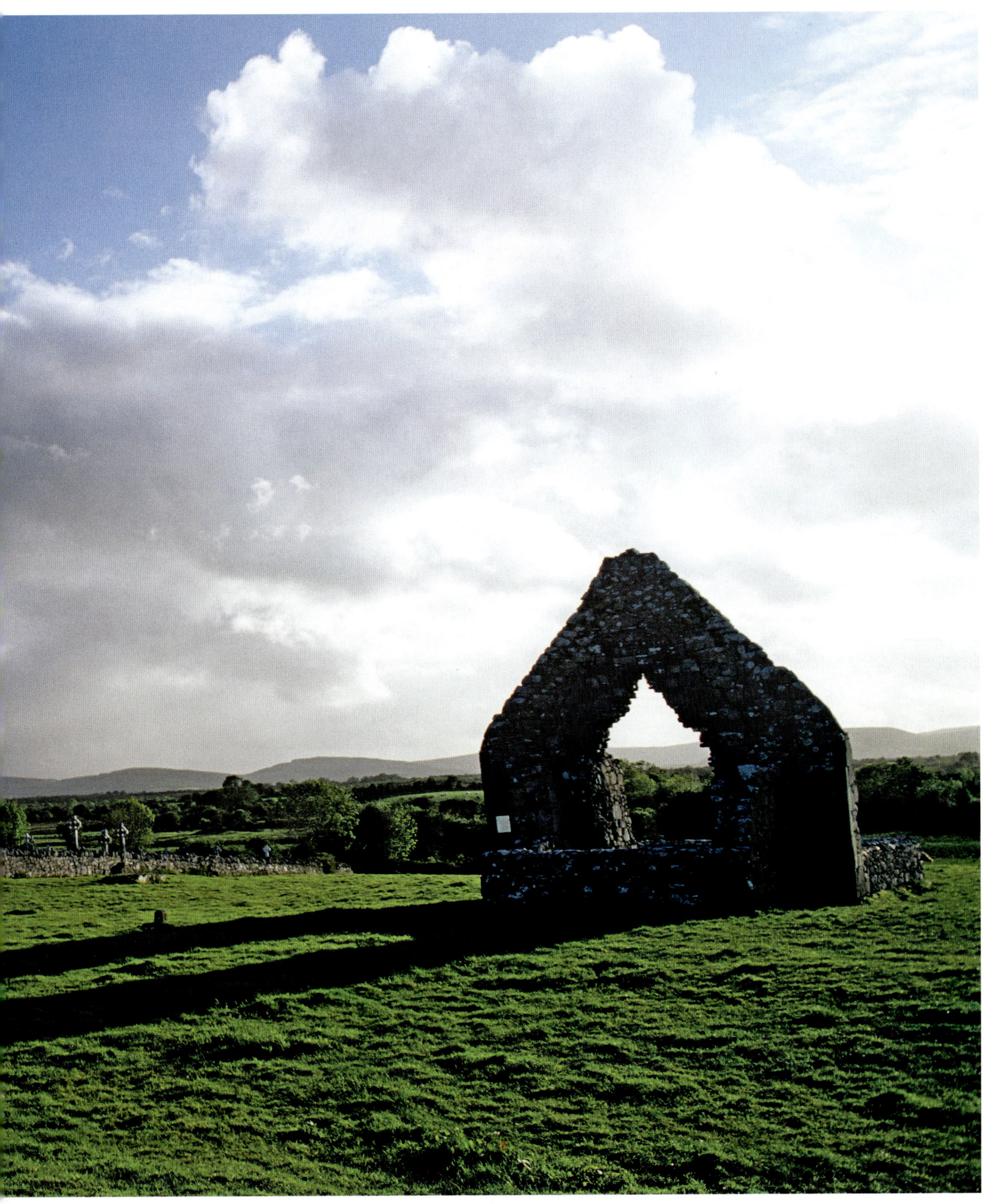

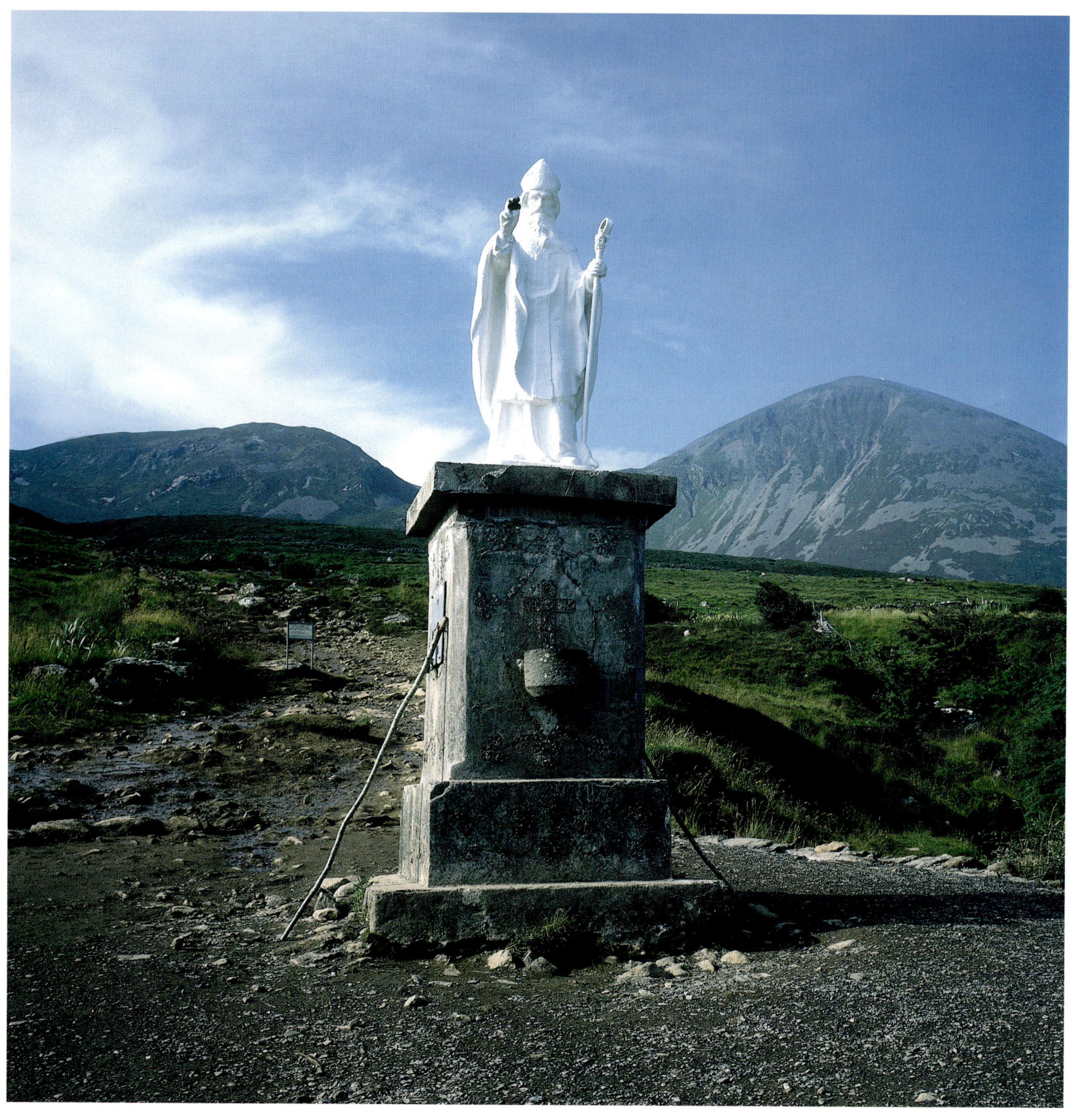

A marble statue of St Patrick stands on a stone plinth on the summit of the conical peak of Croagh Patrick; it commemorates the legend of the saint banishing all the snakes from Ireland.

Pages 36–37: the monastic remains at Kilmacduagh, in County Galway, show a good example of the distinctive round towers found only in Ireland. St Colman, son of Duagh, founded the monastery.

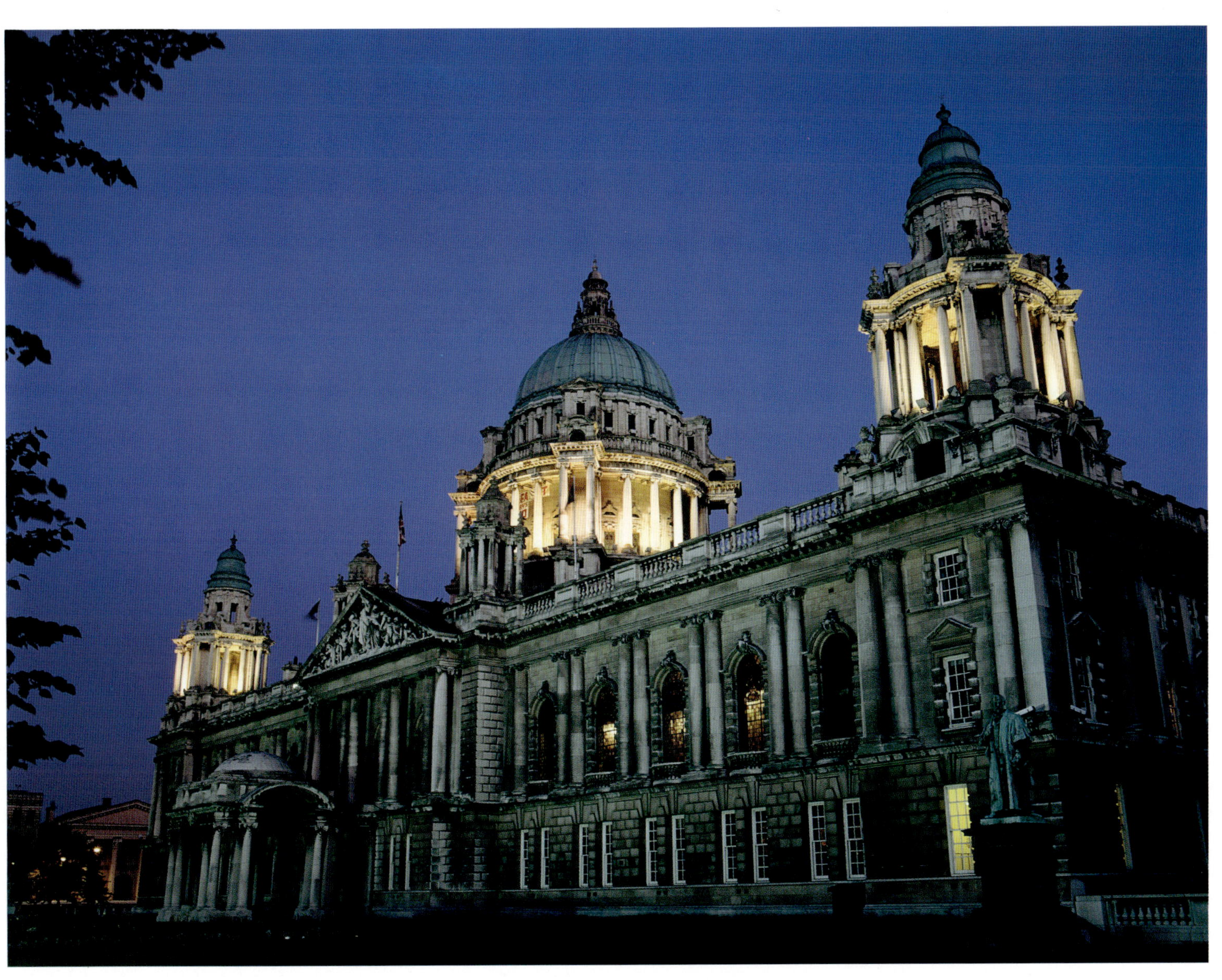

Belfast's City Hall in Donegall Square is the civic building of the Belfast City Council. Built between 1898 and 1906 from Portland stone with towers at each of the four corners, it features a central copper-coated dome that rises to nearly 174 feet. The building covers an area of one-and-a-half acres and has an enclosed courtyard. There is limited access to the interior, but the surrounding gardens are open to the public.

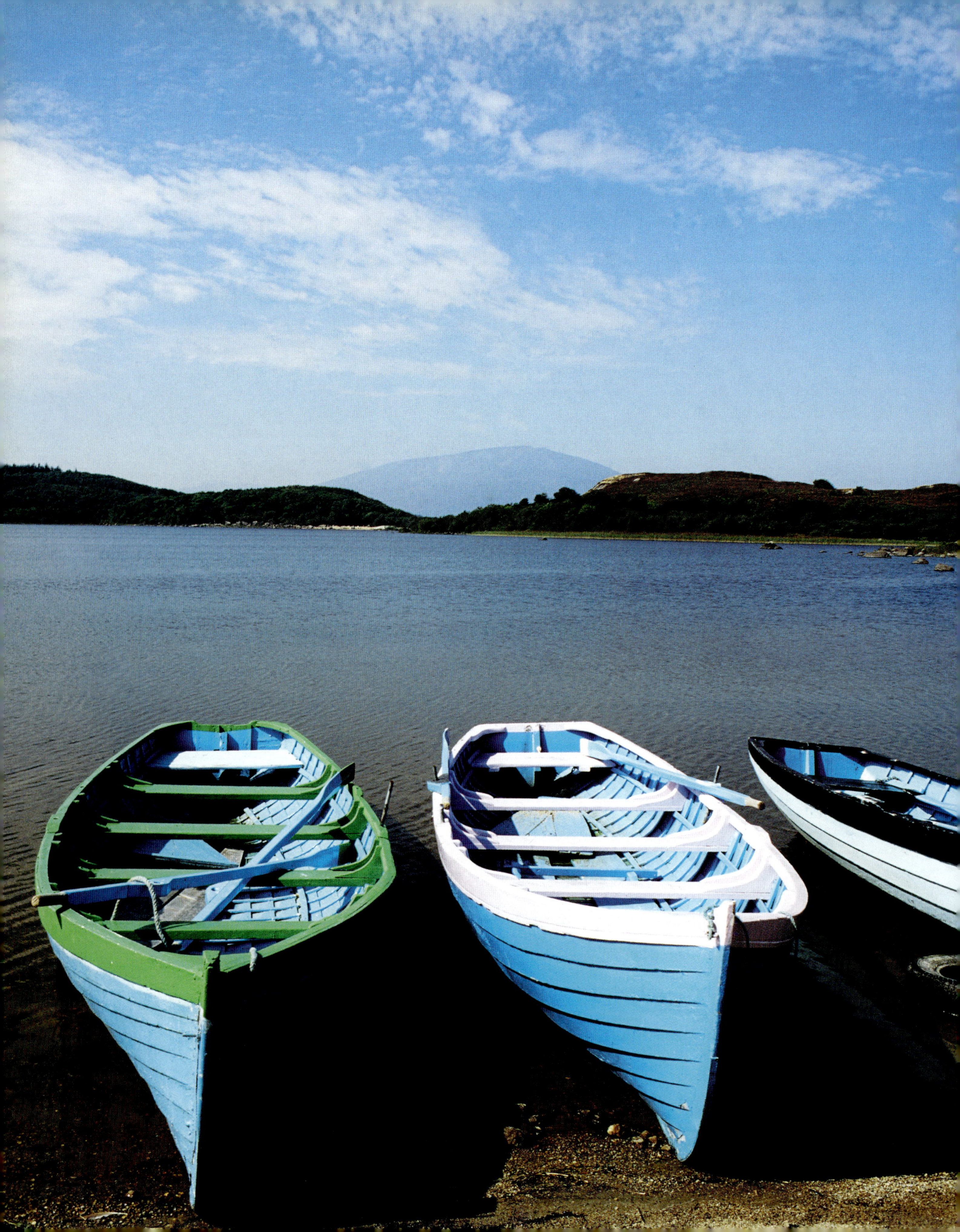

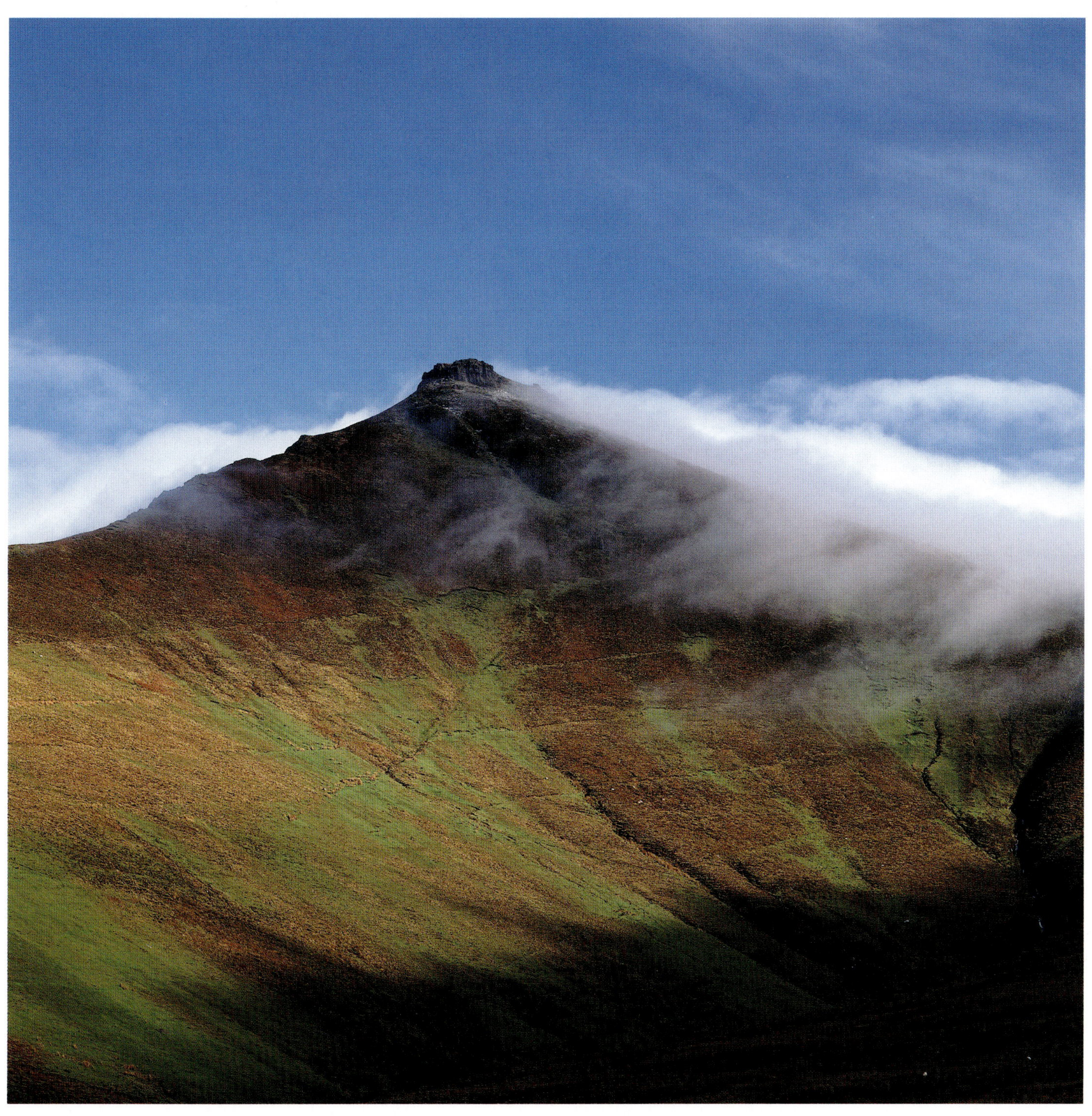

Mount Baurtregaum in the Slieve Mish Mountain Range overlooks Tralee Bay on the Dingle Peninsula. The county of Kerry claims Ireland's highest mountains and is its most westerly point. Opposite: Lough Conn in County Mayo covers about 14,000 acres and is noted for its trout and salmon fishing. With Lough Cullin just to the south, Conn is linked to the sea by the River Moy.

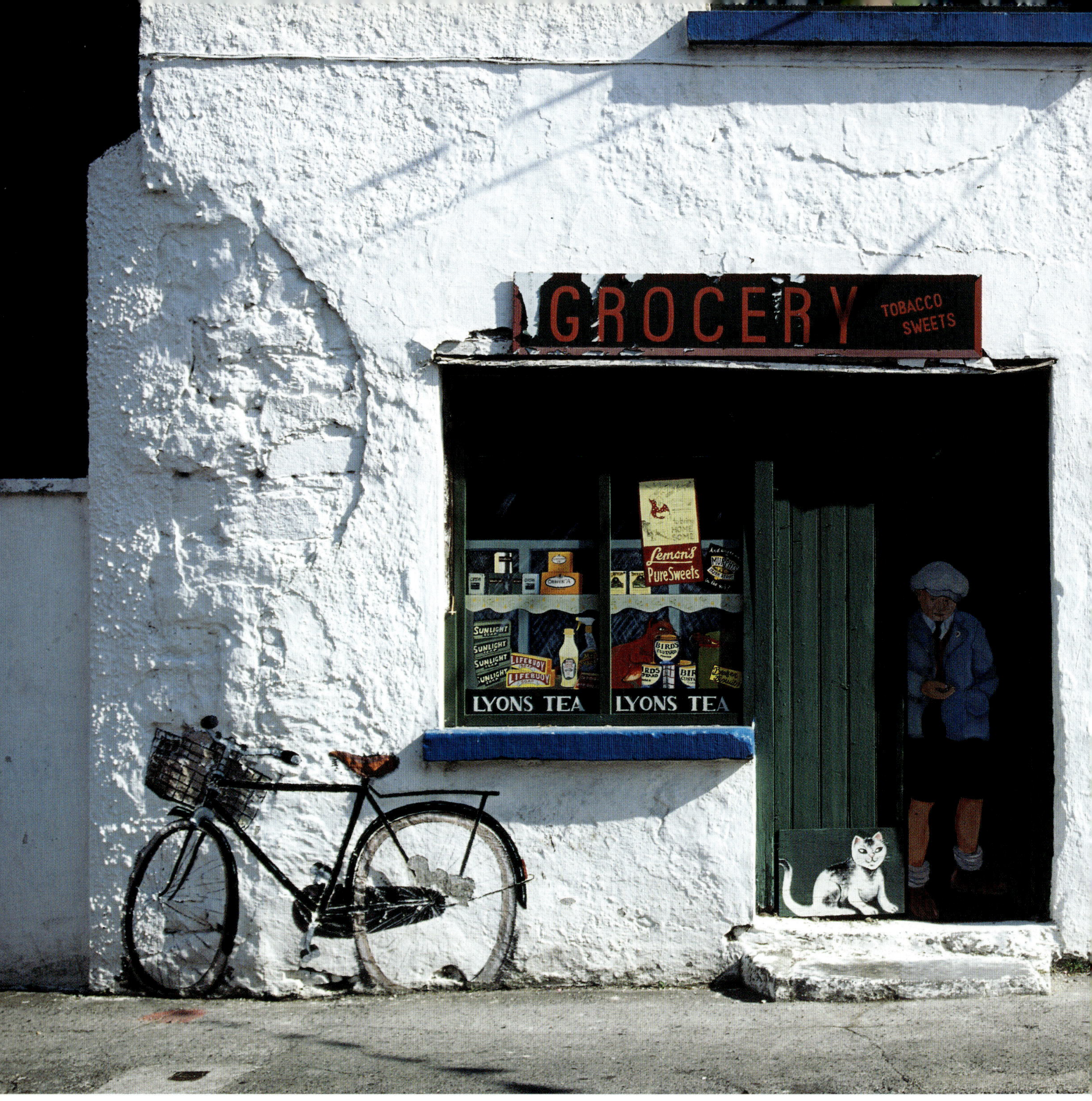

A simple form of trompe-l'oeil in Kinvara (Kinvarra in English), in the southeast corner of Galway Bay. Customer, shopkeeper, and provisions are all painted onto the shop front: even the bicycle leaning against the wall, and the cat sitting on the doorstep are not what they seem.

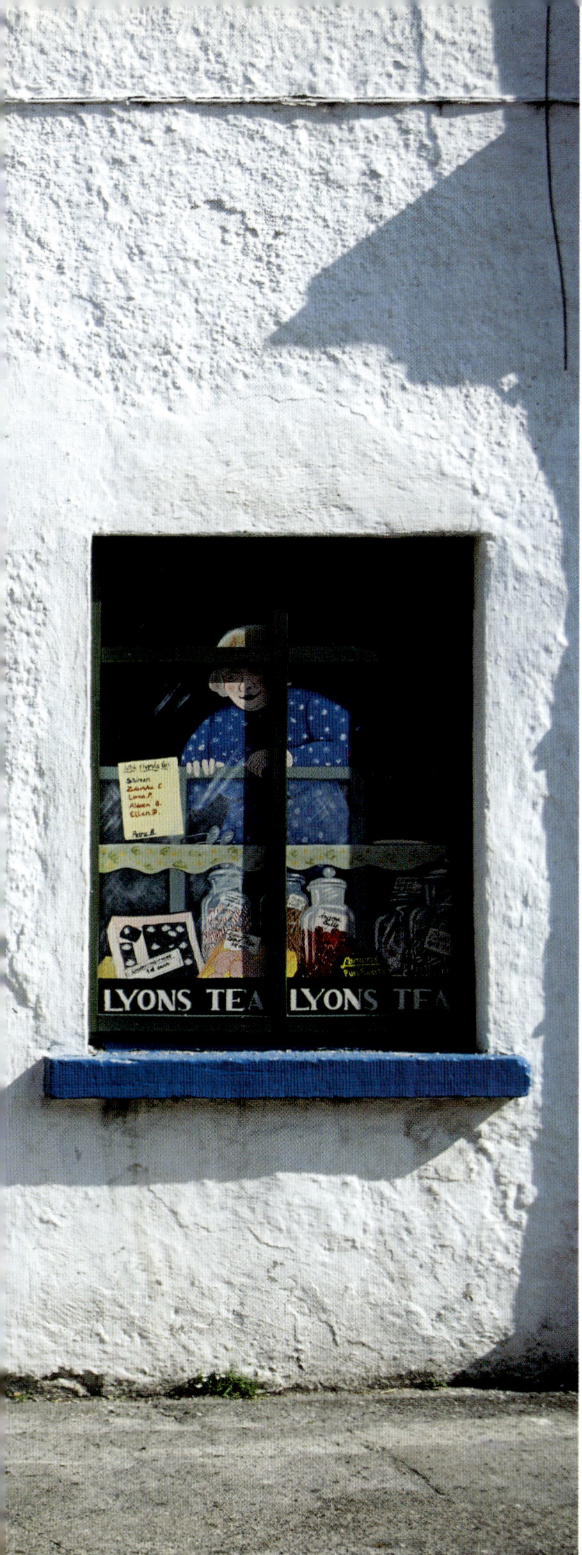

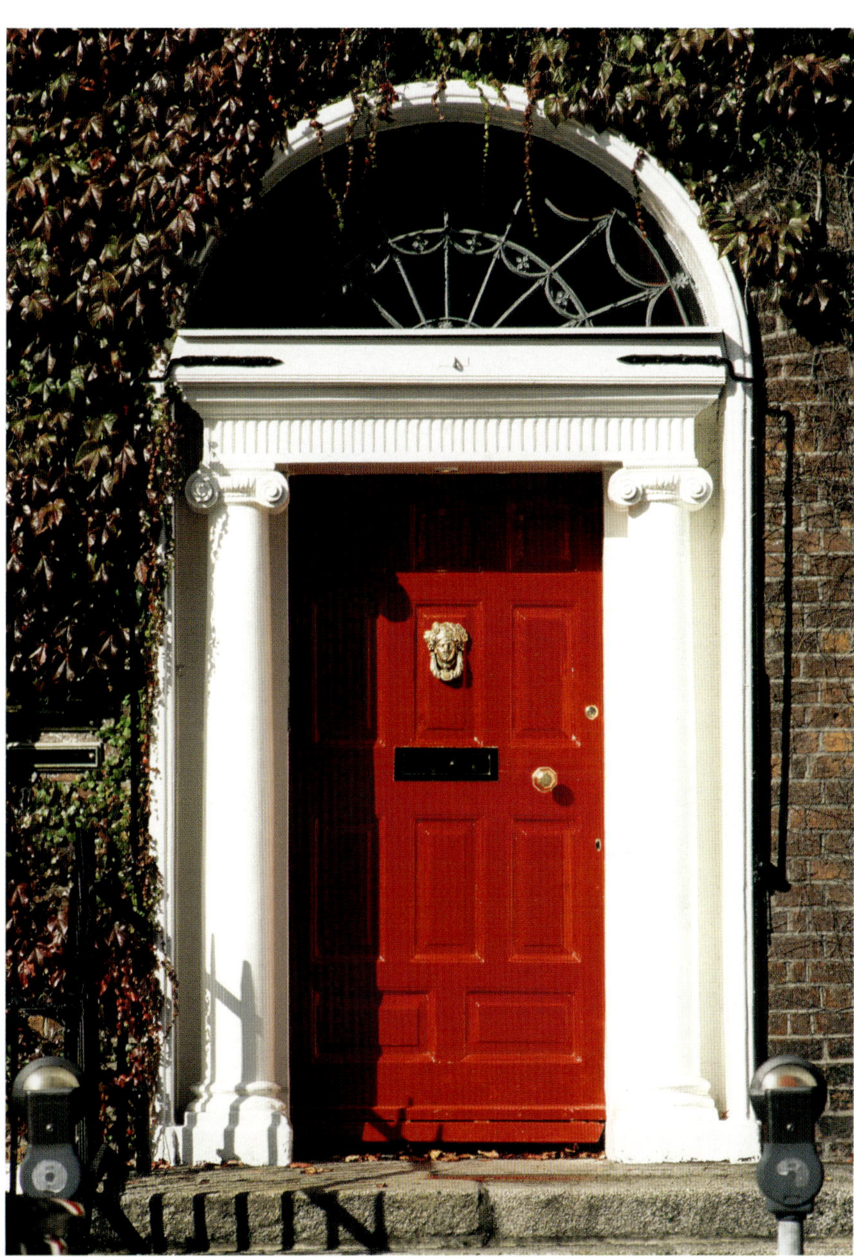

Pillars in front of the house and a fanlight above the front door are typical features of Georgian architecture, a period that ran from 1730–1800. This private house in Fitzwilliam Square in Dublin is a classic example.

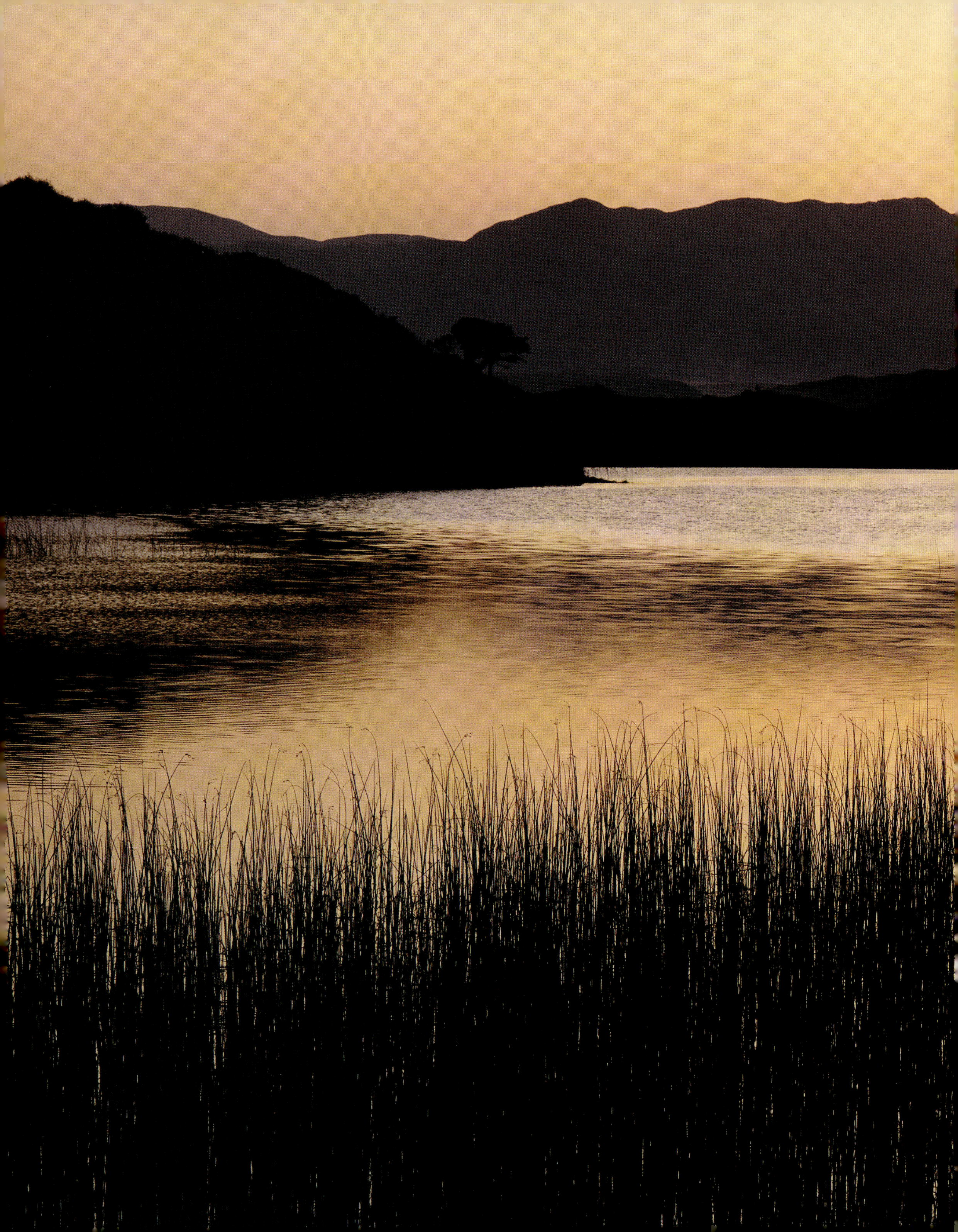

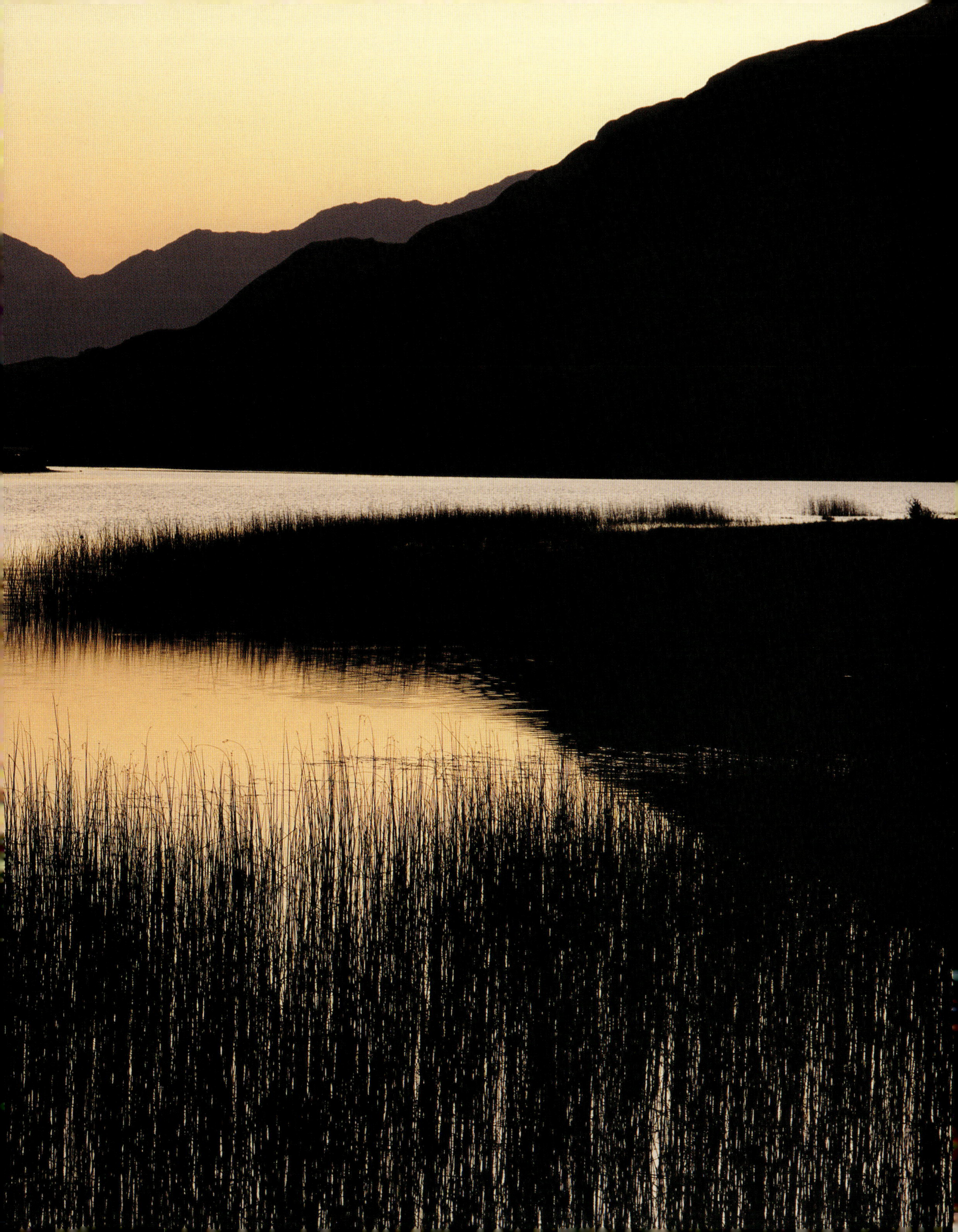

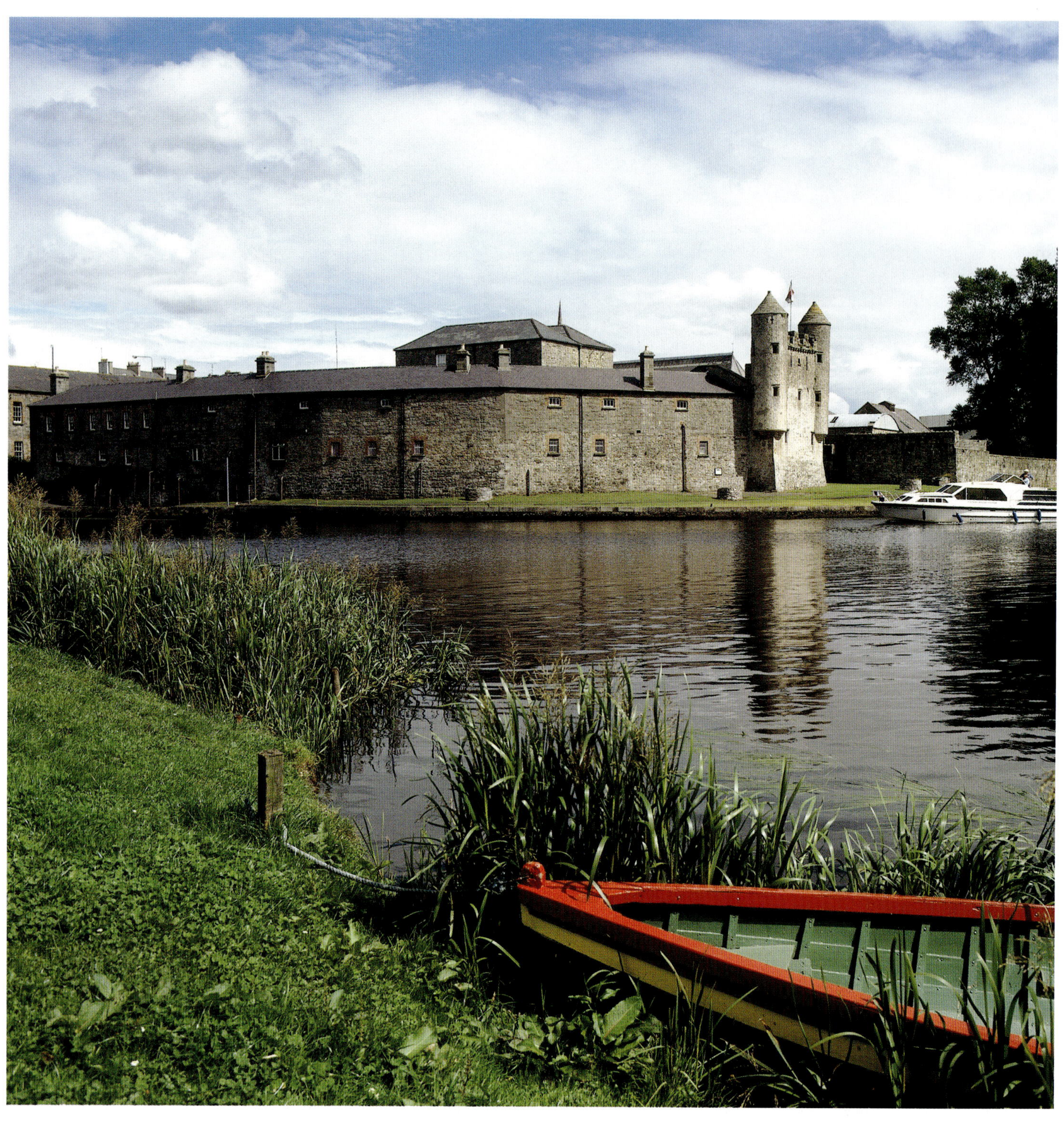

Enniskillen Castle, beside the River Erne in County Fermanagh, became an English garrison fort in the 17th century and later served as part of a military barracks. It now houses two museums. Opposite: these monastic remains are at Glendalough (Glen of the Two Lakes) in County Wicklow. St Kevin sought solitude here in the 6th century and later set up a large religious settlement. Pages 44–45: dawn breaks over the rushes at the edge of Kylemore Lough, which lies at the foot of the Twelve Bens Mountain range in Connemara in County Galway.

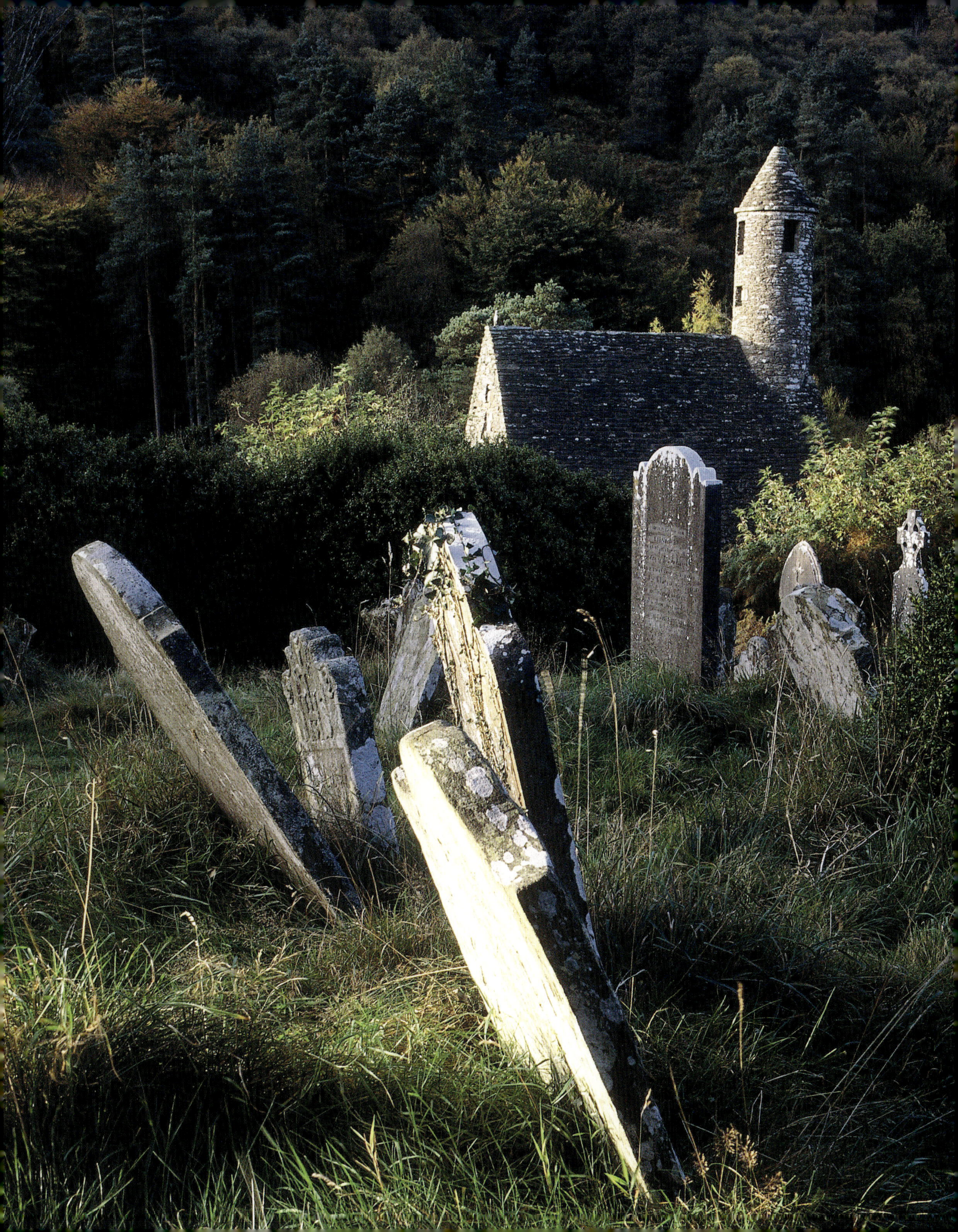

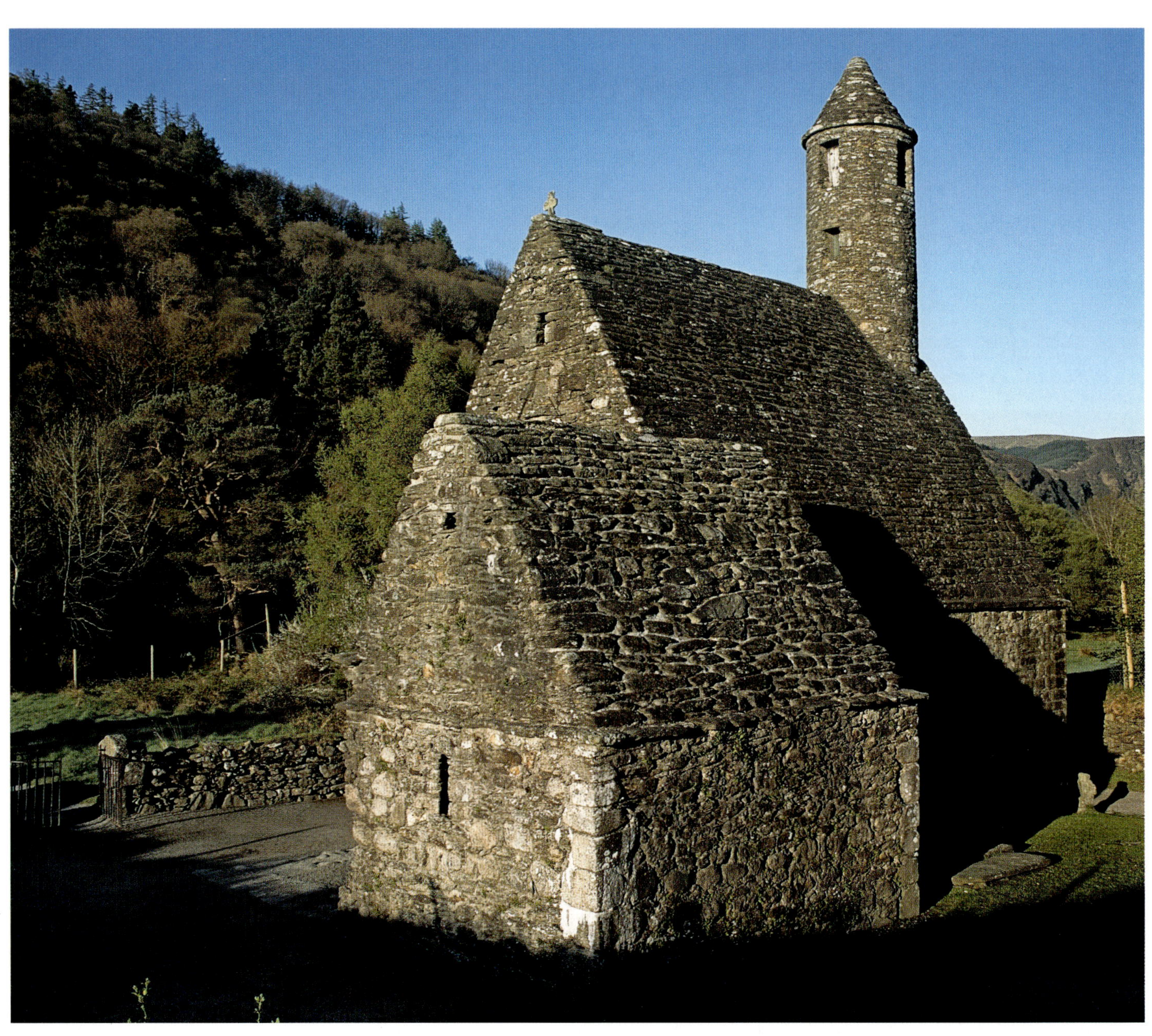

The Chapel of St Kevin is at Glendalough. There are many fanciful and unsubstantiated legends about the saint, but a common theme is his ability to communicate with animals and his preference for their company over that of human beings – especially women's. Opposite: the Government Buildings in Merrion Street Upper, Dublin. Edward VII laid the foundation stone in 1904 but the building was not finally completed until 1922. It was formerly used by the Royal College of Science and then by University College Dublin.

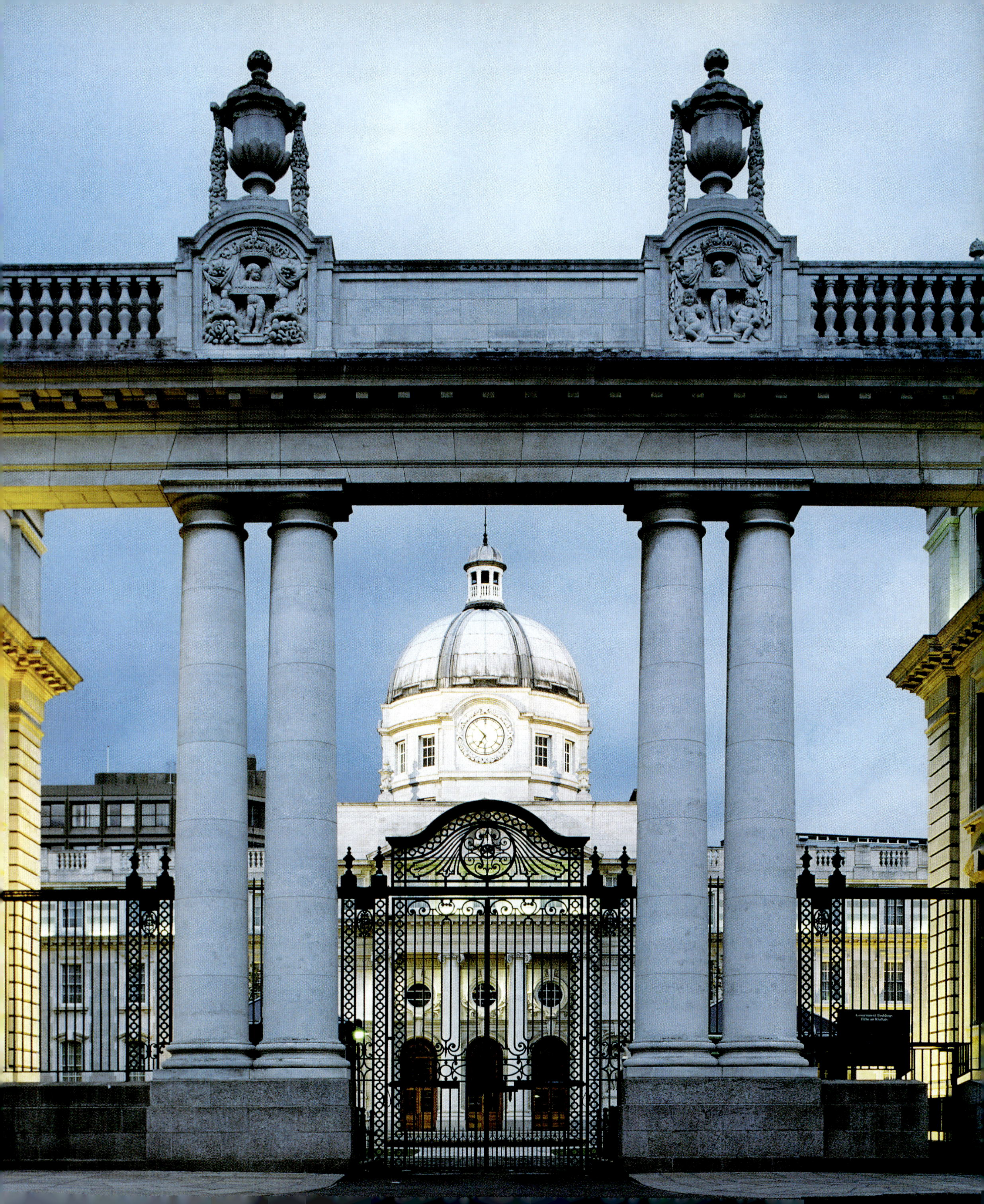
Government Buildings

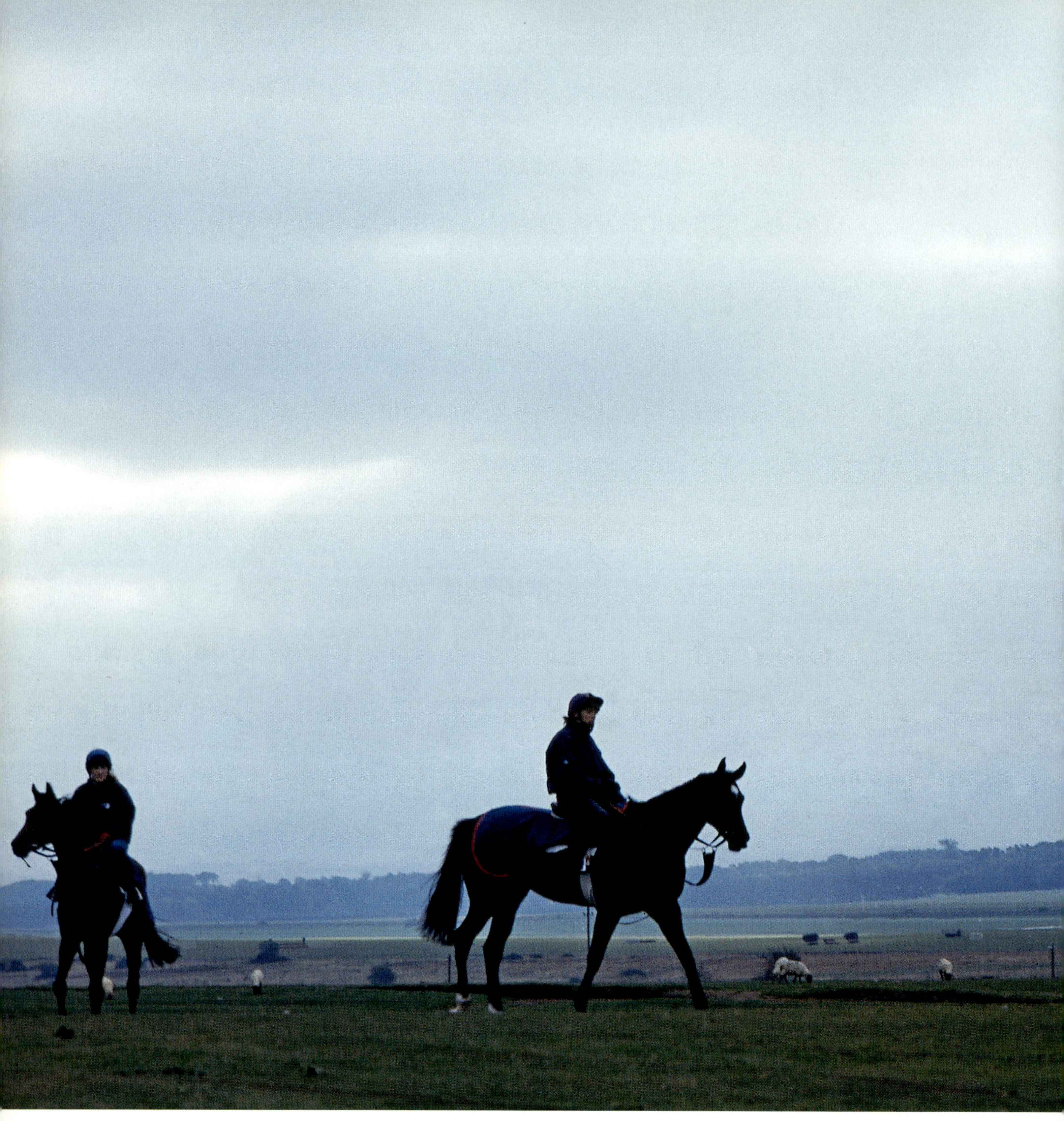

Horses are exercised at the Curragh, Ireland's flat-racing headquarters in County Kildare. The course hosts all five of the Classic Races, including the Irish Derby. Curragh means 'place of the running horse'.

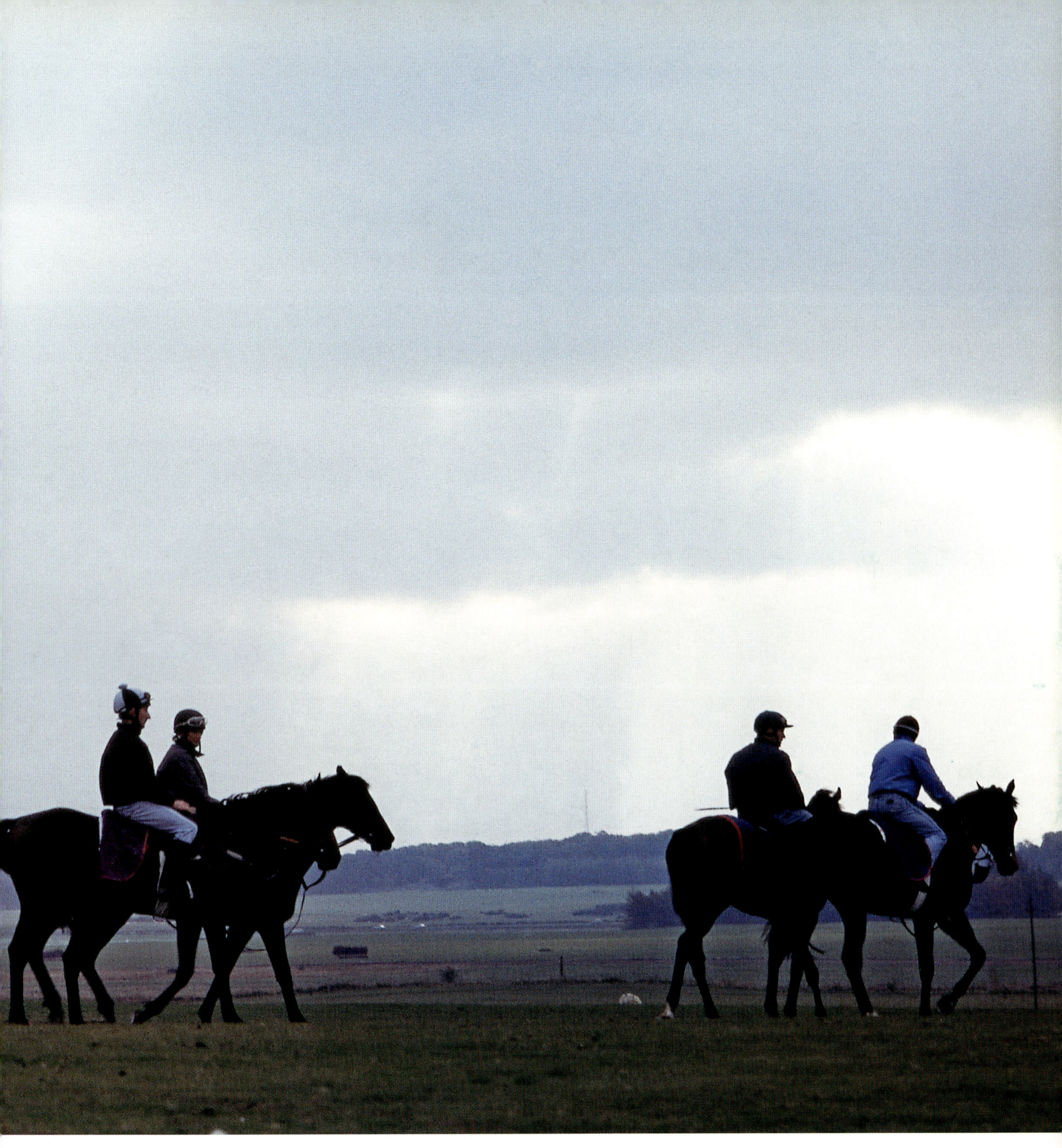

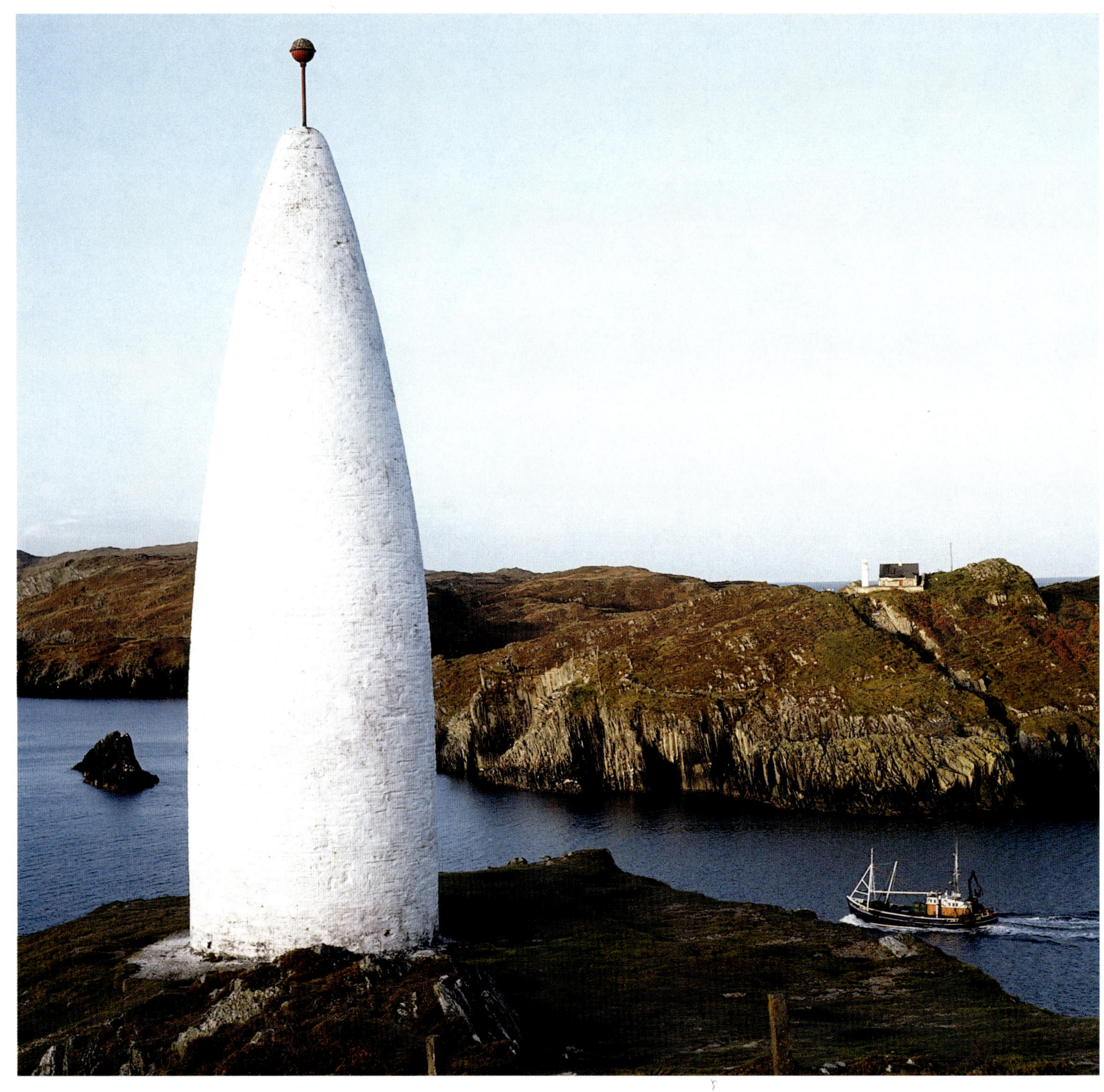

The Baltimore Beacon (also known as Lot's Wife – in a biblical story, Lot's wife is turned into a pillar of salt) stands at the entrance to Baltimore Harbour in County Cork. The town's long tradition of boat-building is celebrated in the annual Wooden Boat Festival, held in May.

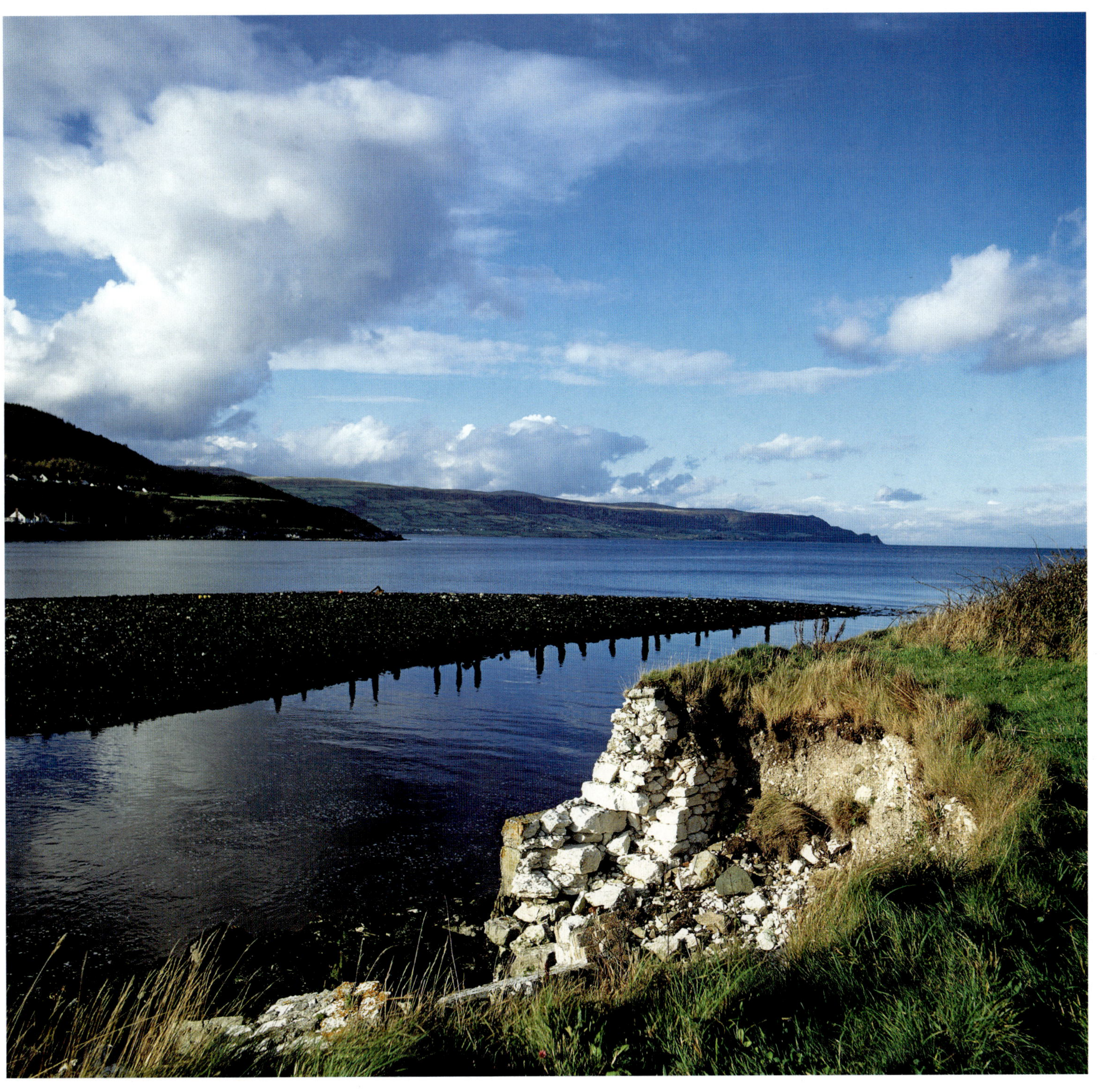

Glenarm village takes its name from the glen in which it lies, one of the nine Glens of Antrim in Northern Ireland that radiate inward from the coast towards Lough Neagh. Its limestone harbor has been restored and attractions nearby include Glenarm Forest Park, Glenarm Castle, and a salmon fishery.

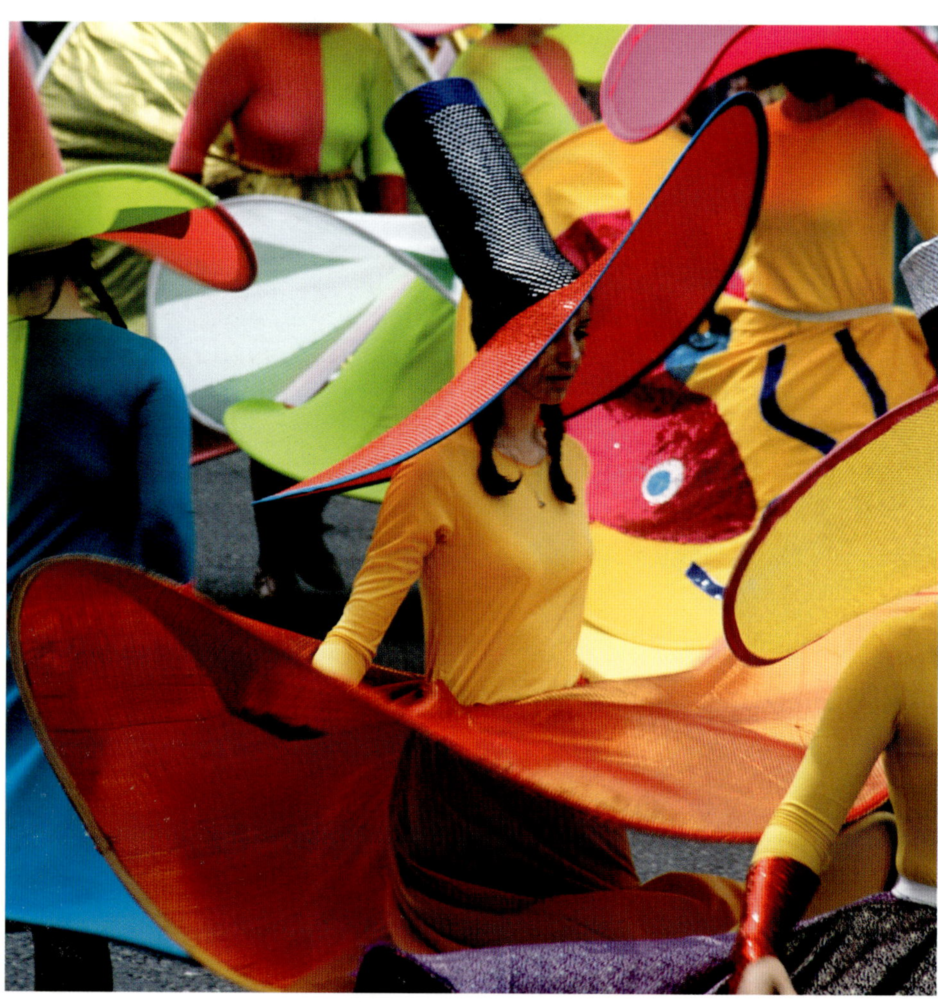

The annual St Patrick's Day parade in Dublin is just one of hundreds of celebrations that takes place among the Irish diaspora around the world on March 17, Patrick's religious feast day. Opposite: traditional Irish dancing is a highlight of the Galway International Oyster Festival, a three-day round of parties, music, entertainment, and gourmet feasting held every September.

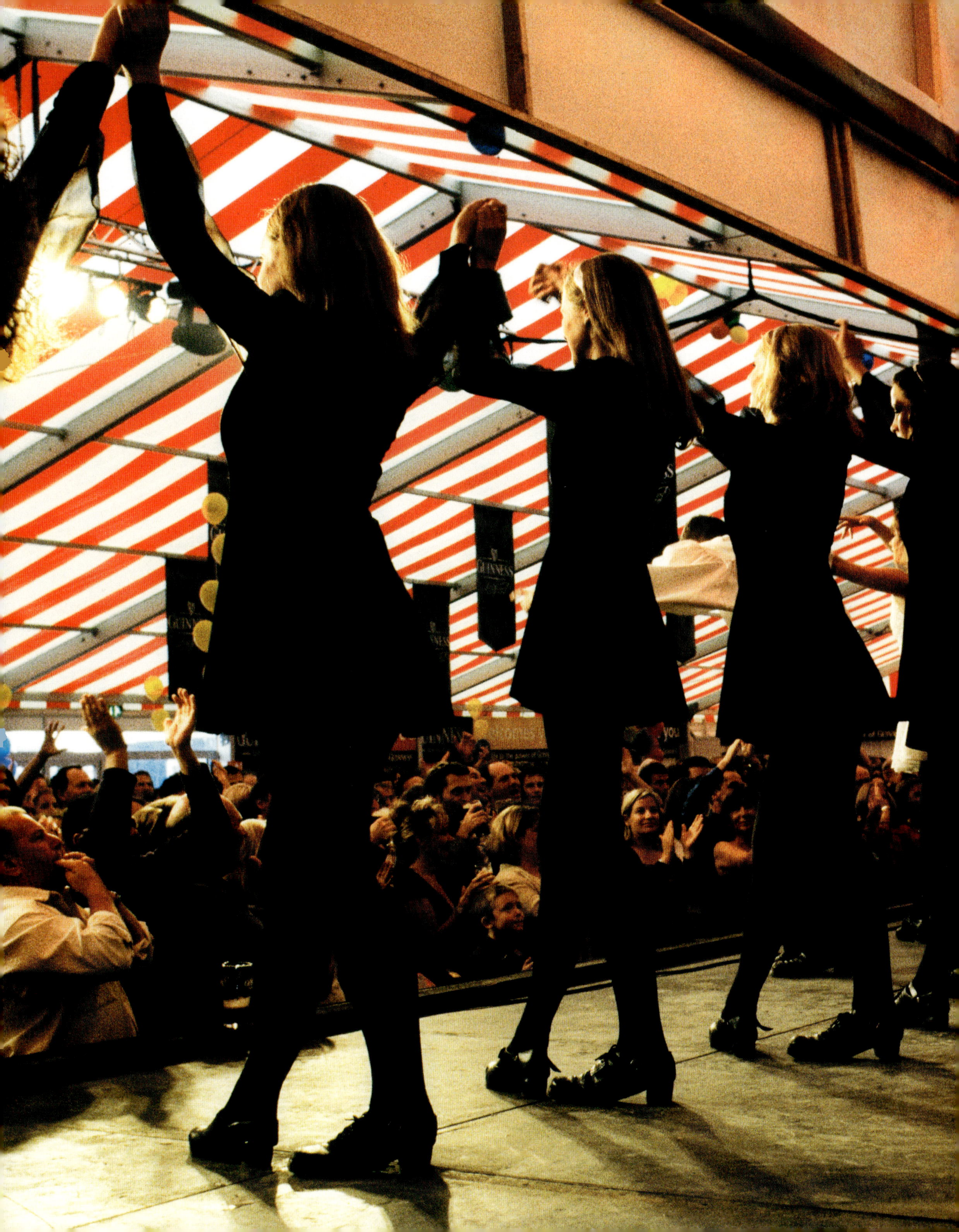

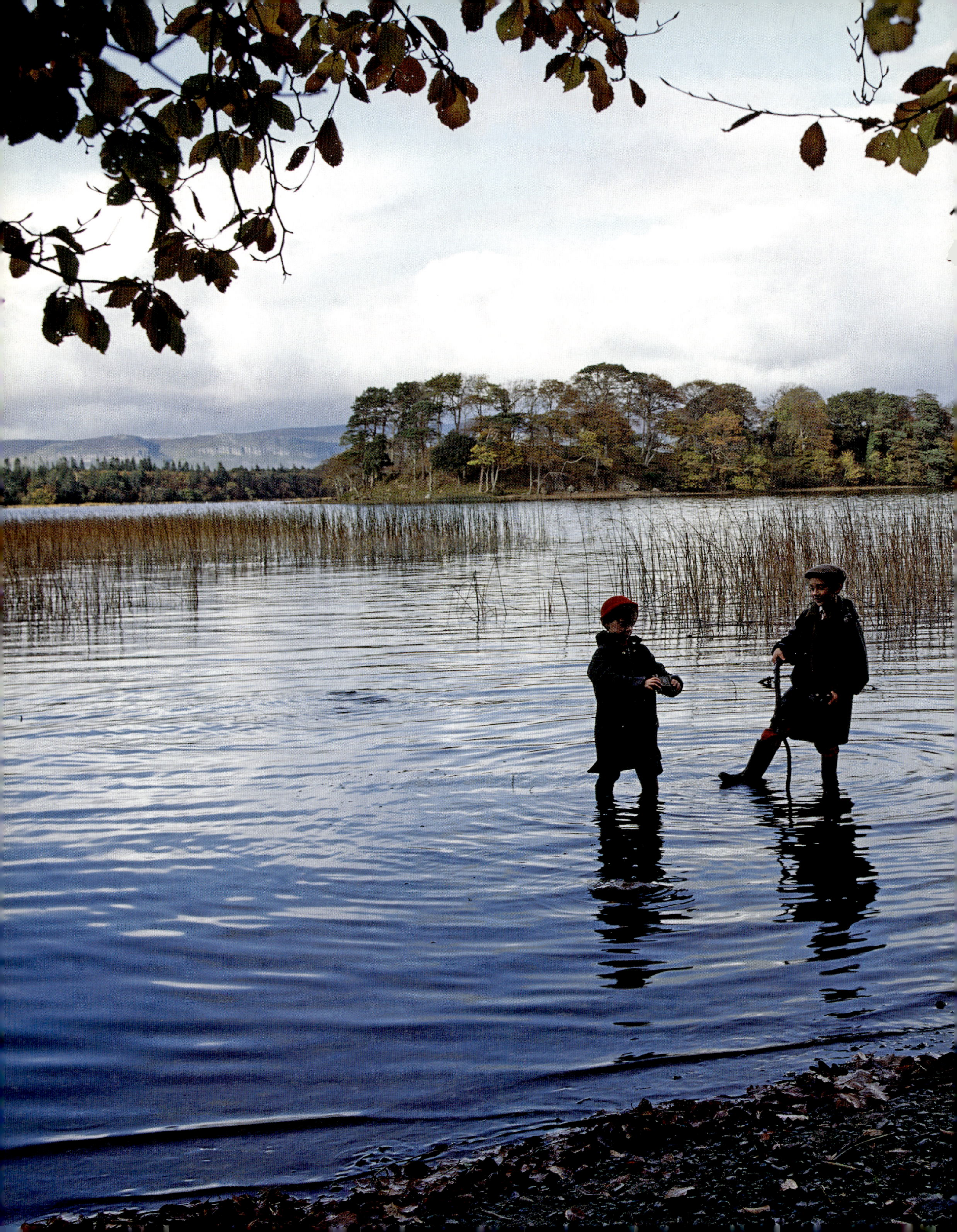

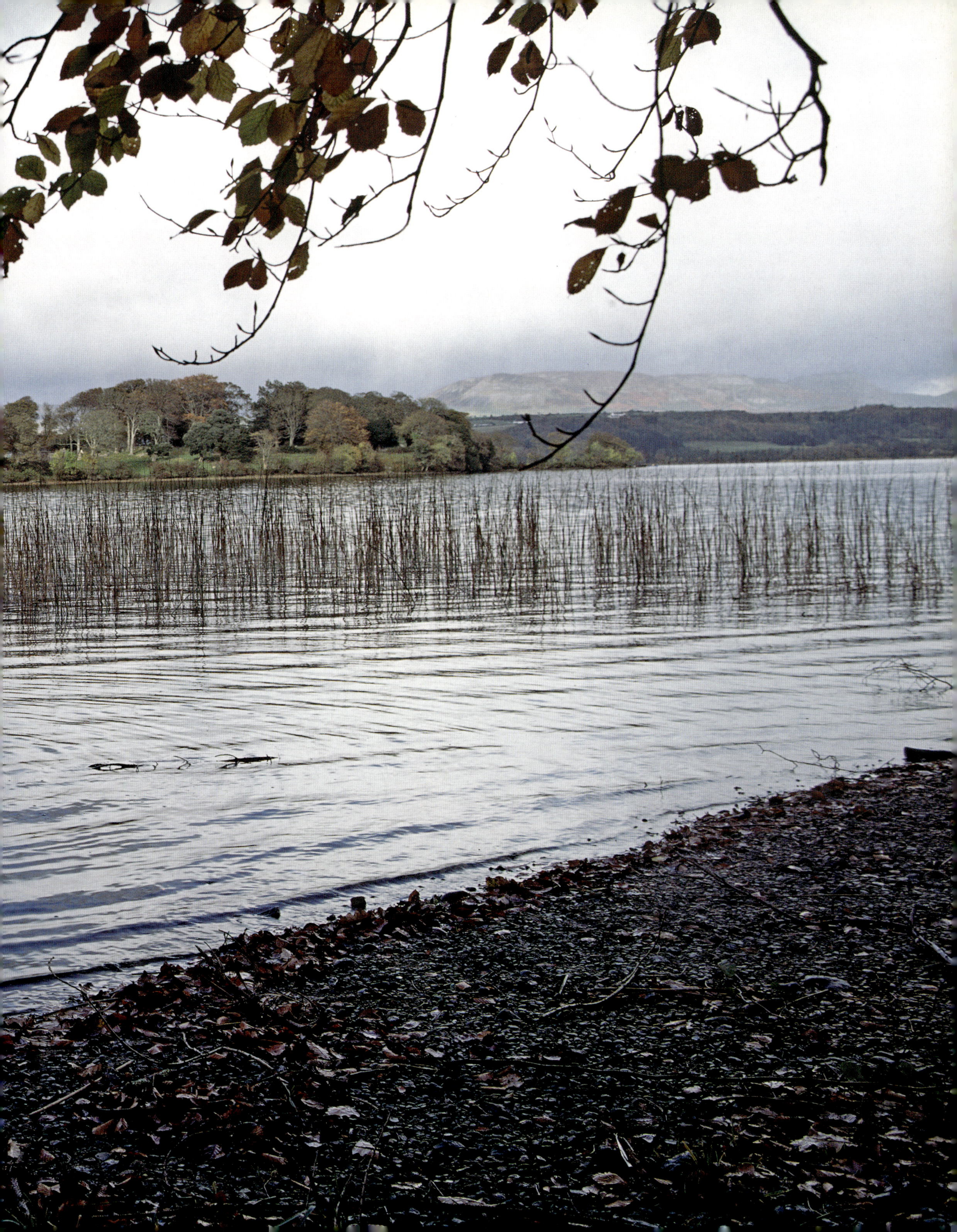

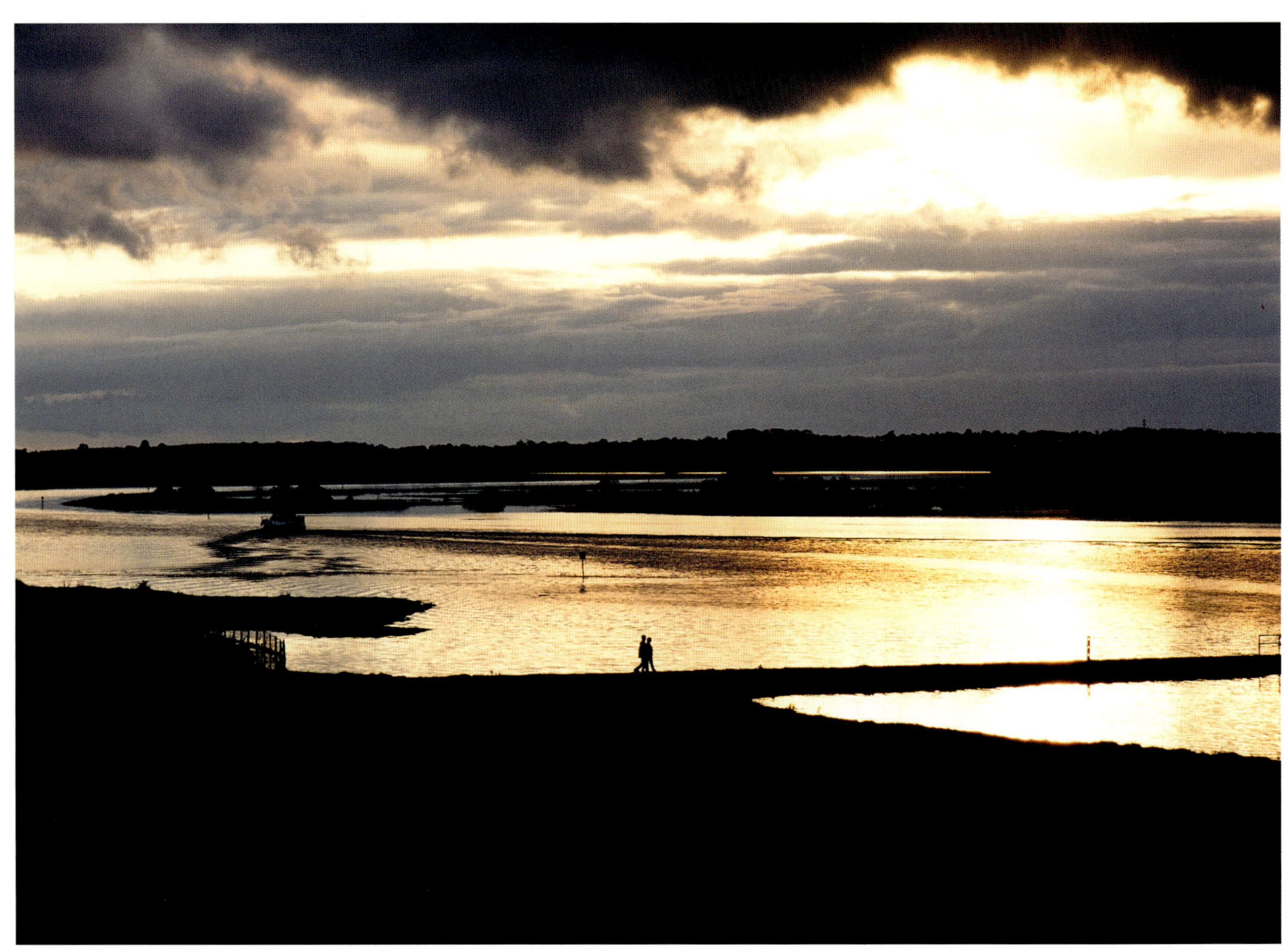

Looking out over the River Shannon off Clonmacnois as the sun sets over the village, casting a golden glow over the waters.
Opposite: around 40,000 hexagonal-shaped basalt columns make up the Giant's Causeway in County Antrim. It was formed about 62 to 65 million years ago by volcanic action – not as legend has it, by the giant Finn MacCool, who was trying to reach the Scottish coast.
Previous page: Lough Gill in County Sligo. One of the lake's many islands, Lake Isle of Innisfree, was made famous by the Irish poet William Butler Yeats (1865–1939) in his poem of the same name. A good view of the whole lake can be seen from Dooney Rock.

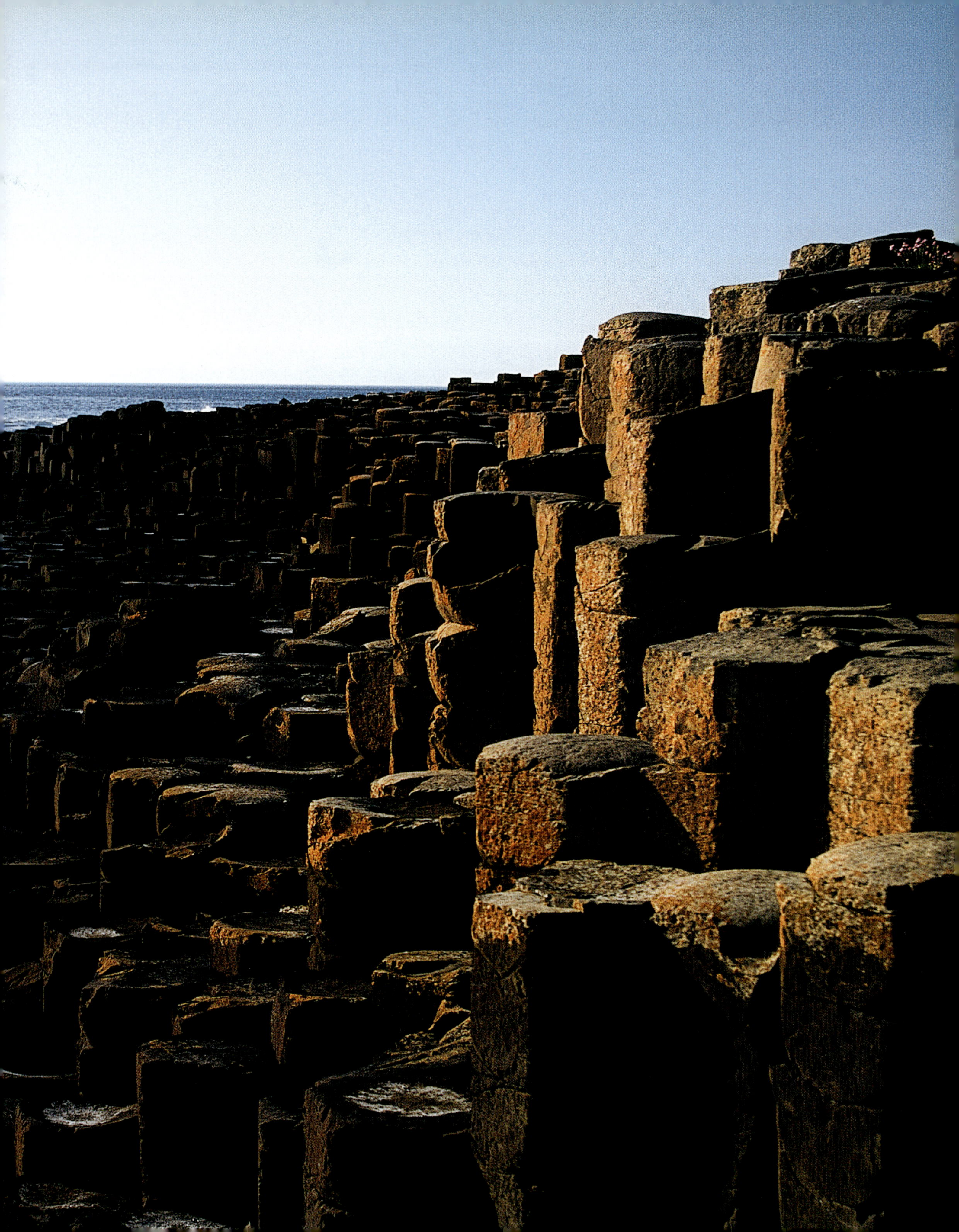

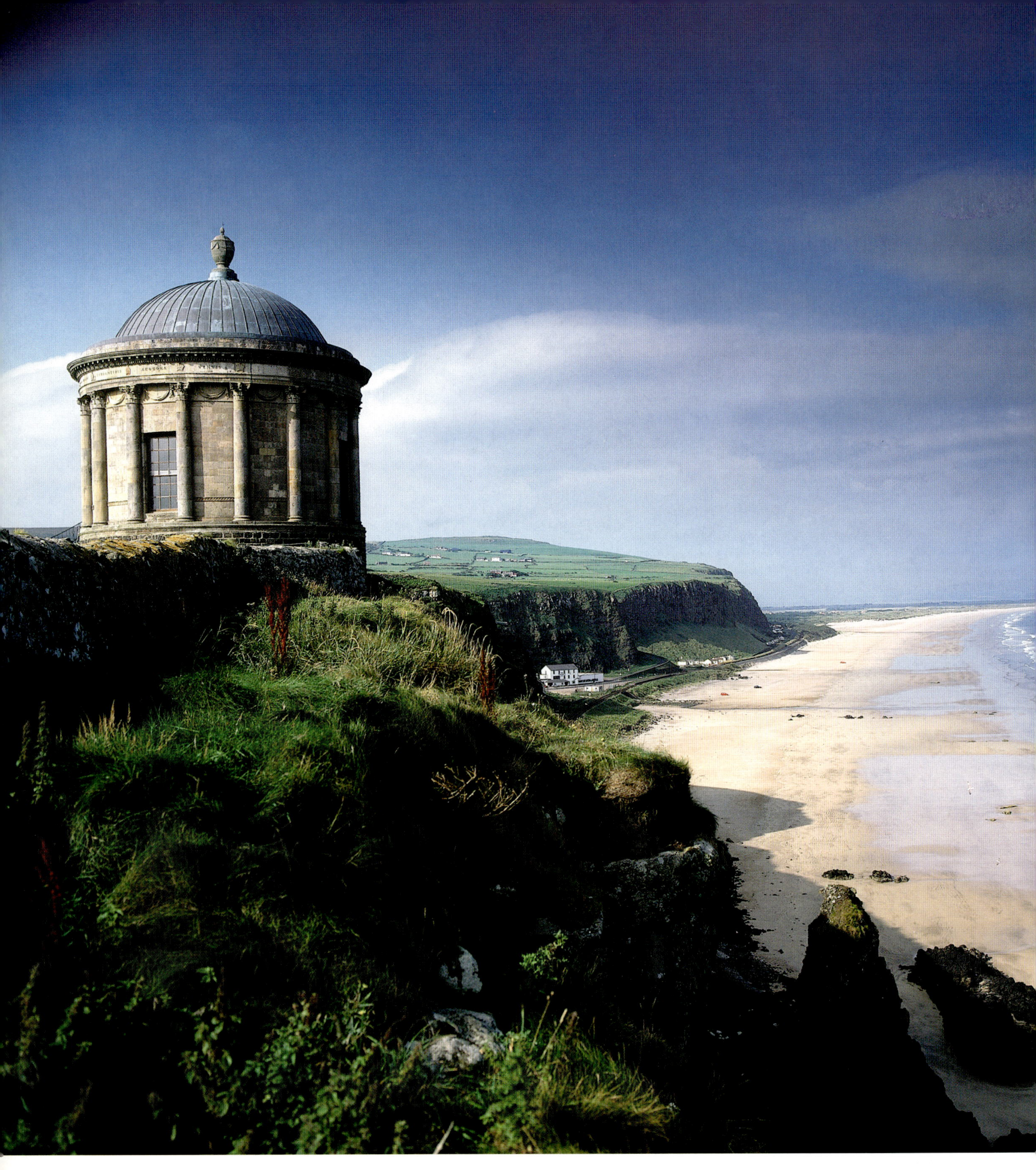

The classical-style Mussenden Temple, built in the 18th century as a library by the eccentric Earl Bishop Hervey of Derry, is just one of the attractions on the Downhill Estate in Northern Ireland.

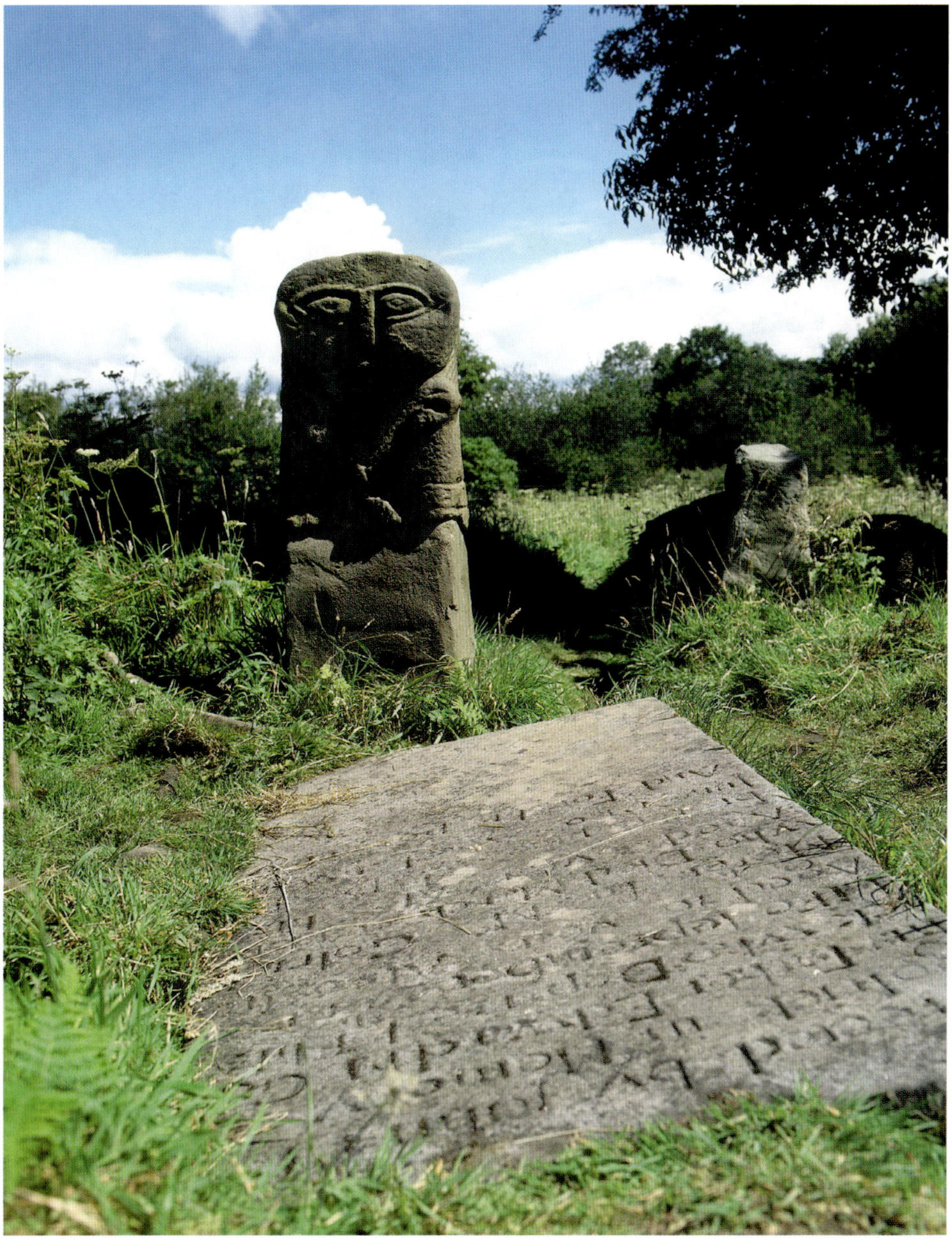

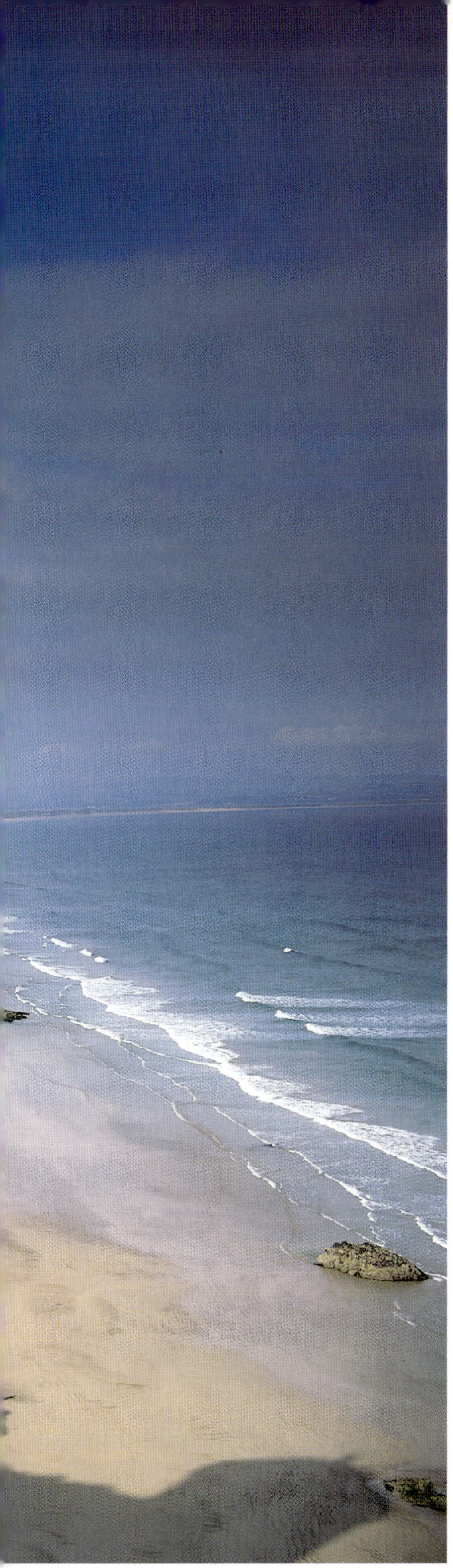

A strange, two-sided Janus figure stands in an ancient Christian graveyard on Boa Island, on the north shore of Lower Lough Earne. The carving stands so that its faces look due east and west and the sun rises and sets directly above it at the vernal equinox.

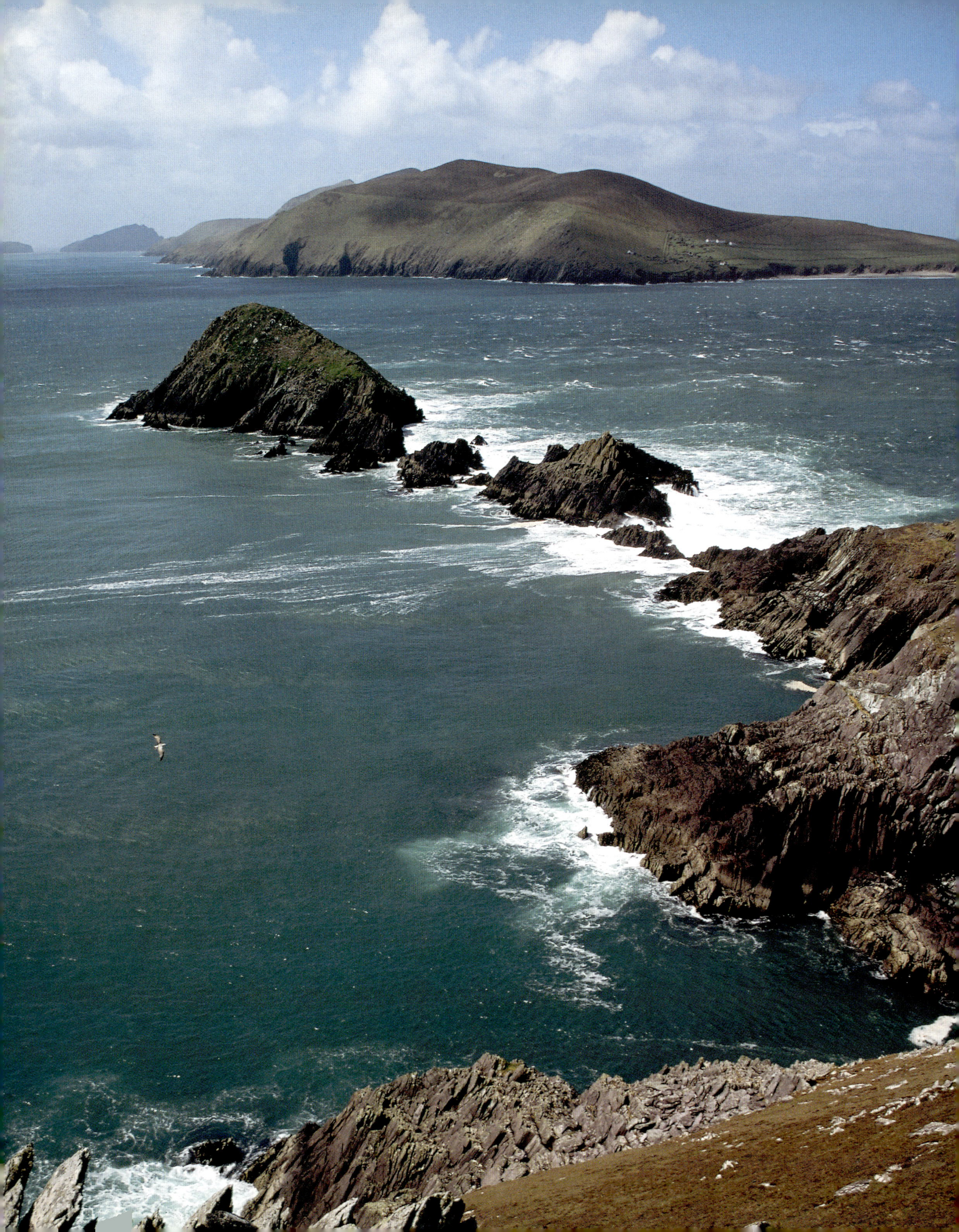

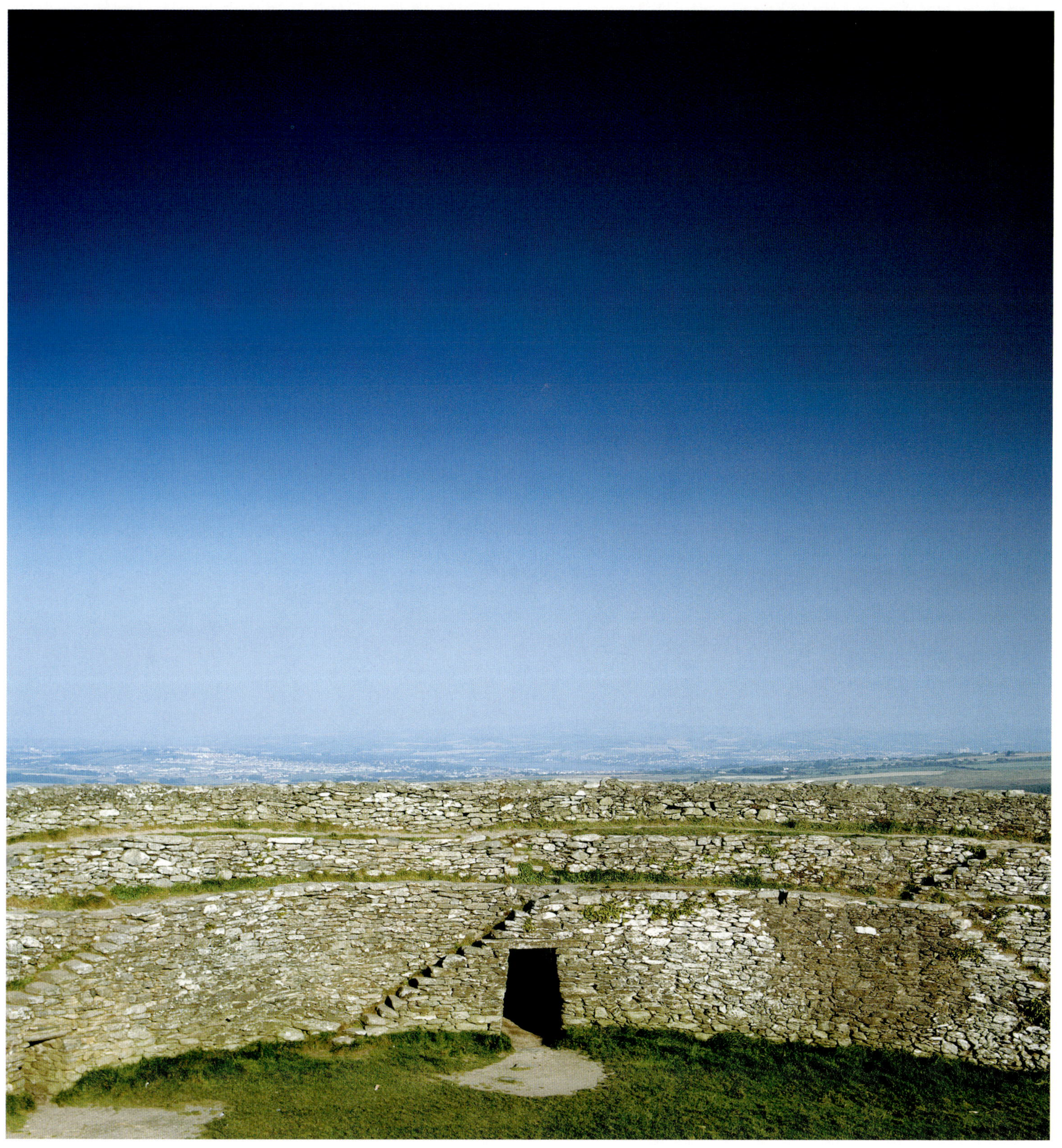

The circular stone fort of Grianan of Aileach in County Donegal, built in the early Christian era, served as the royal seat of the O'Neill clan from the 5th to the 12th century. It was reconstructed in the 1870s. Opposite: a view of the Blasket Islands off the Dingle Peninsula on the southwest coast. Uninhabited today, the islands were once home to a thriving community. Boats take visitors to and fro across the Sound.

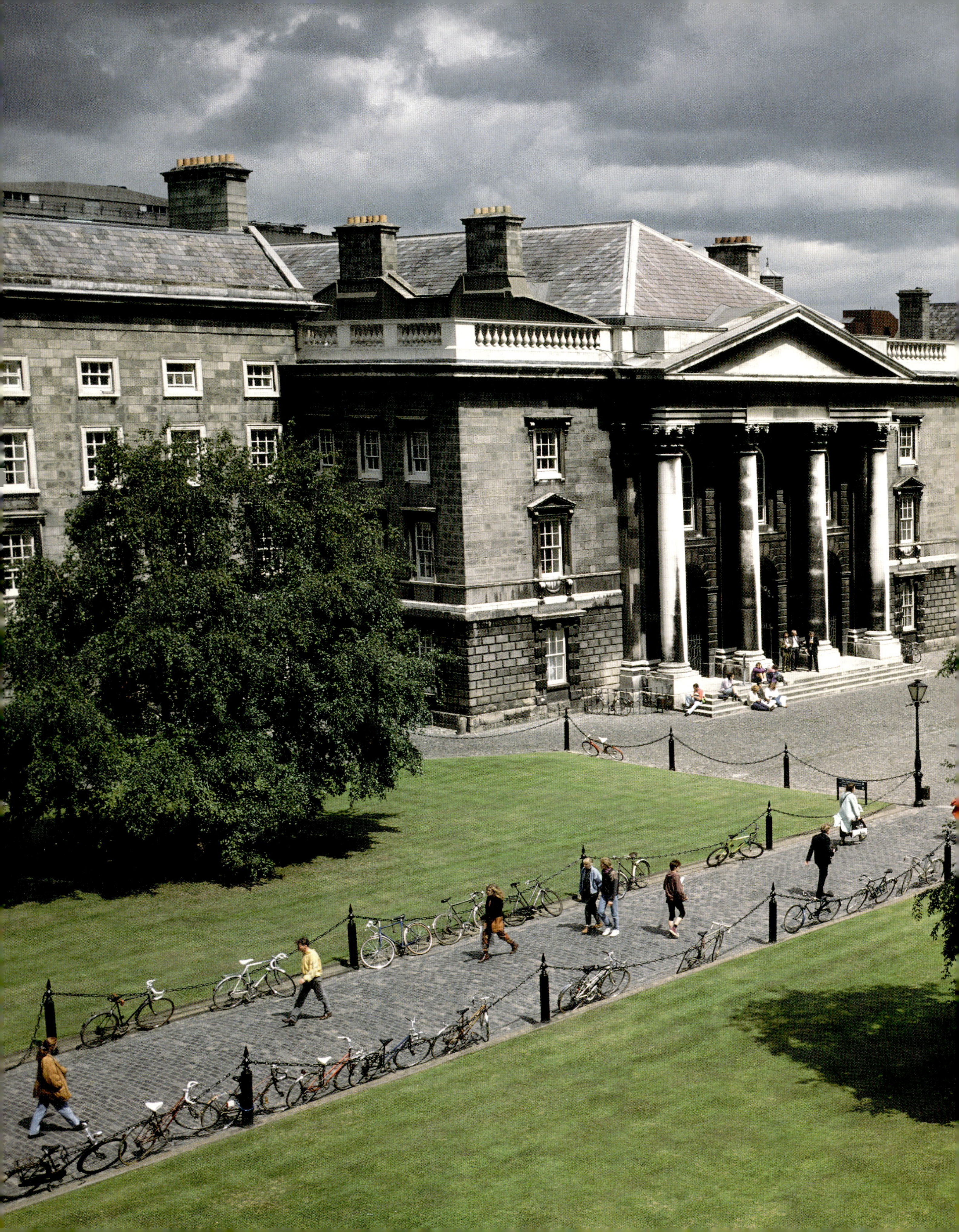

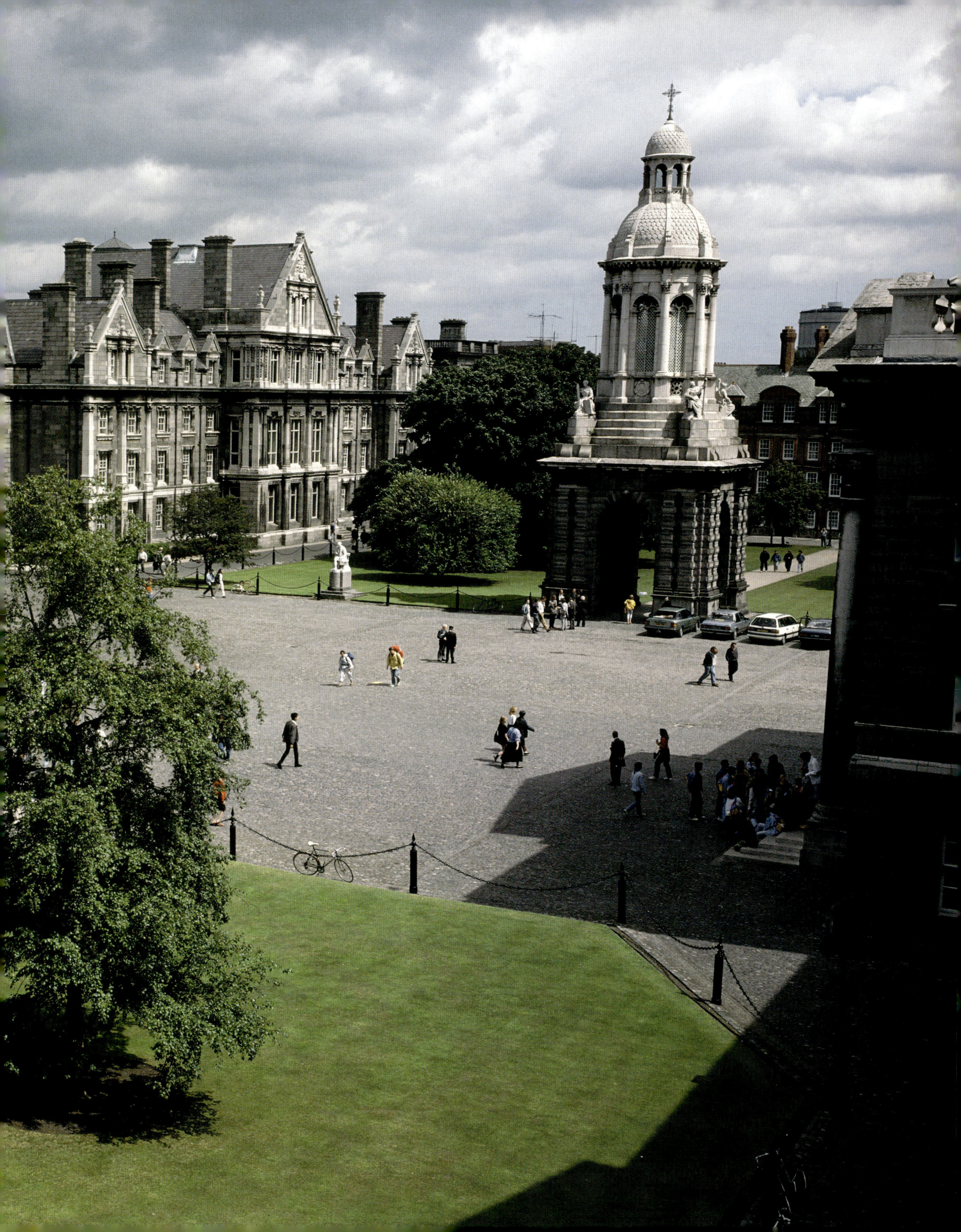

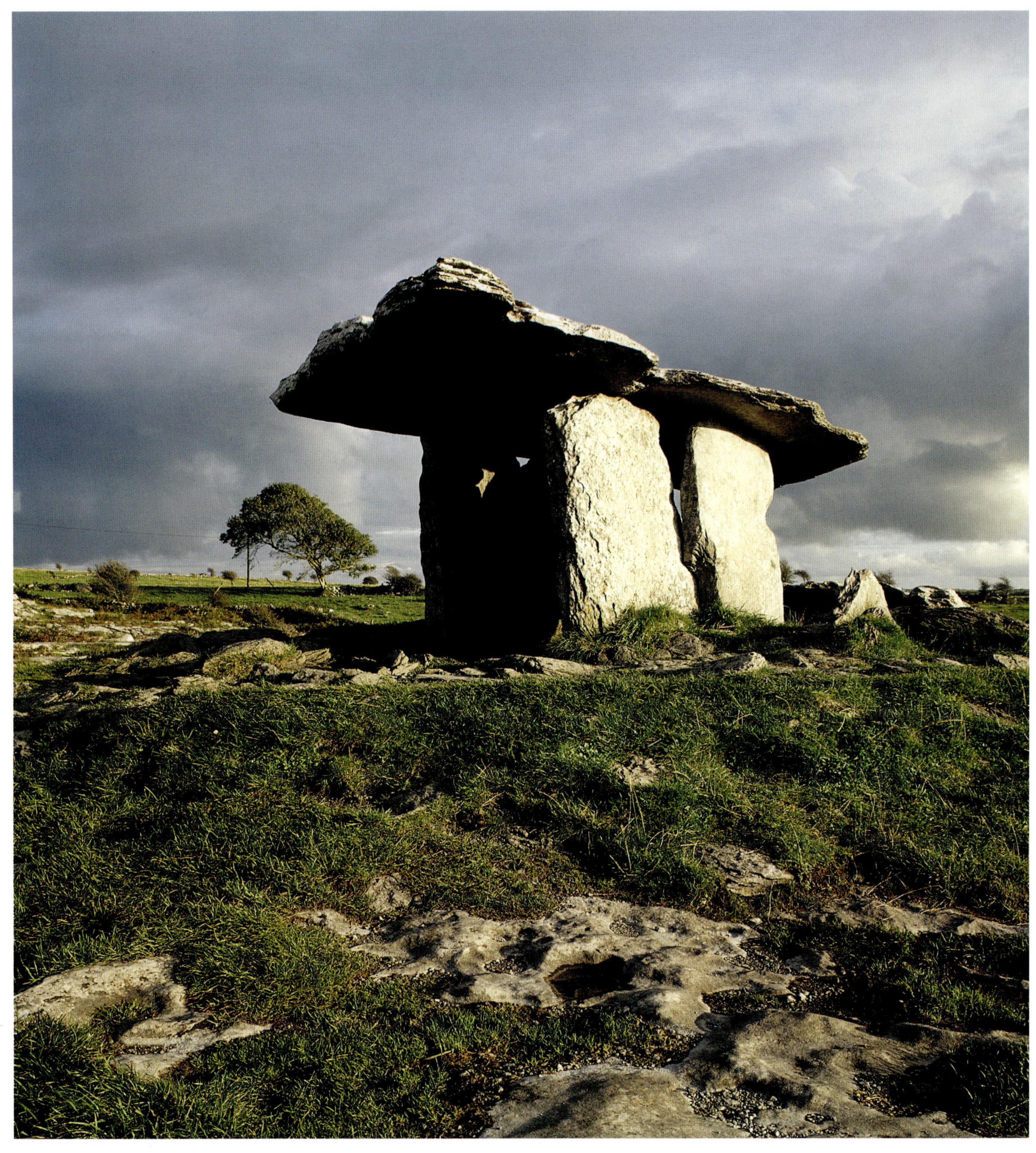

Dozens of ancient dolmens, or portal tombs, are scattered over the Burren in County Clare.
Pages 64–65: the principal buildings of Trinity College, Dublin, were founded in 1592 by Elizabeth I on the site of an Augustinian monastery. The college is set in its own grounds, known as College Park.

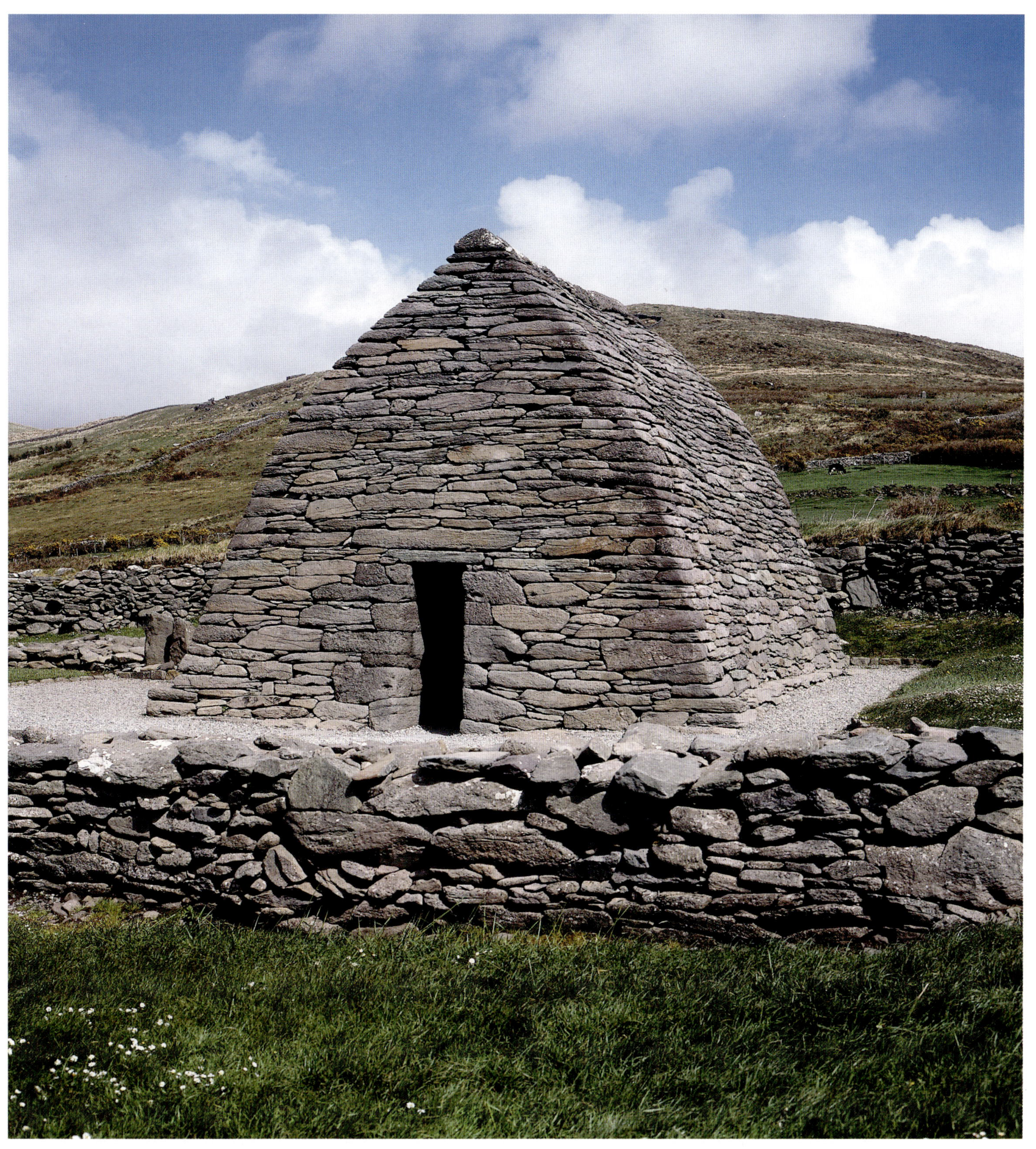

Gallarus Oratory, a very early Christian church on the Dingle Peninsula, is a classic example of the art of dry-stone corbelling, a building technique first developed by Neolithic tomb-makers. The horizontal stones were layed at a slight angle, with the lower edge on the outside, to allow water to run off.

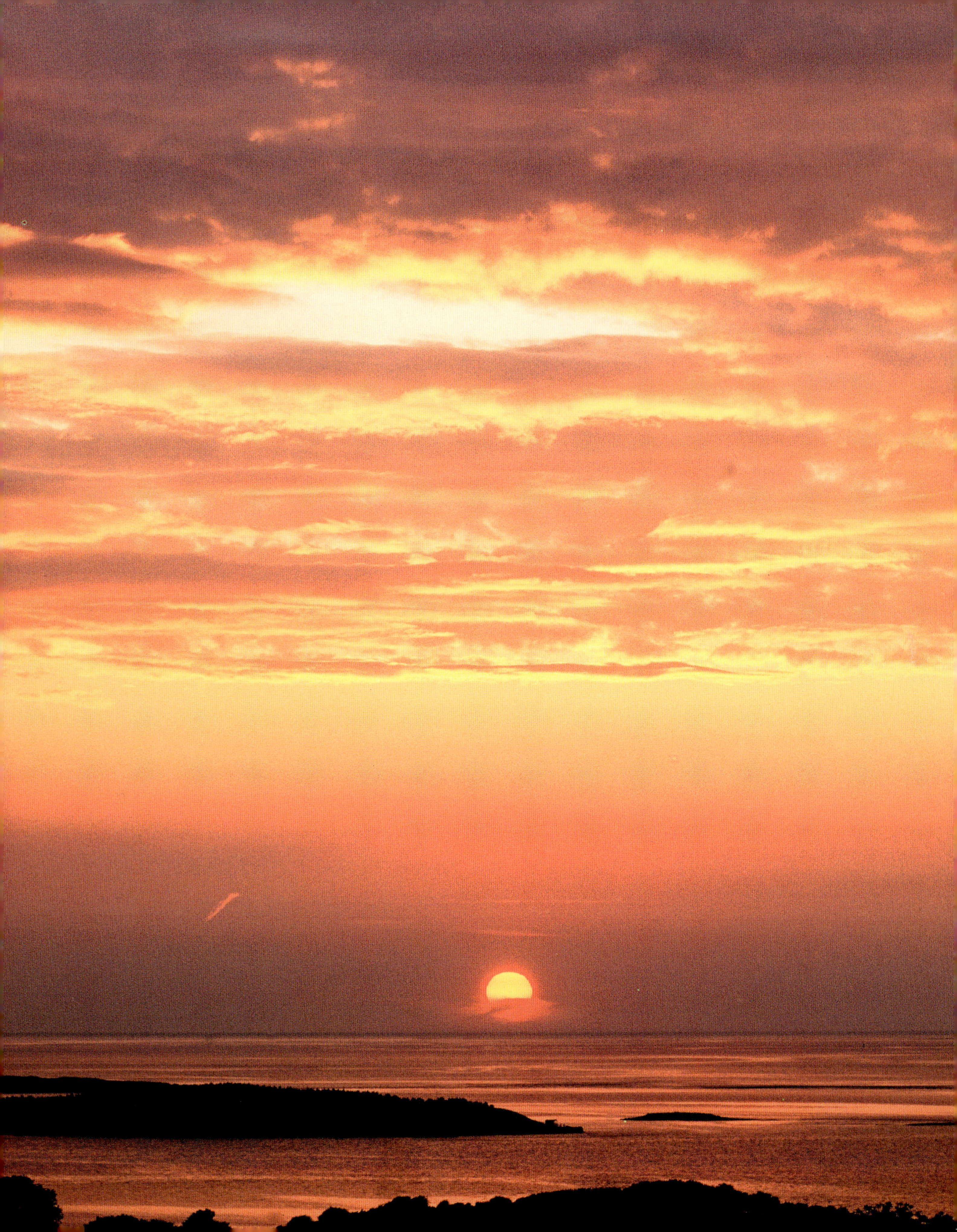

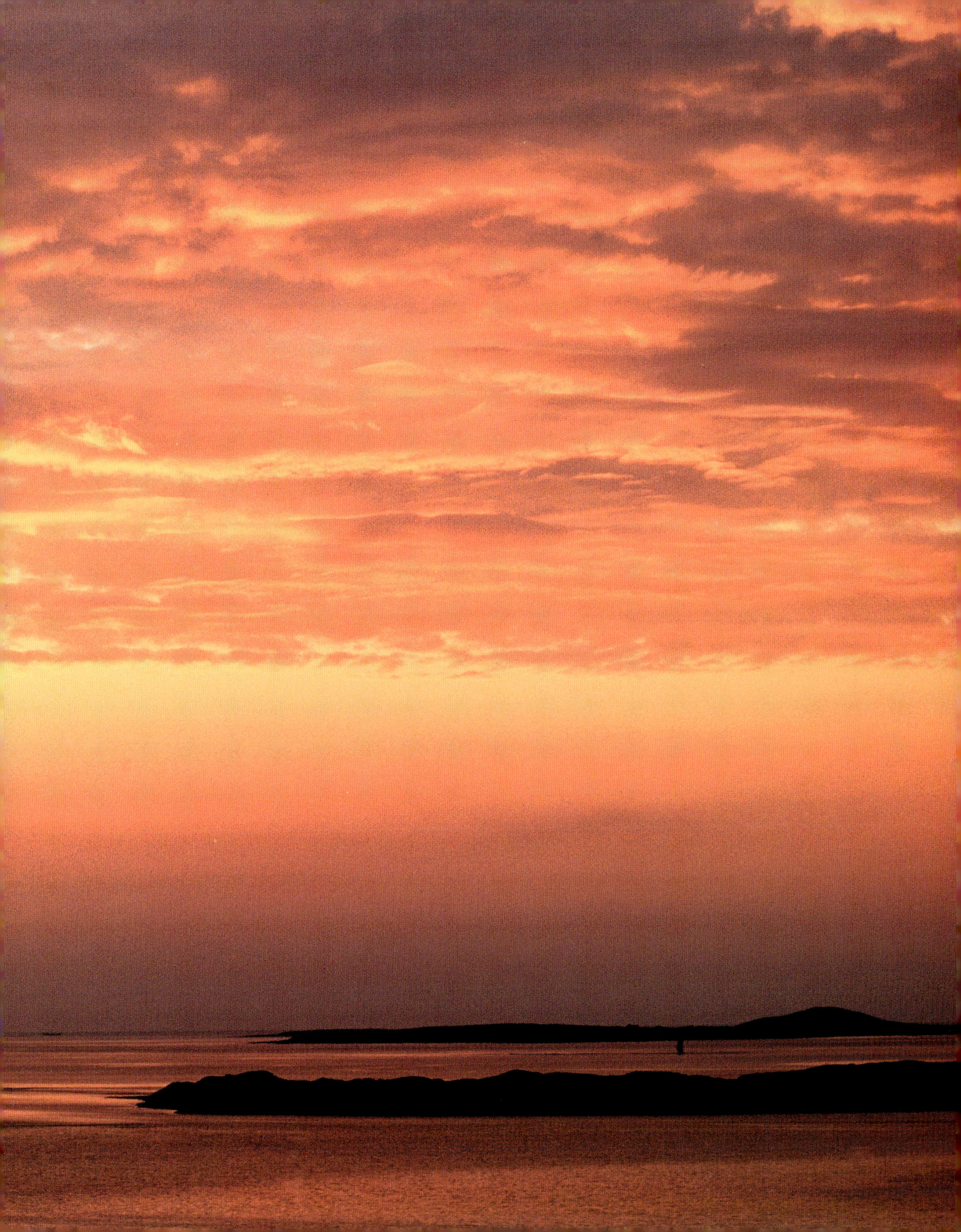

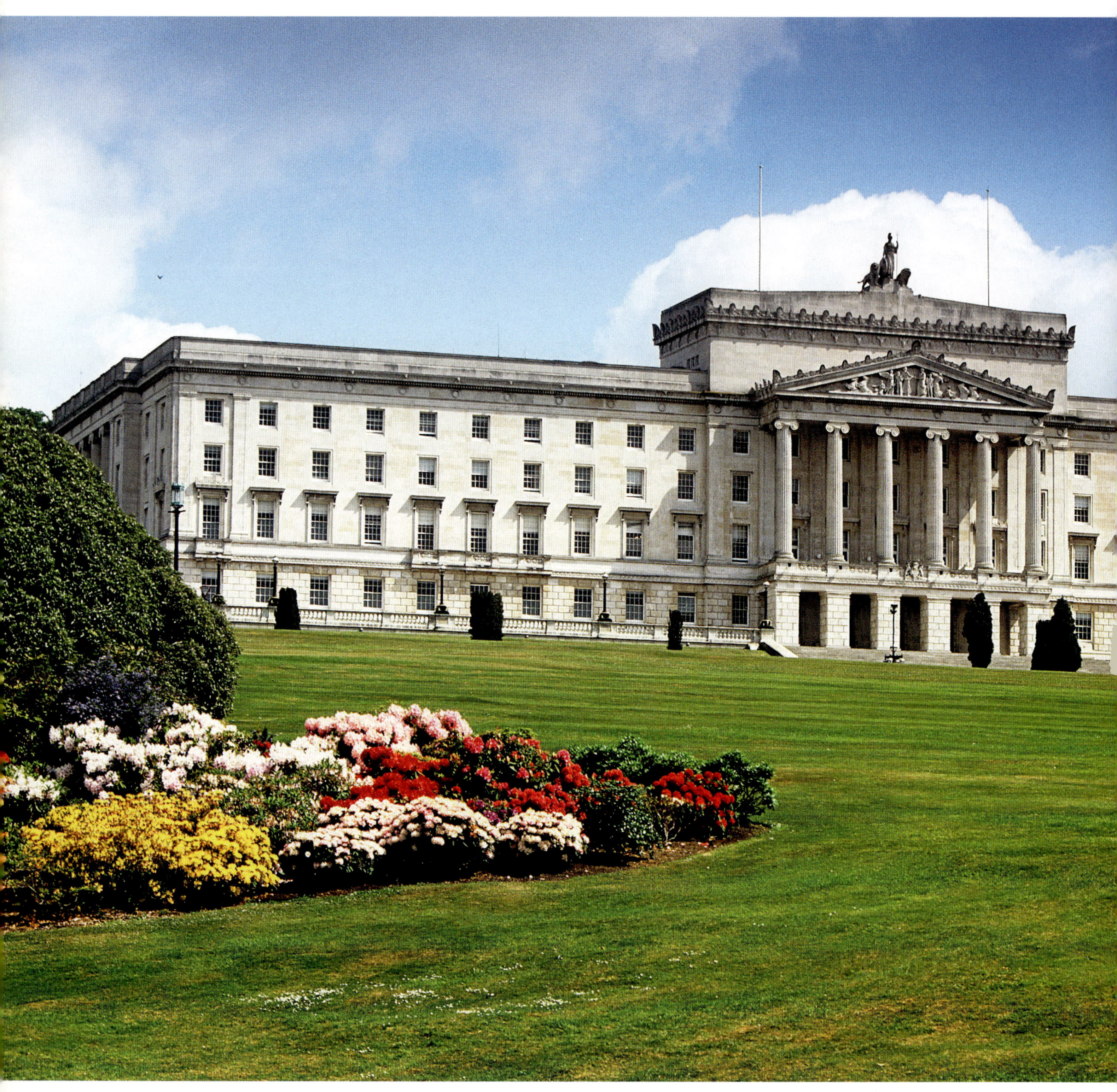

The Parliament Building in Belfast has been the home of the Northern Ireland Assembly since 1998. It was built from English Portland stone and has a granite base quarried from the Mountains of Mourne. Pages 68–69: Sligo Bay on the west coast of Ireland. The town of Sligo (its name means 'place of shells') stands on the bay at the mouth of the Garavogue River.

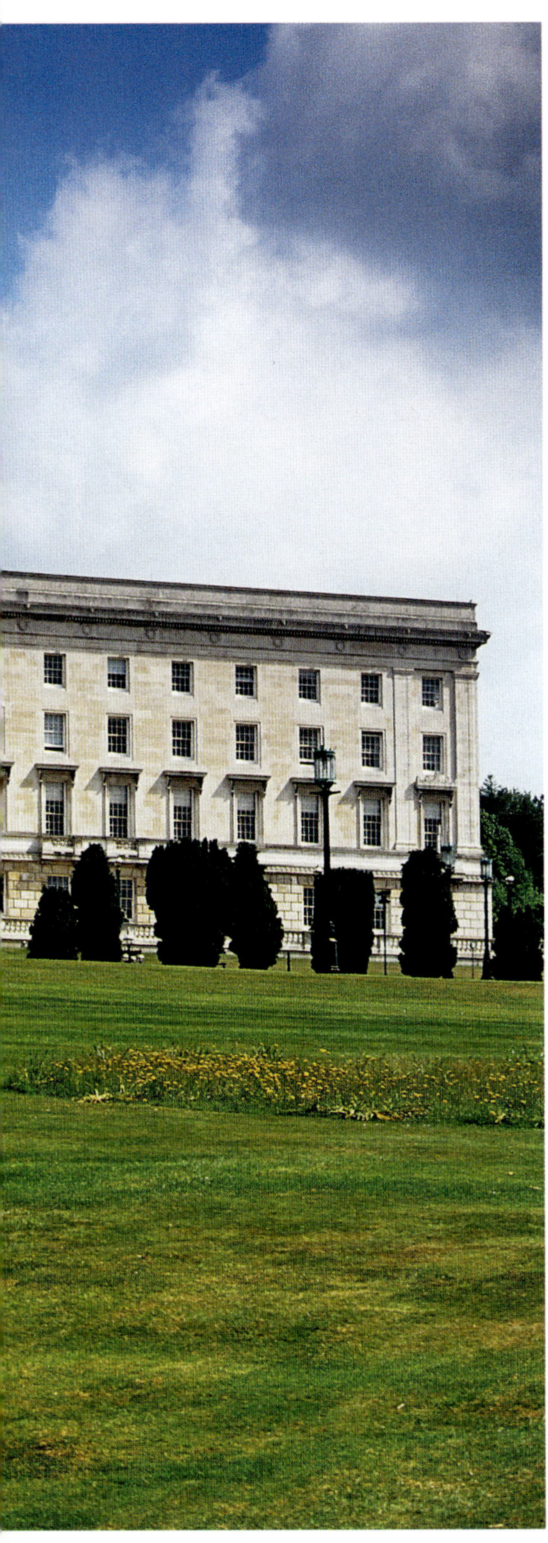

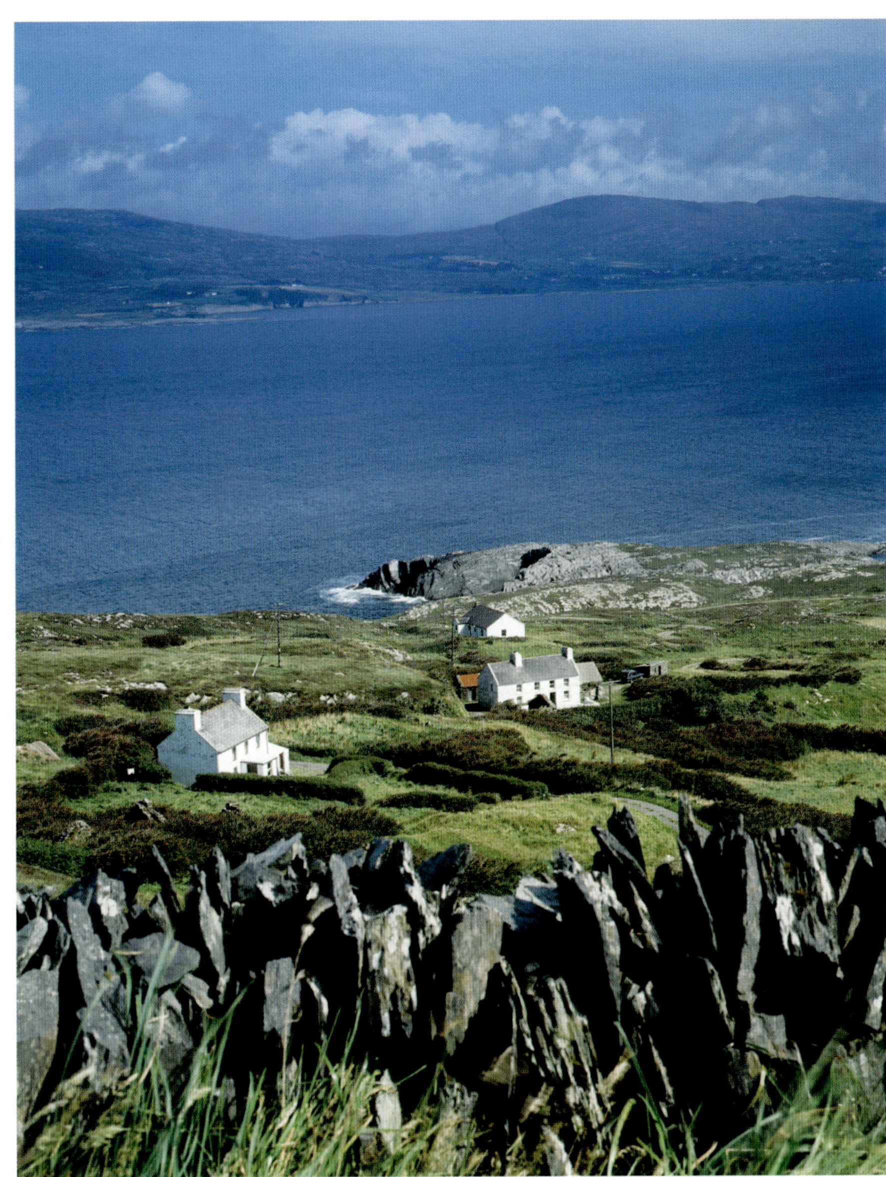

Dunmanus Bay is one of the deep inlets in western Cork. It is bounded on the northern side by the Sheep's Head Peninsula and on the southern side by the Mizen Peninsula. Bantry Bay lies on the other side of Sheep's Head.

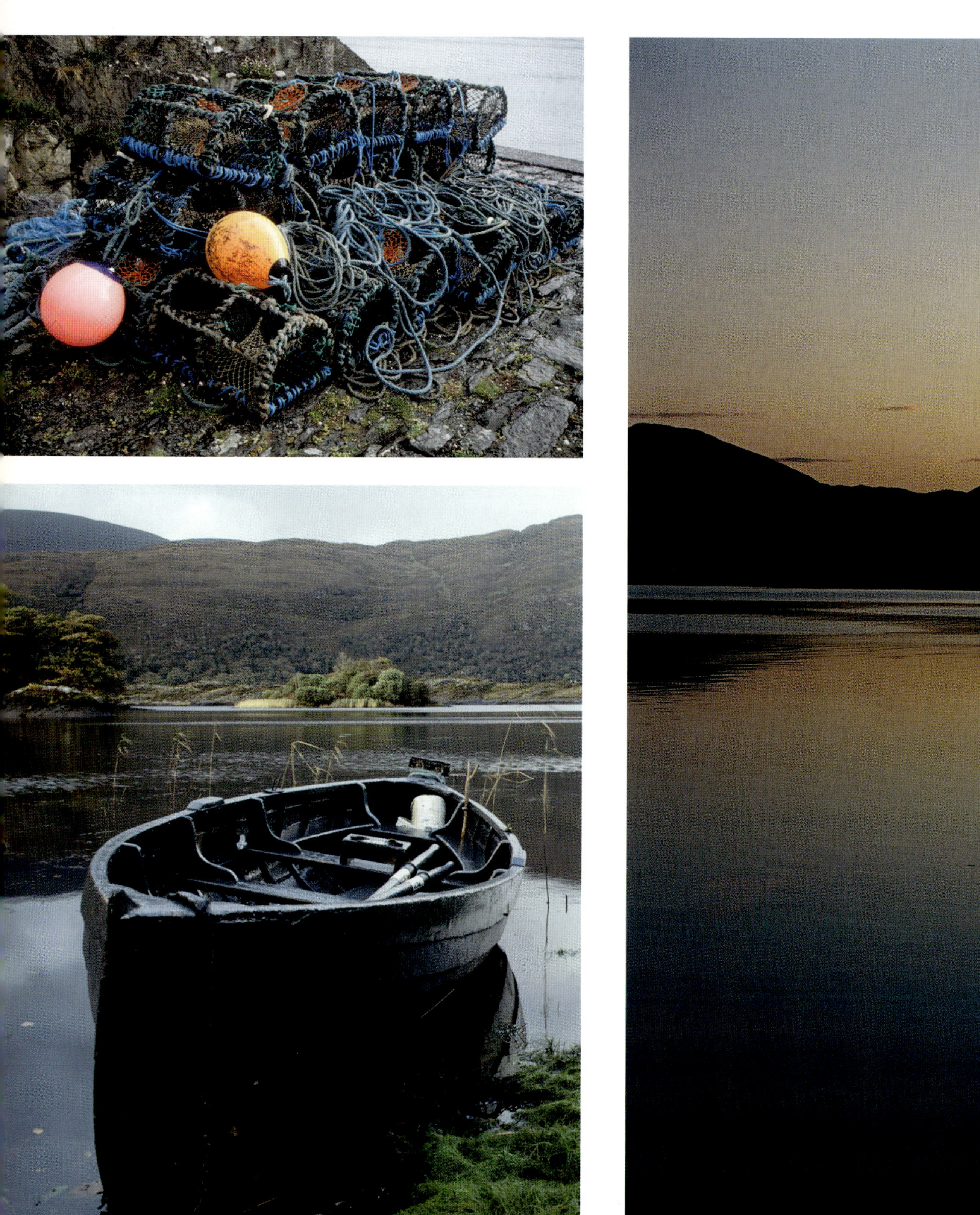

A boat moured by the shore in Lough Leane, part of the Killarney National Park.
Top: lobster pots are stacked on Dooneen Pier on Sheep's Head Peninsula in County Cork.

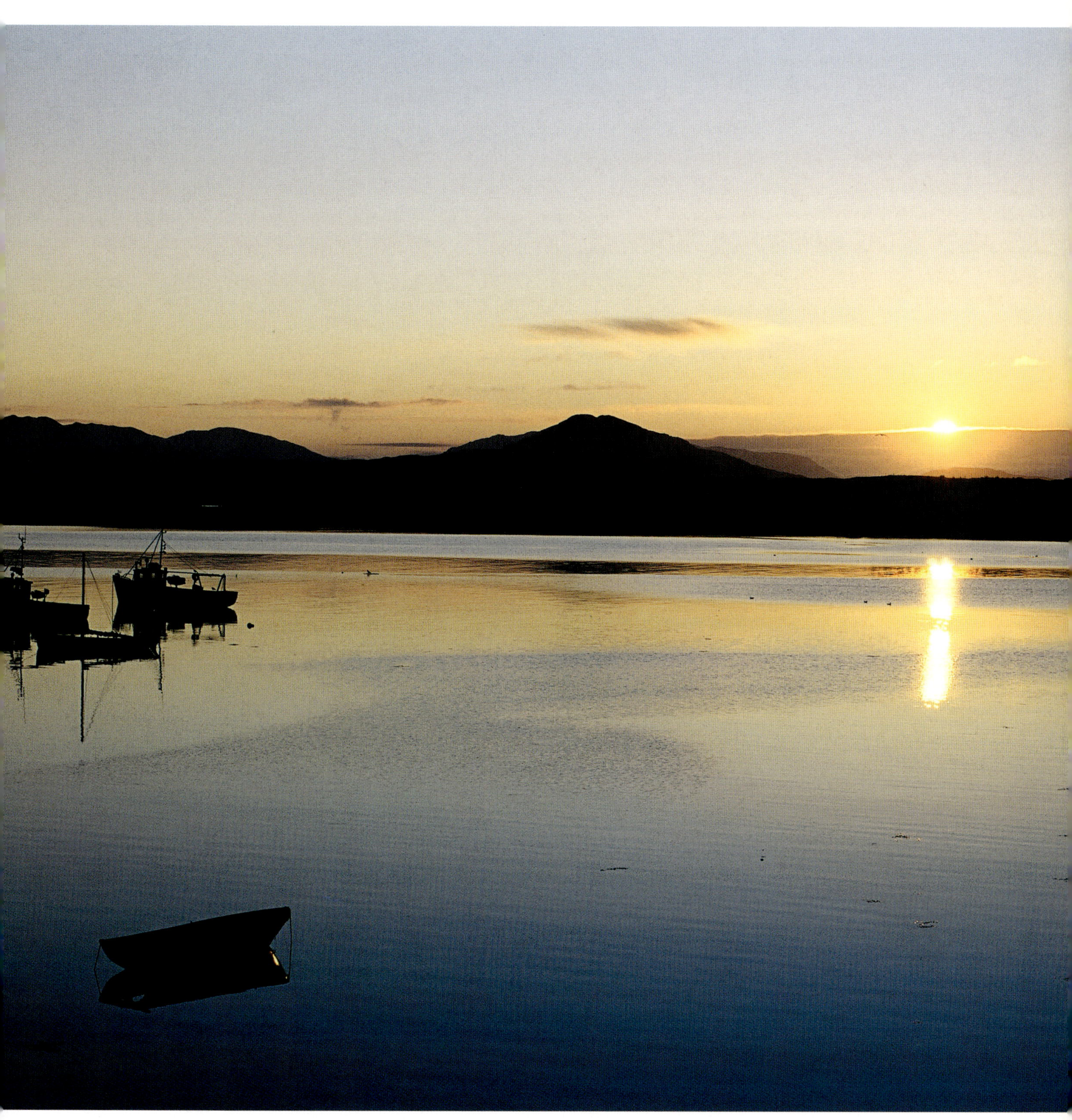

Island-studded Clew Bay in County Mayo is overlooked by Croagh Patrick, Ireland's holy mountain, and the mountains of North Mayo. Clare Island marks the entrance of the bay.

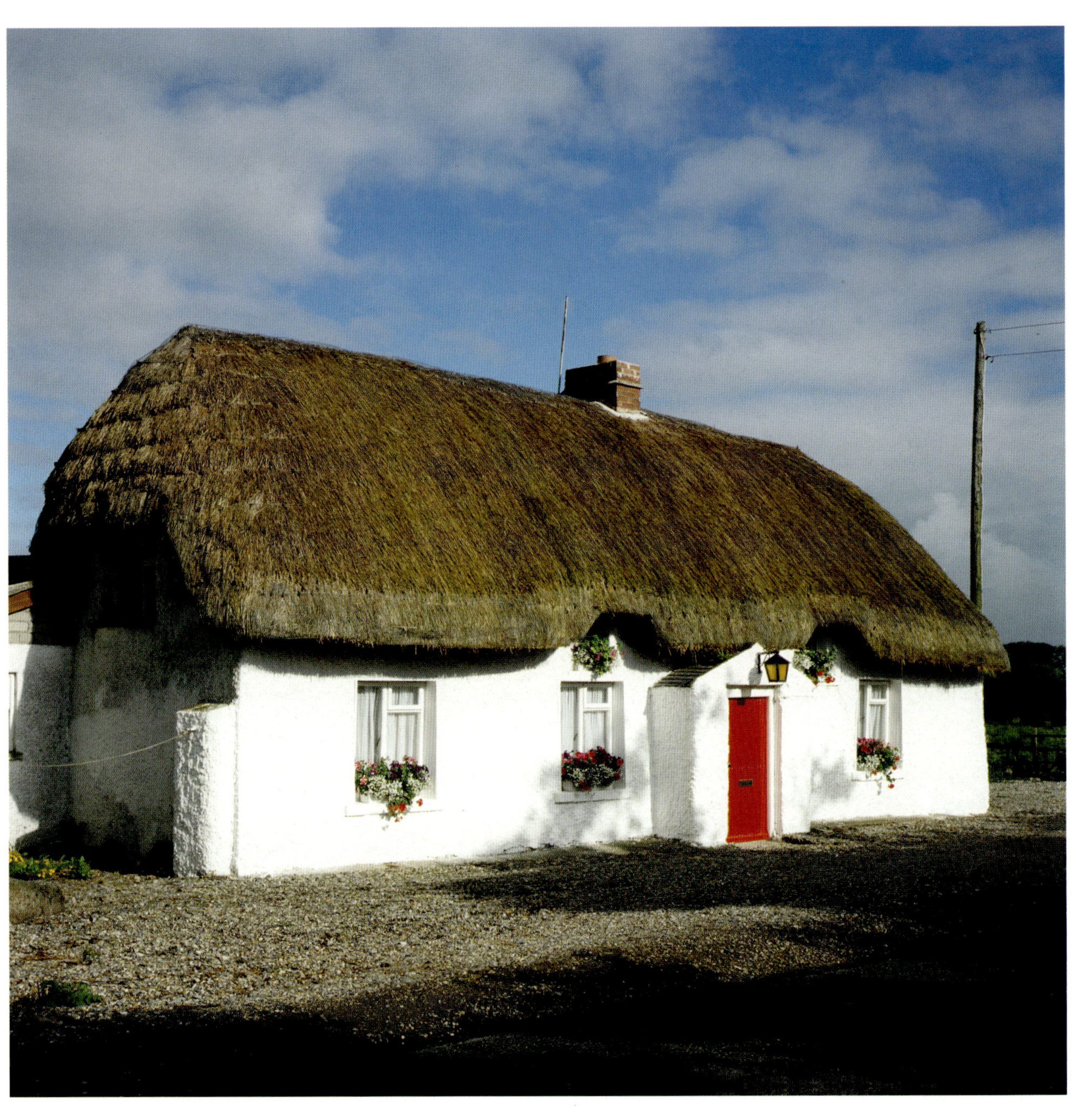

A row of thatched cottages runs through the small fishing village of Kilmore Quay on the eastern side of Ballyteige Bay, about 12 miles from the international ferryport of Rosslare. Noted for its lobster and deep-sea fishing, the village holds a Seafood Festival in the second week of July.

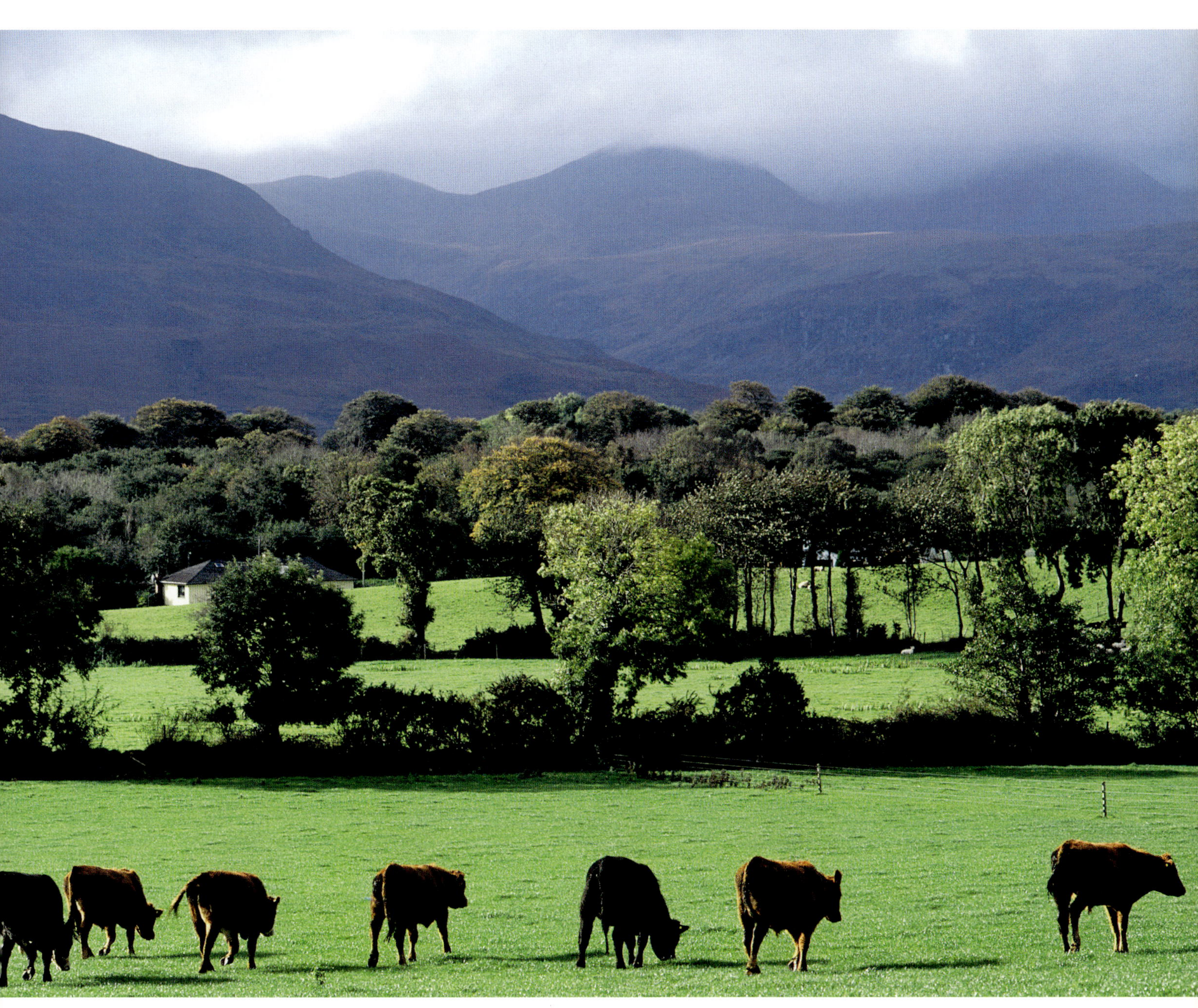

Cattle graze near Killarney, with the Aghadoe Hills beyond. The national park has the country's only herd of red deer, which are native to Ireland. Japanese Sika deer were introduced in the mid-19th century and they pose a potential threat to the pedigree of the red deer should cross-breeding occur.

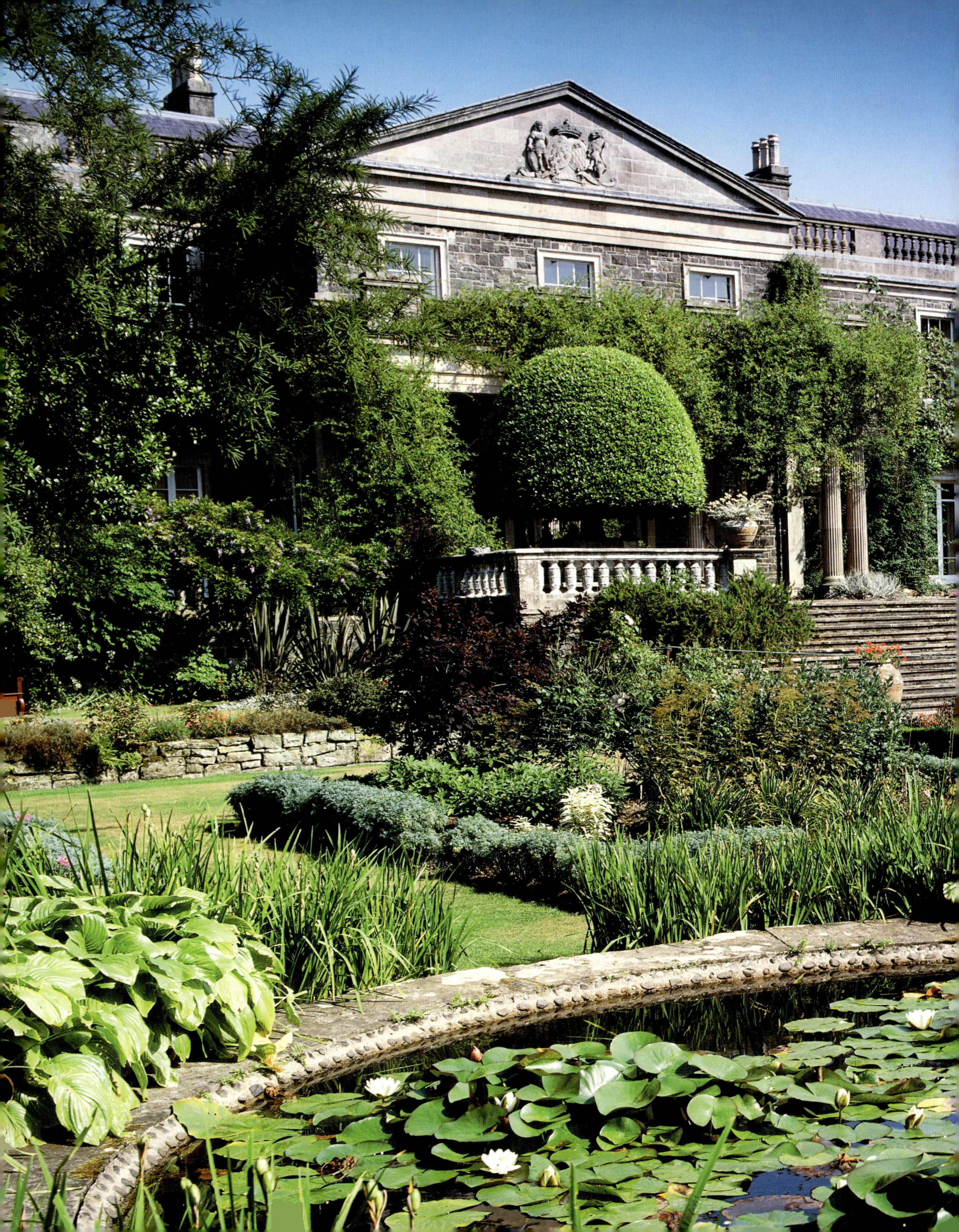

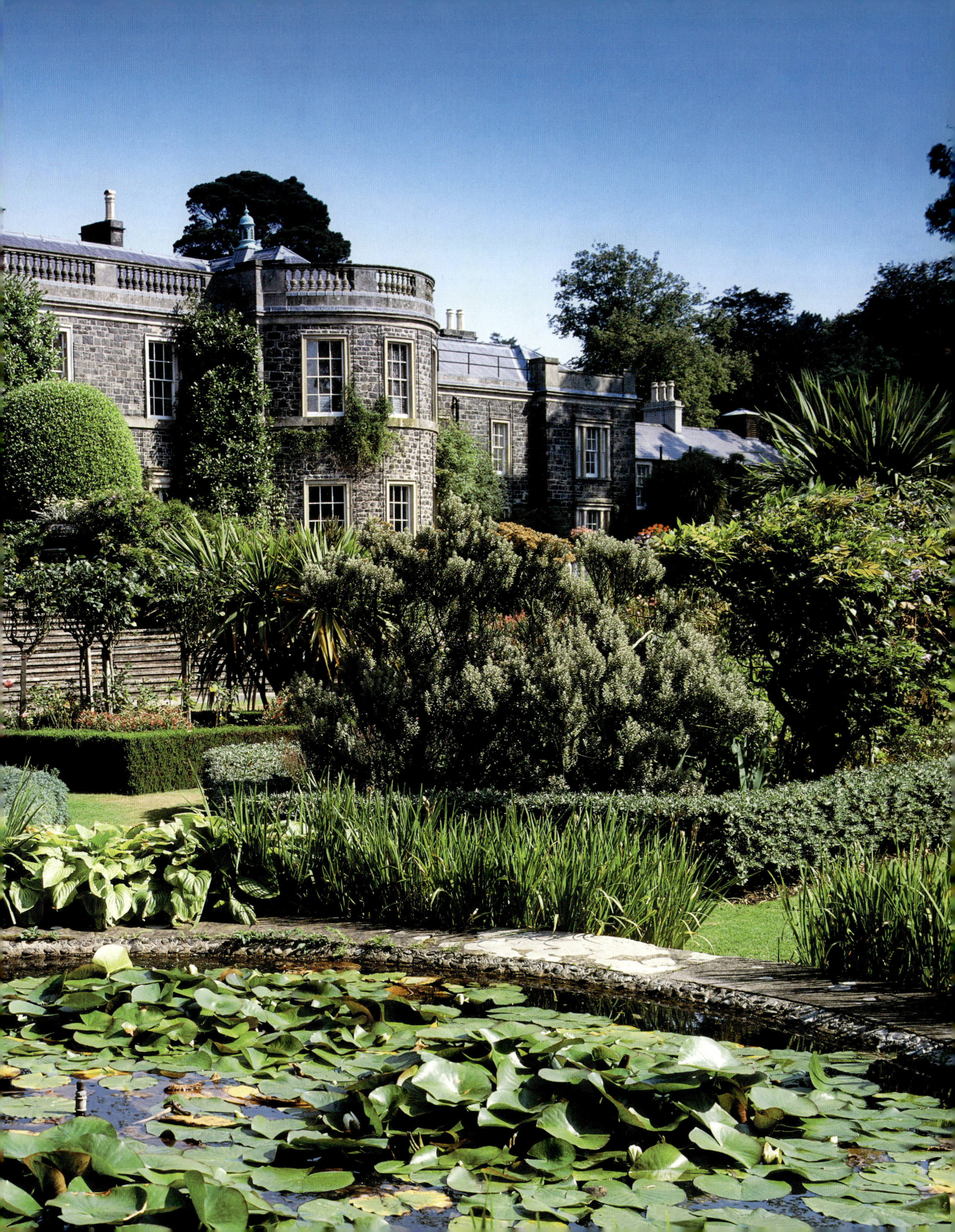

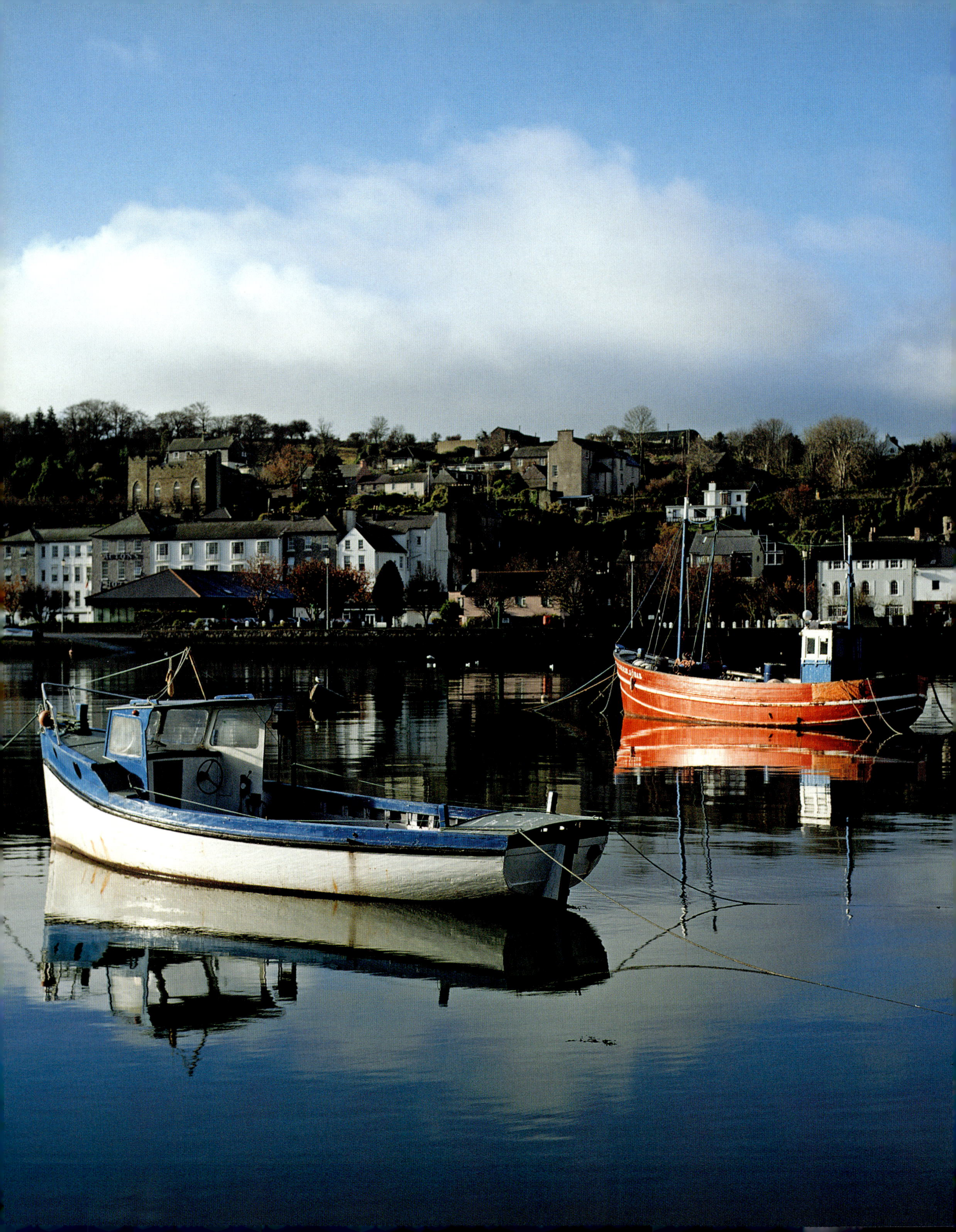

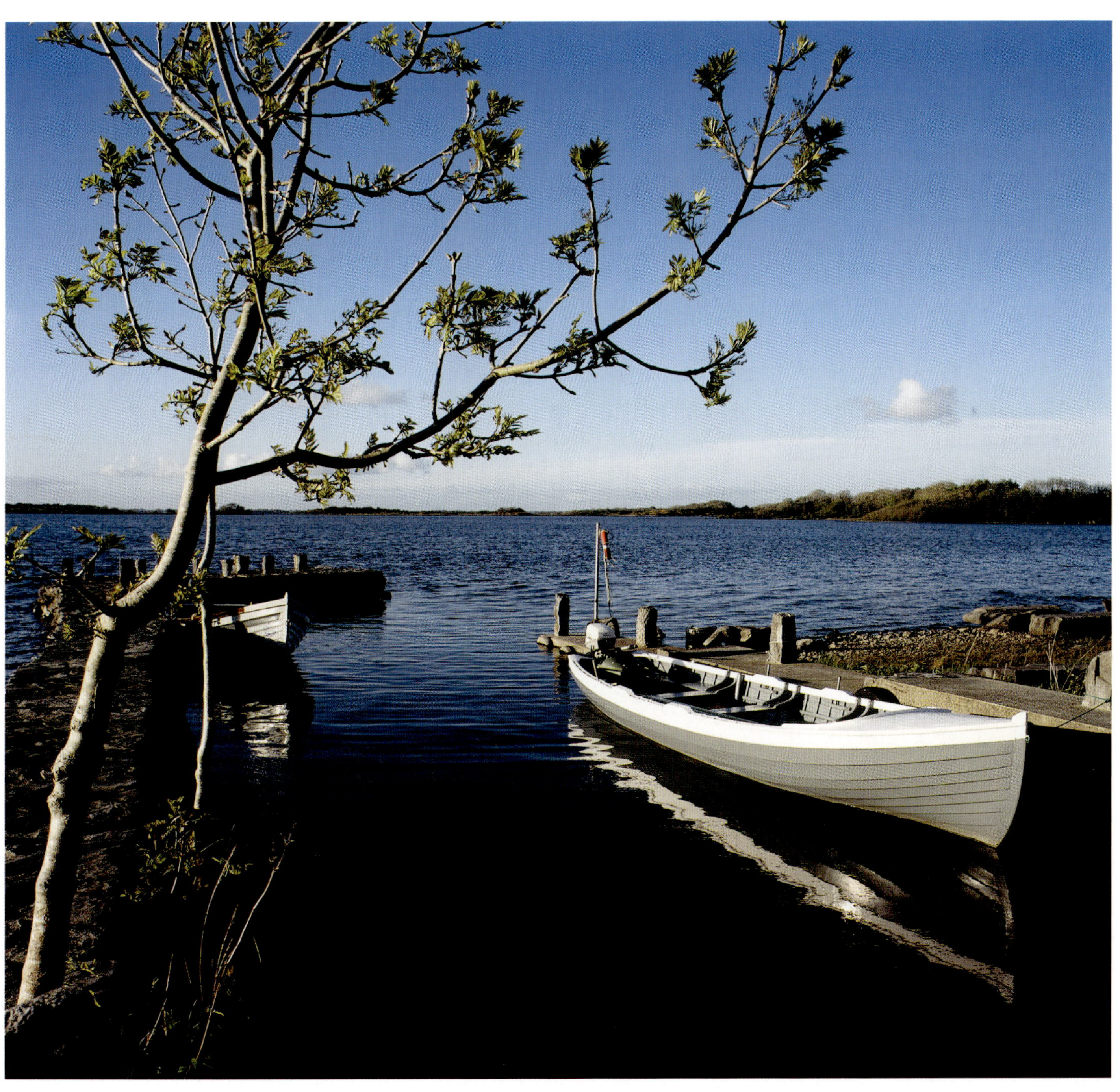

Lough Corrib, in the west, is the largest lake in the Republic of Ireland at nearly 42,000 acres and is full of islands. The River Corrib and the Galway River connect it to the sea at Galway.
Opposite: the harbour town of Kinsale in County Cork is one of the oldest towns in Ireland.
Pages 76–77: County Down's Mount Stewart House, with its internationally renowned gardens and Temple of the Four Winds, is one of the National Trust's most popular properties in Northern Ireland.

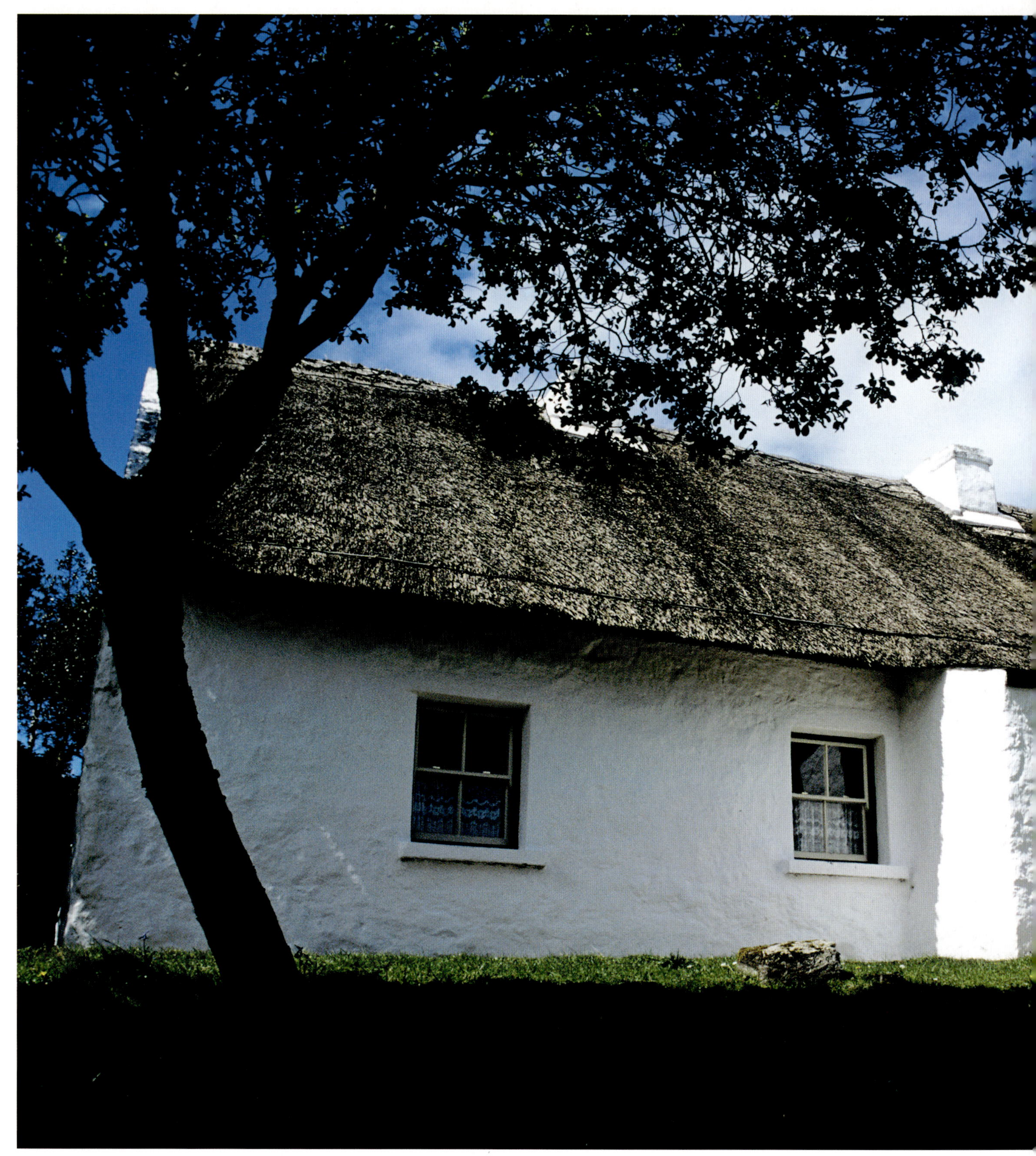

Around 7,400 acres of blanket bog and four of the Twelve Ben peaks are protected as the Connemara National Park. Pádraic Pearse's Cottage stands on the shores of Lough Oiriúlach near Gortmore.

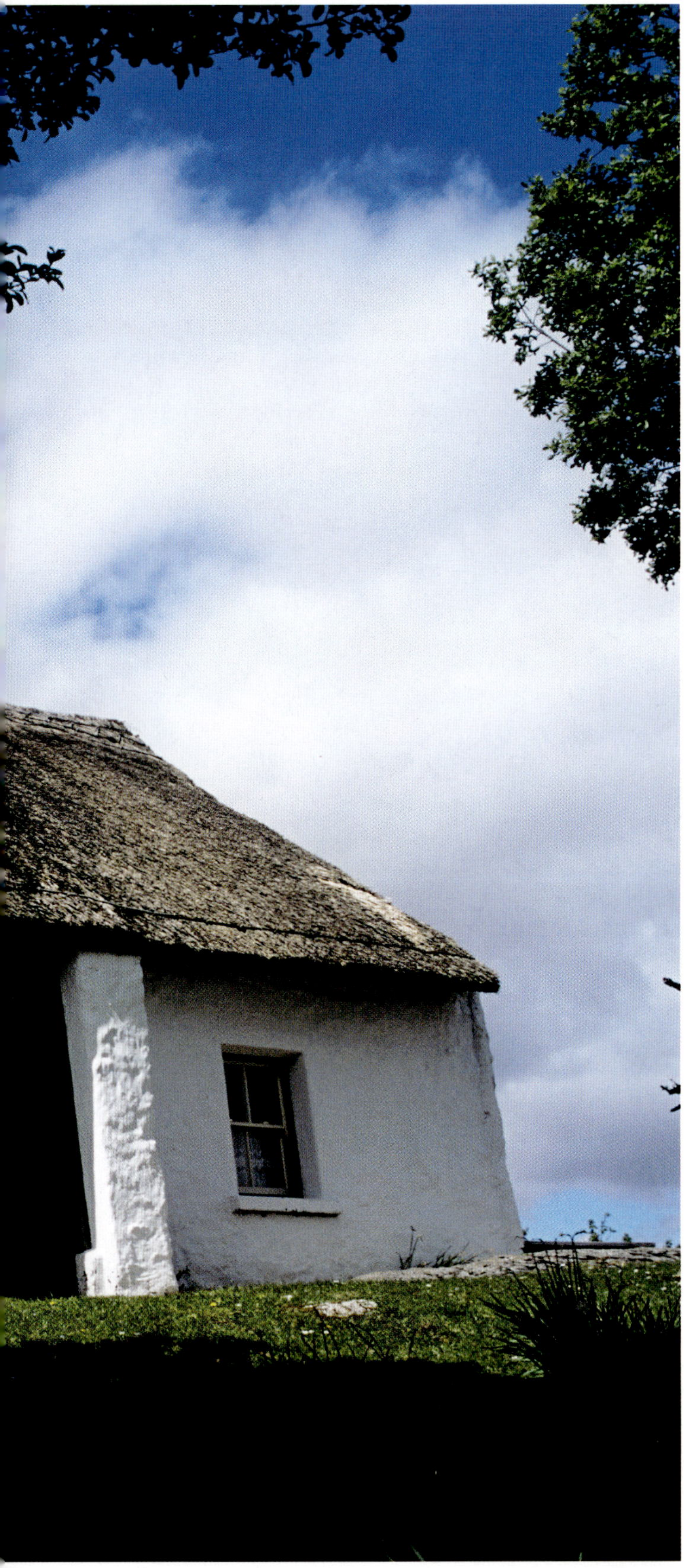

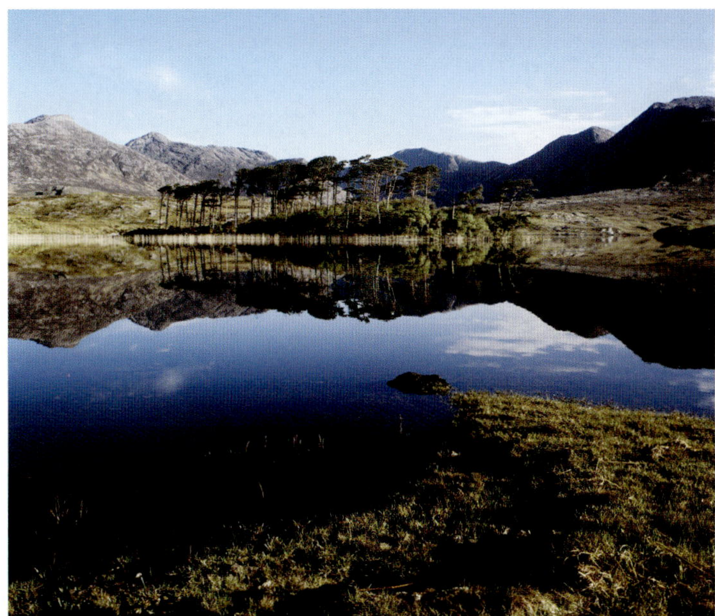

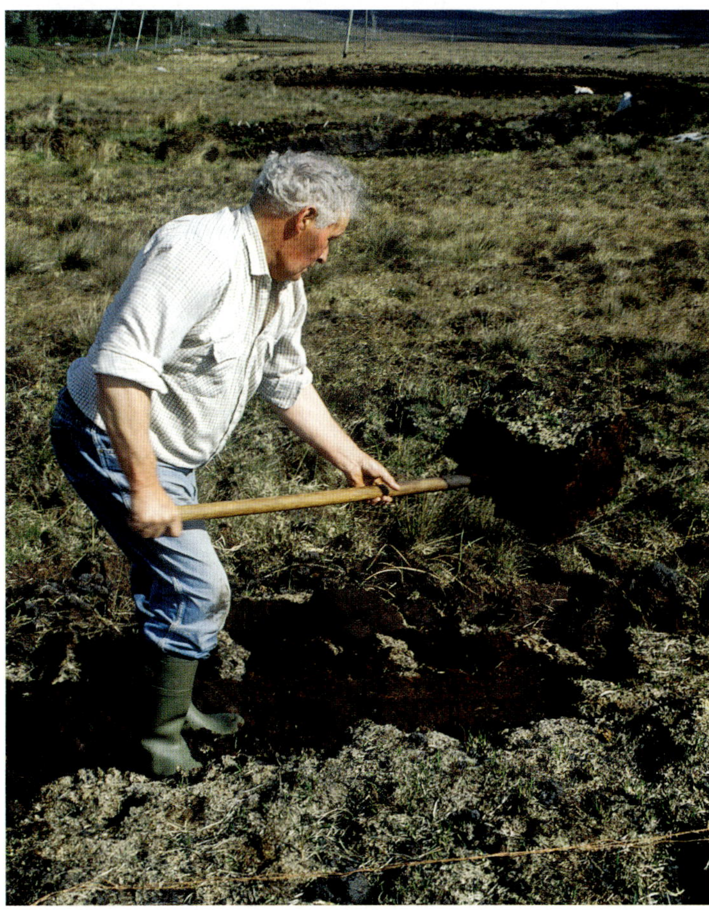

Peat land (bogland) covers much of rural Ireland.
Top: the Twelve Bens mountains are reflected in the blue water of Derryclare Lough in Connemara National Park.

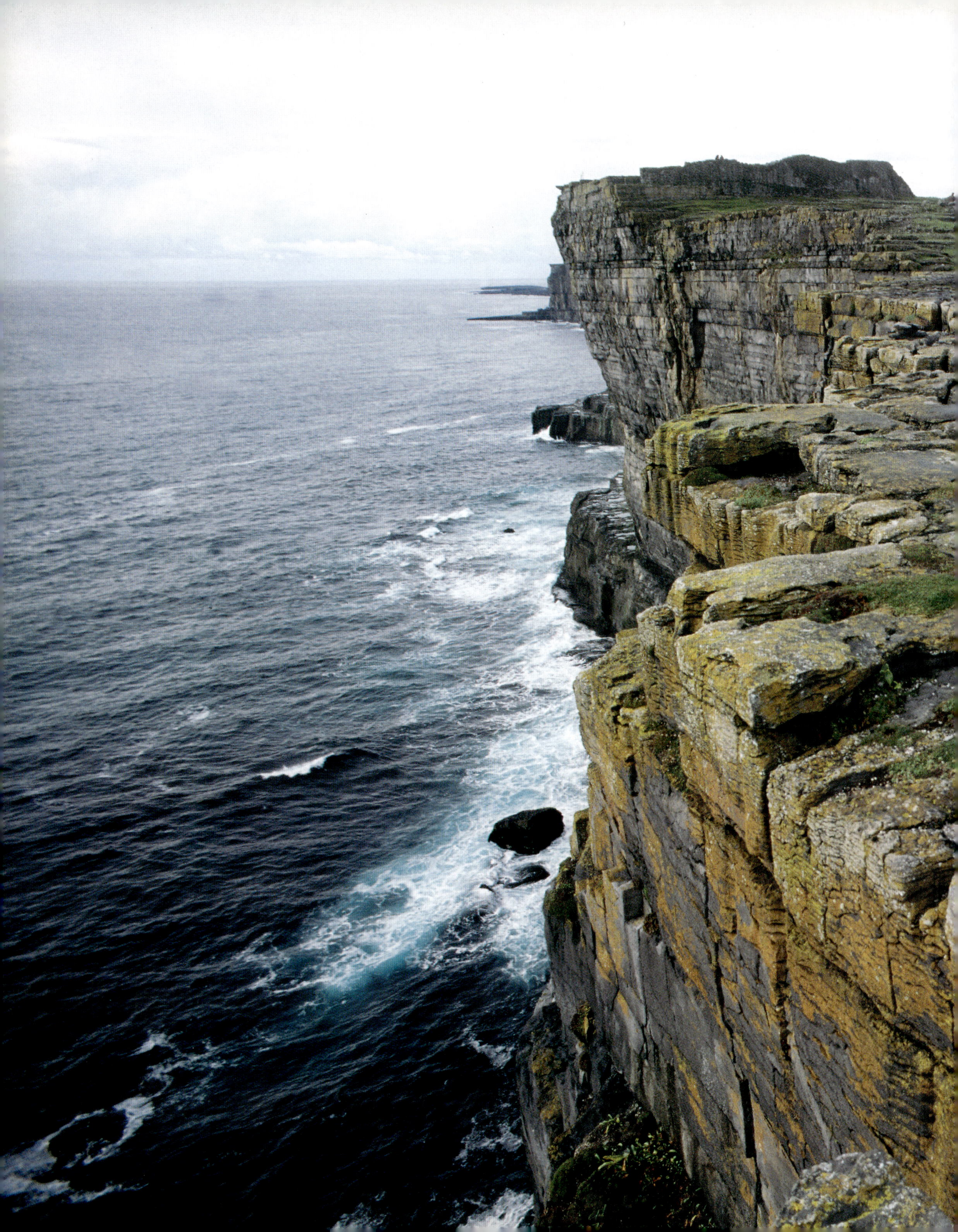

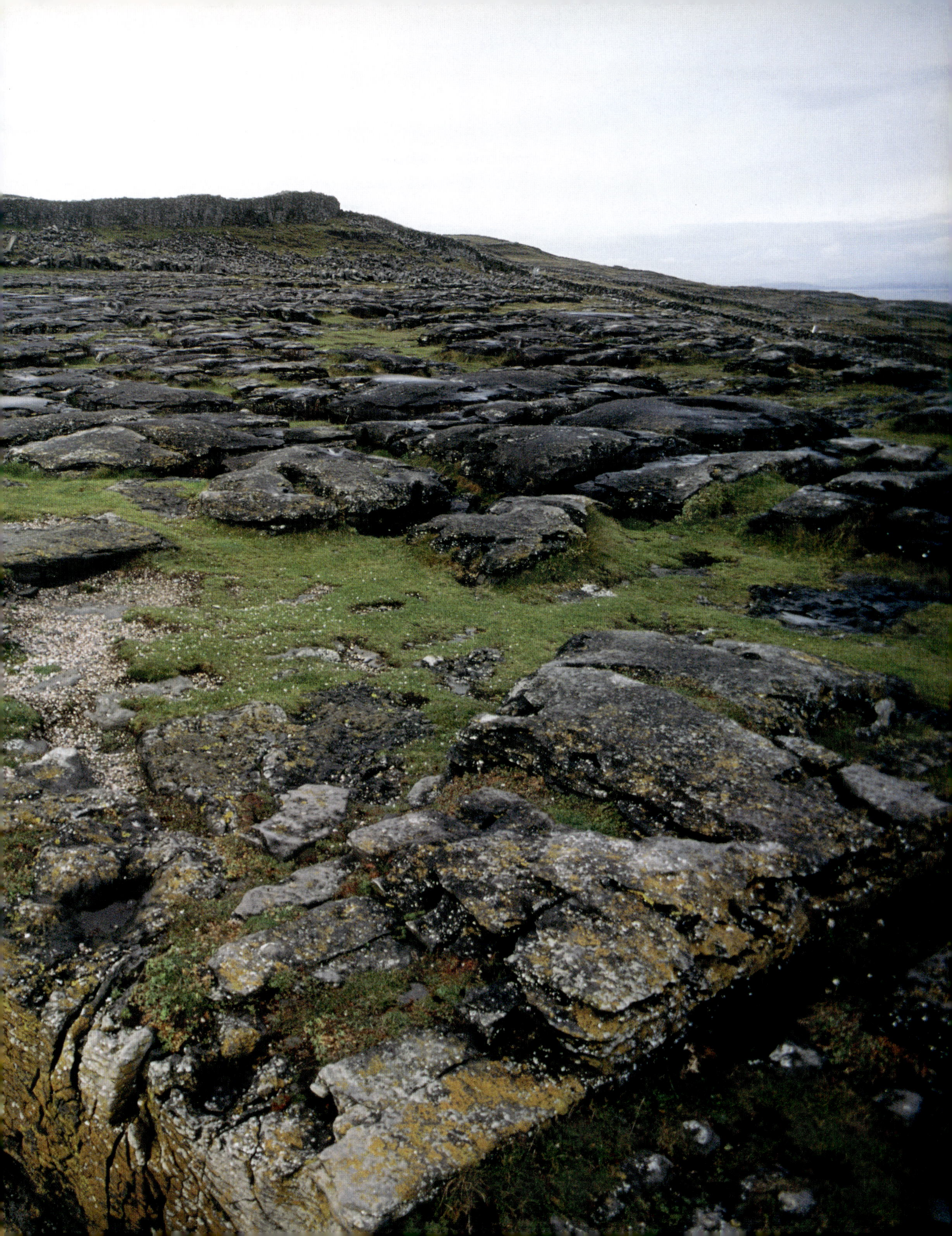

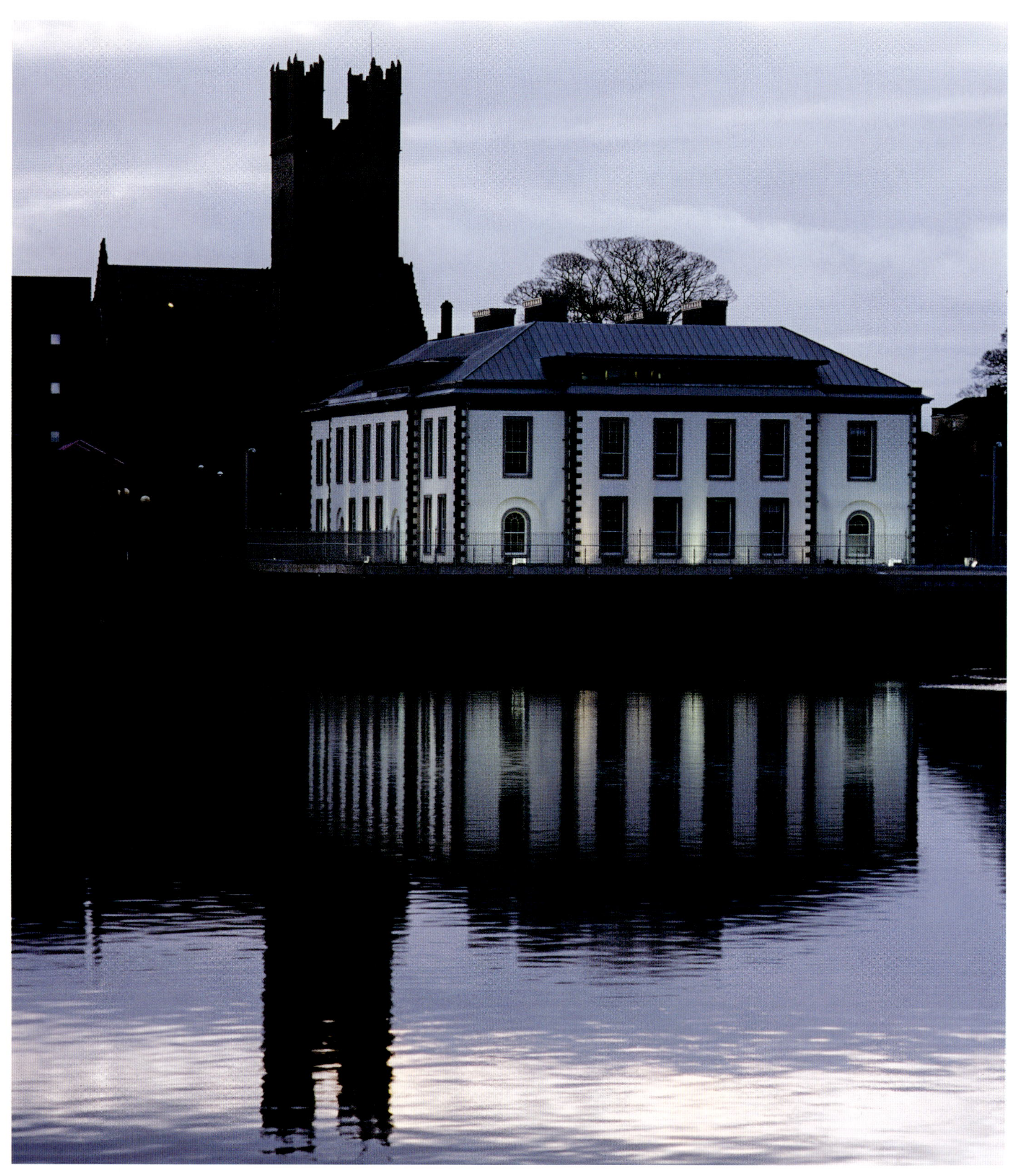

Limerick's Custom House and St Mary's Cathedral can be seen across the River Shannon.
Page 82–83: the remains of fort Dun Aengus are visible on Inishmore Island, largest of the Aran Islands.

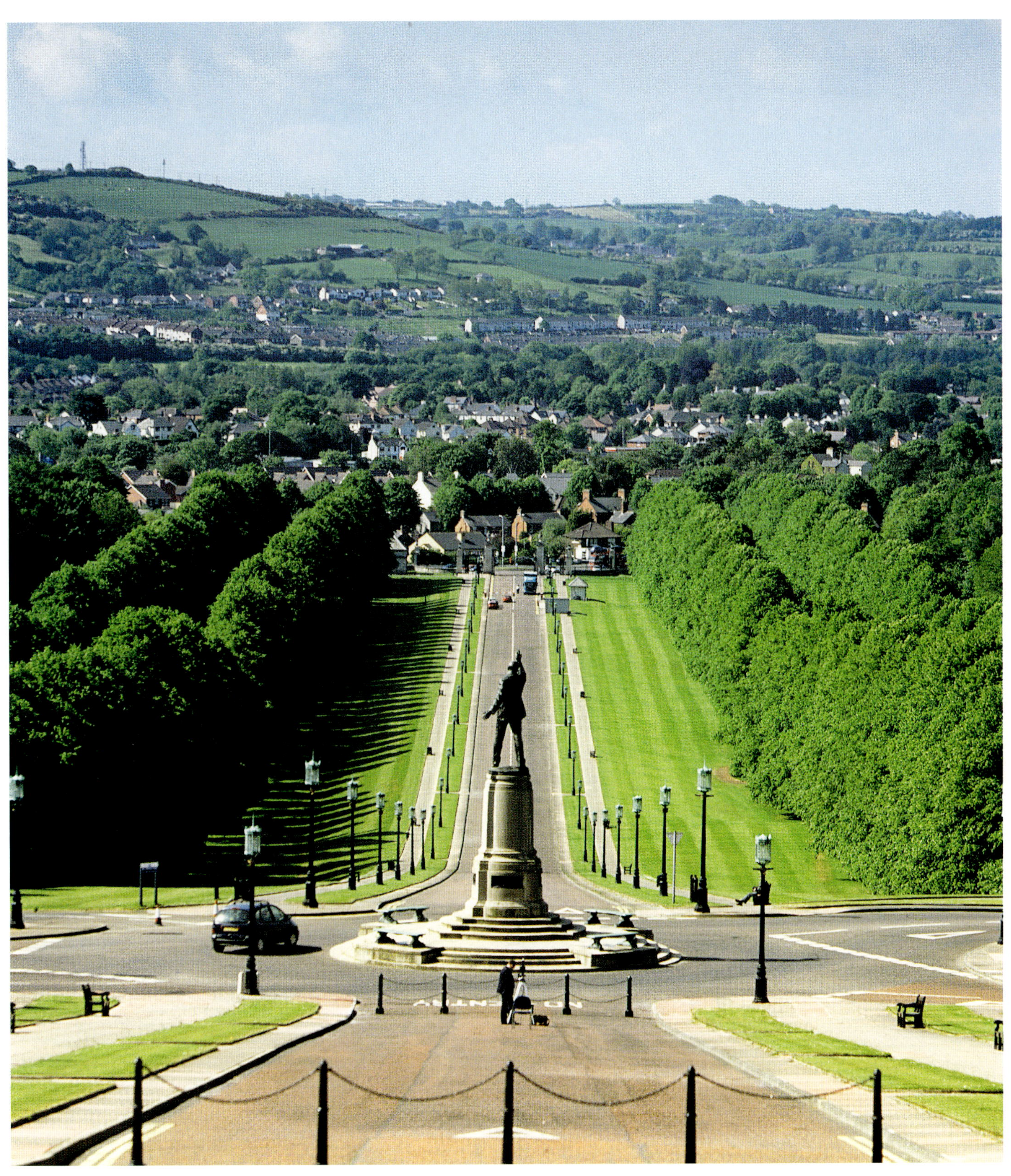

A bronze statue of Lord Edward Carson, Architect of the Northern Ireland State, was erected in 1932 outside the new Parliament Building. It was unveiled by Carson in 1933 two years before his death.

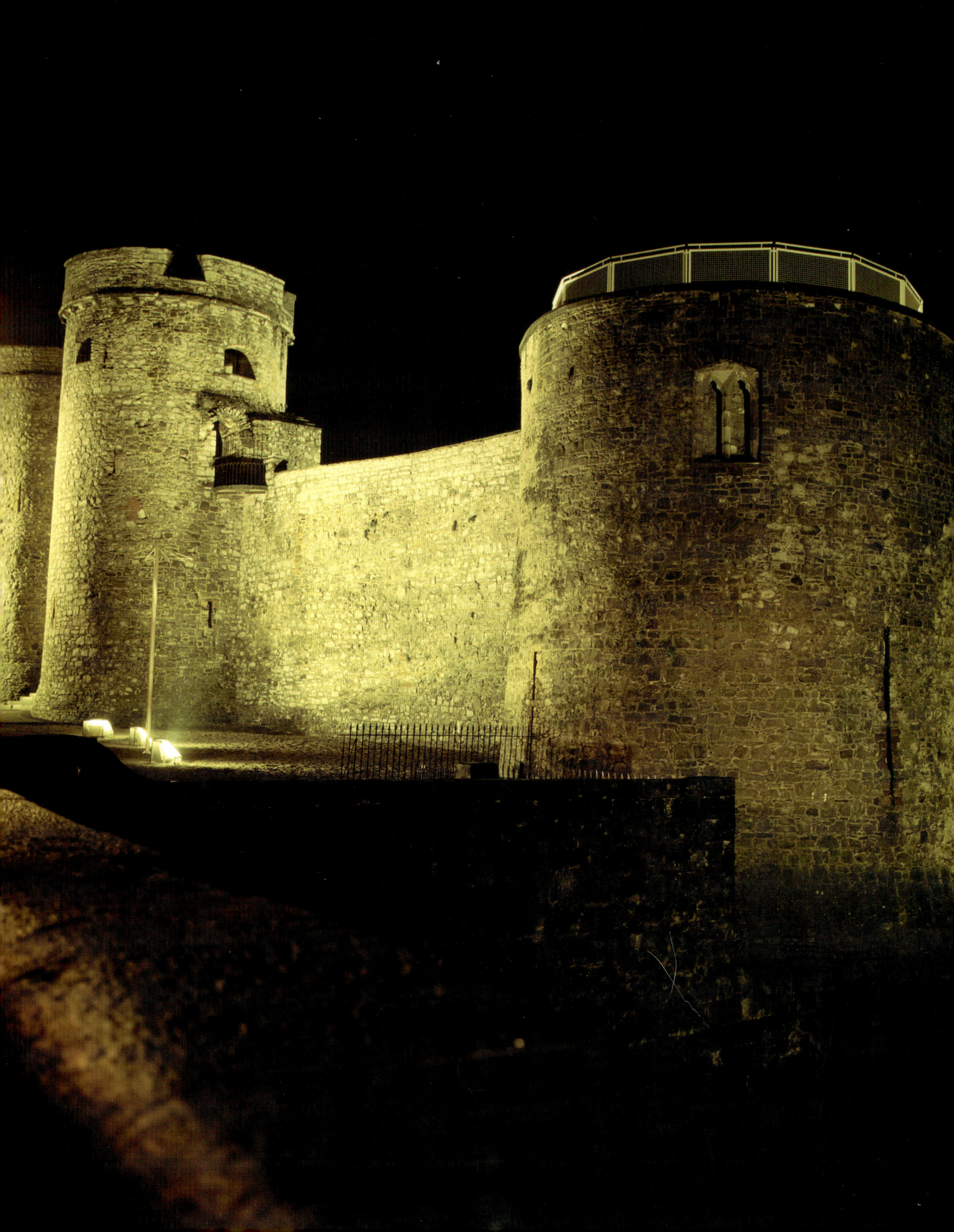

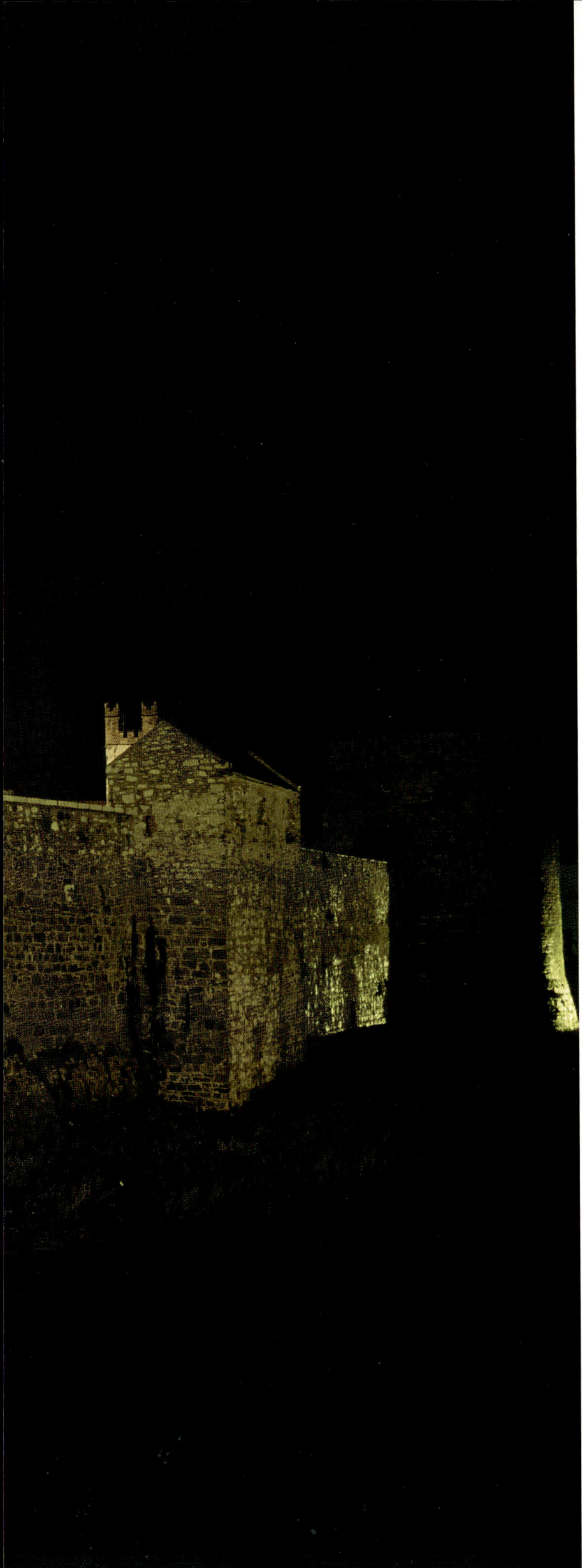

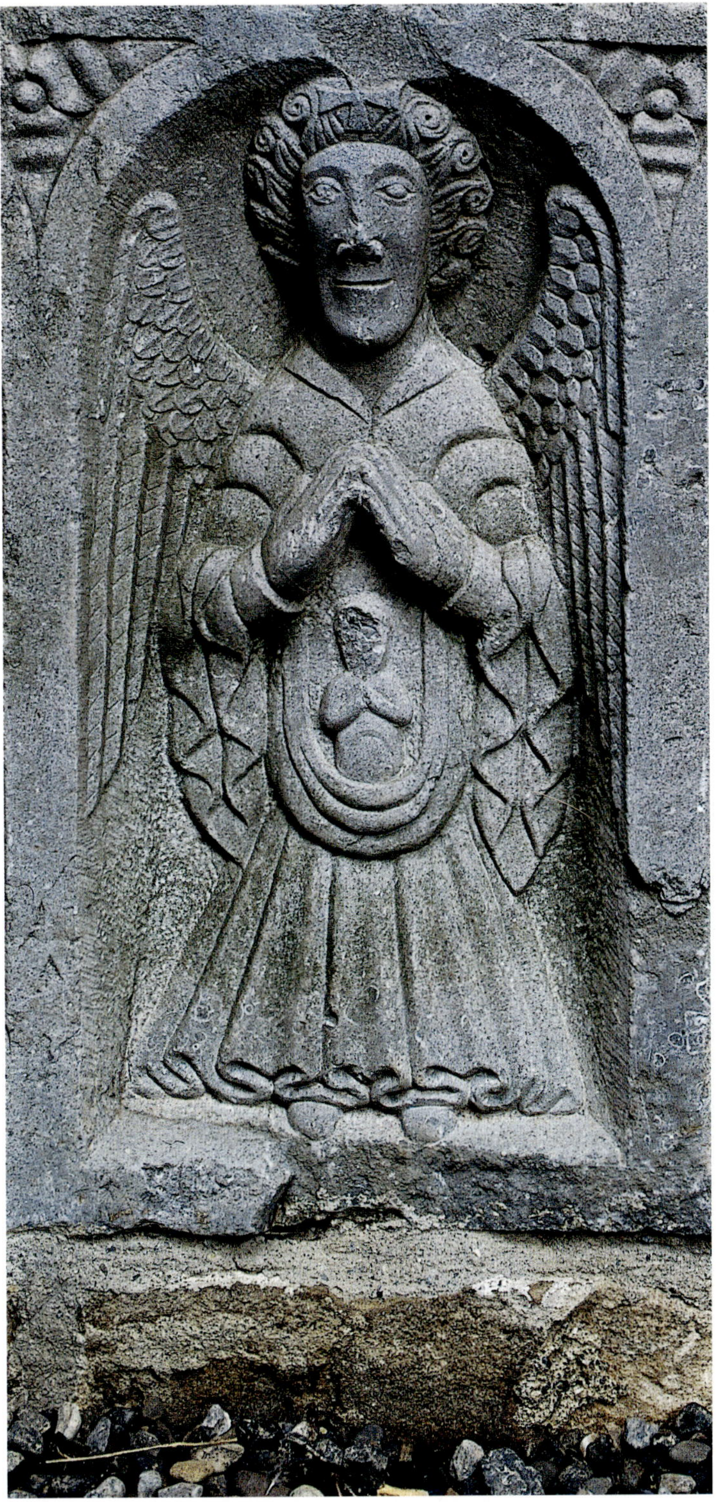

Stone tomb sculpture and a cloistered arcade are highlights of a visit to the Cistercian Jerpoint Abbey in County Kilkenny. Opposite: King John's Castle in Limerick stands on King's Island, next to the River Shannon. It dates from the reign of King John of England (1166–1216).

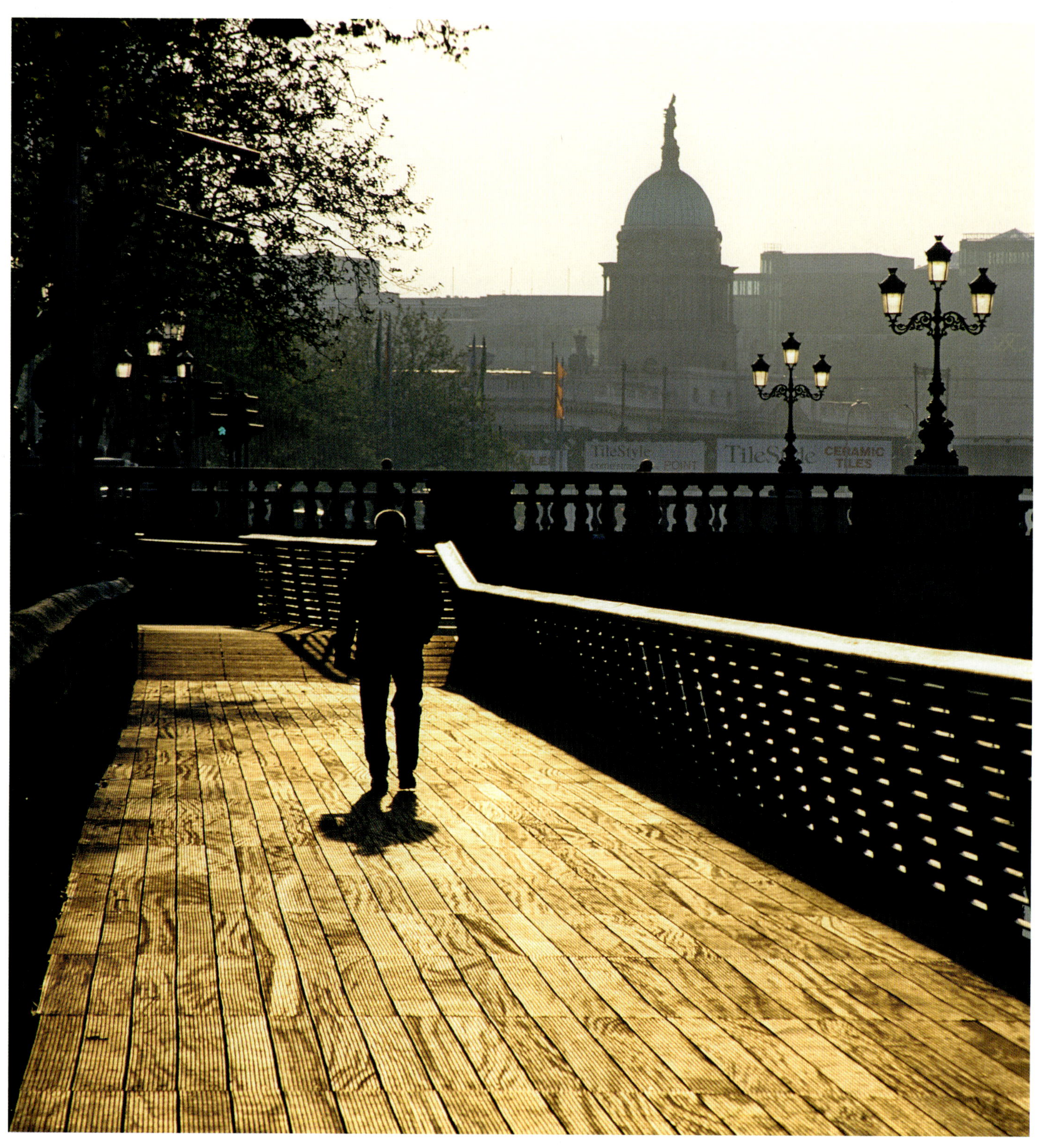

The dome of Dublin's neoclassical Custom House is an unmistakable landmark on the city skyline. It can be seen from both sides of the Liffey thanks to the many bridges.

Opposite: Malahide Castle to the north of Dublin dates largely from the 14th century and houses much of the National Portrait Collection from Dublin's National Gallery.

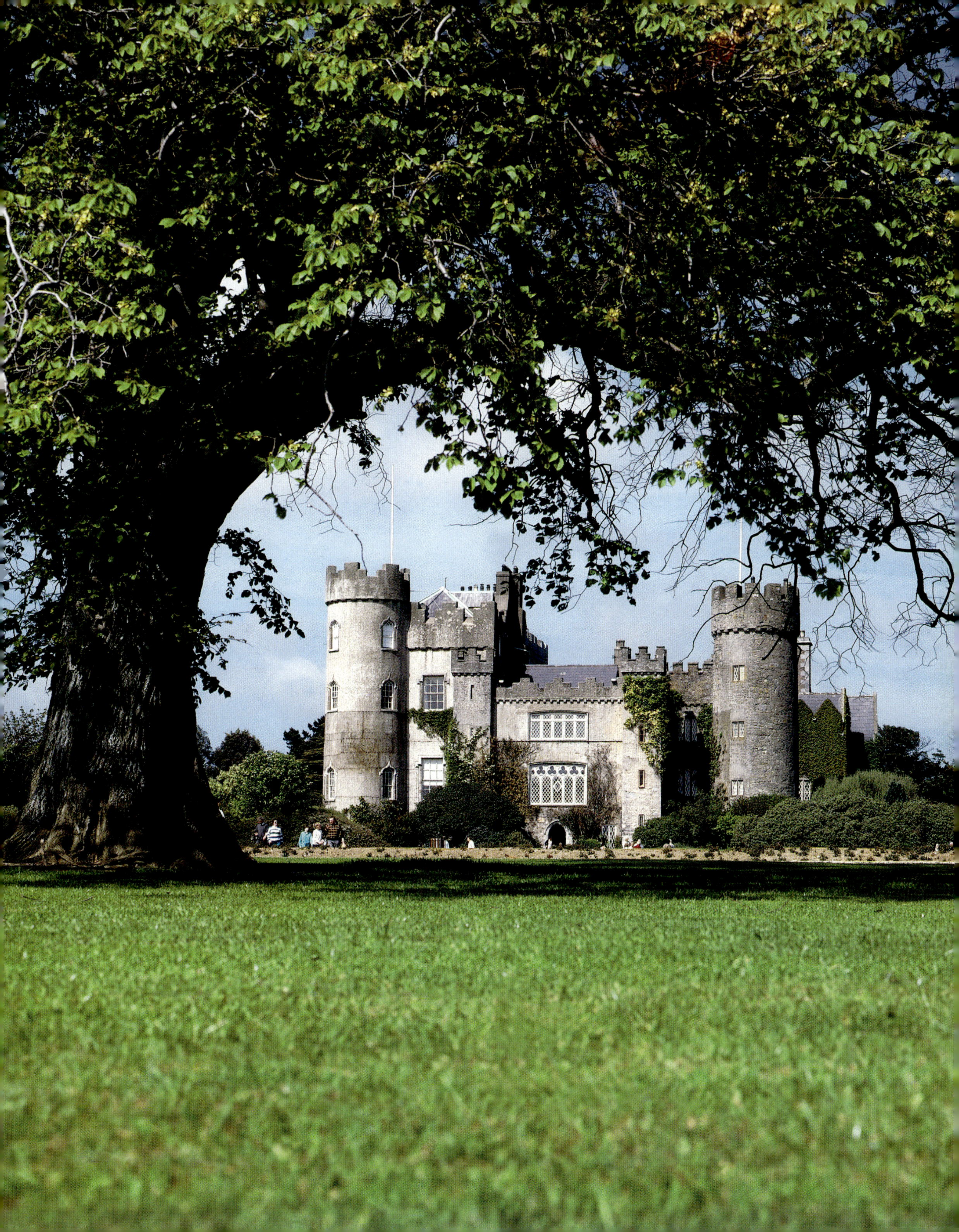

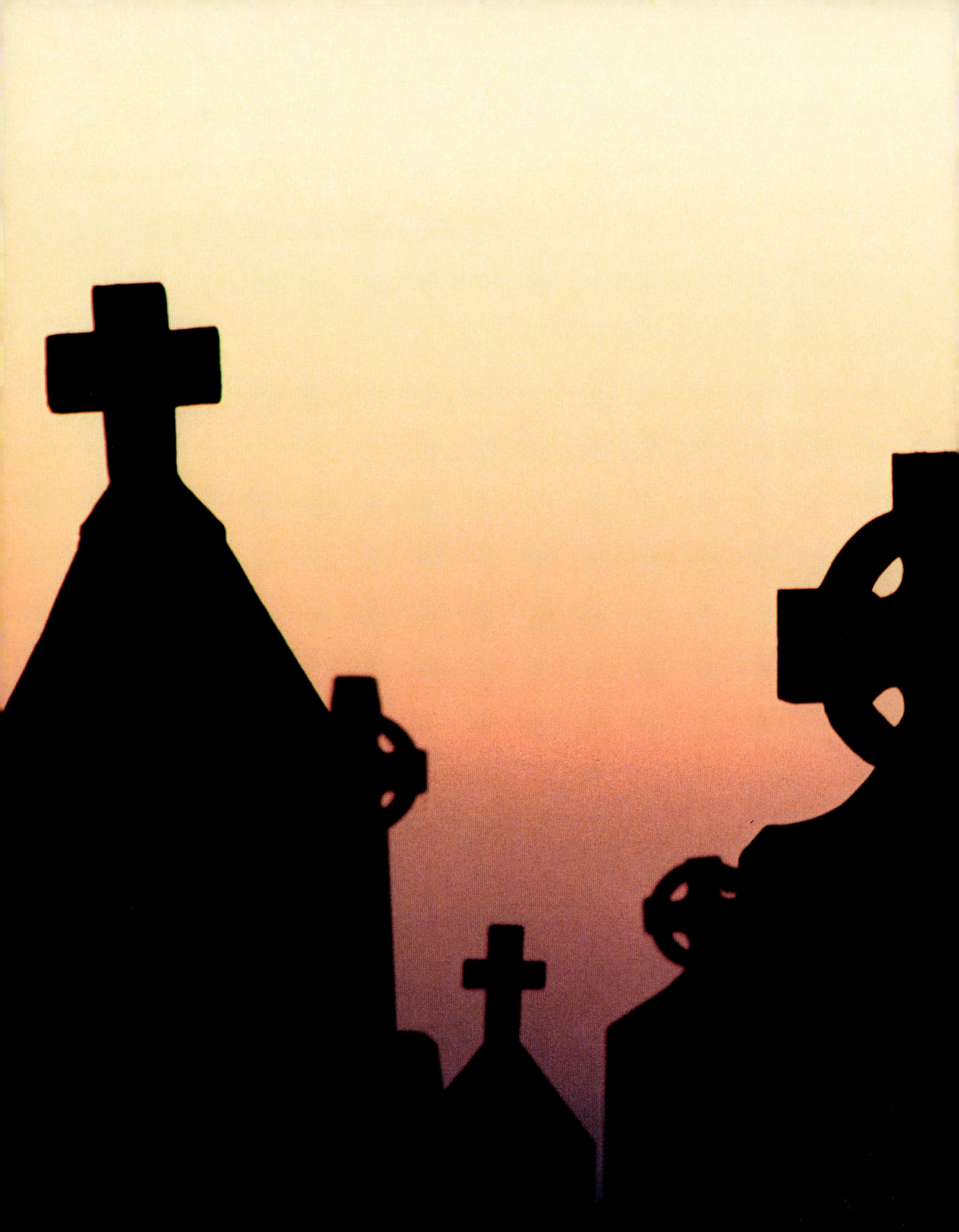

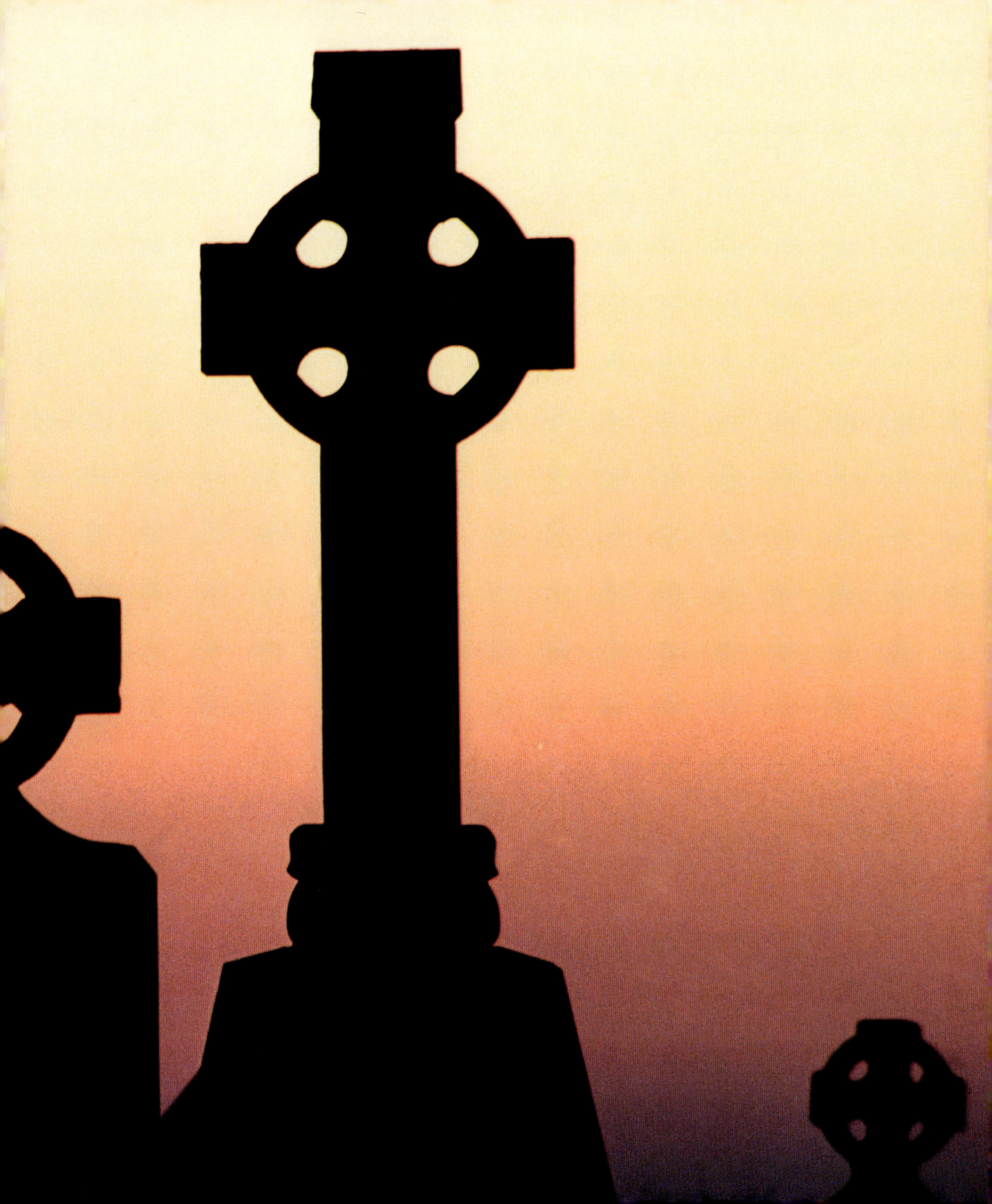

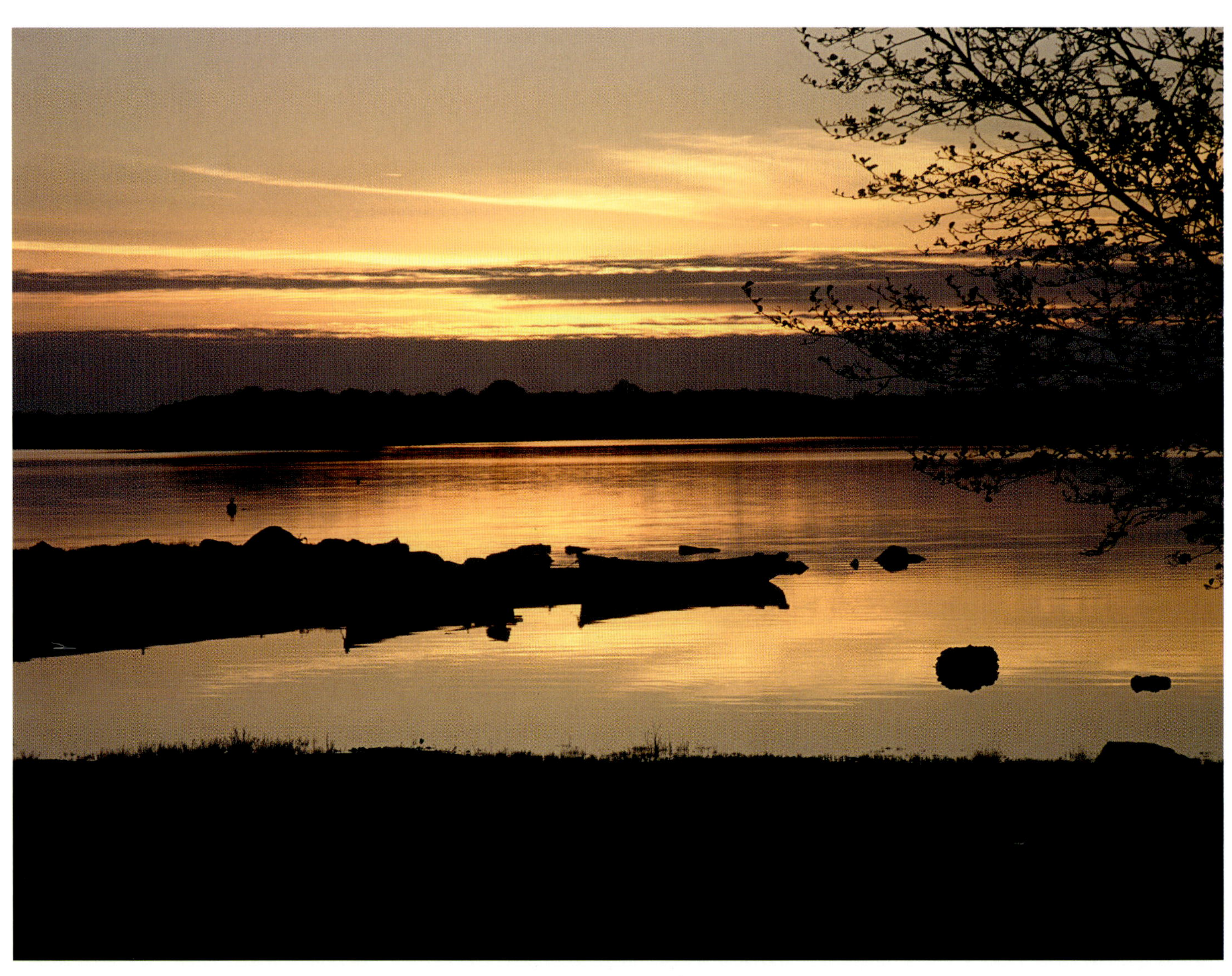

This view of Lough Corrib was taken near Oughterard, often referred to as the gateway to Connemara. The town is a centre for game-fishing on the huge lake, which crosses the border of County Galway into County Mayo. Boat cruises around the many islands are available.

Pages 90–91: Celtic crosses on Inishmore Island, one of the largest Aran islands.

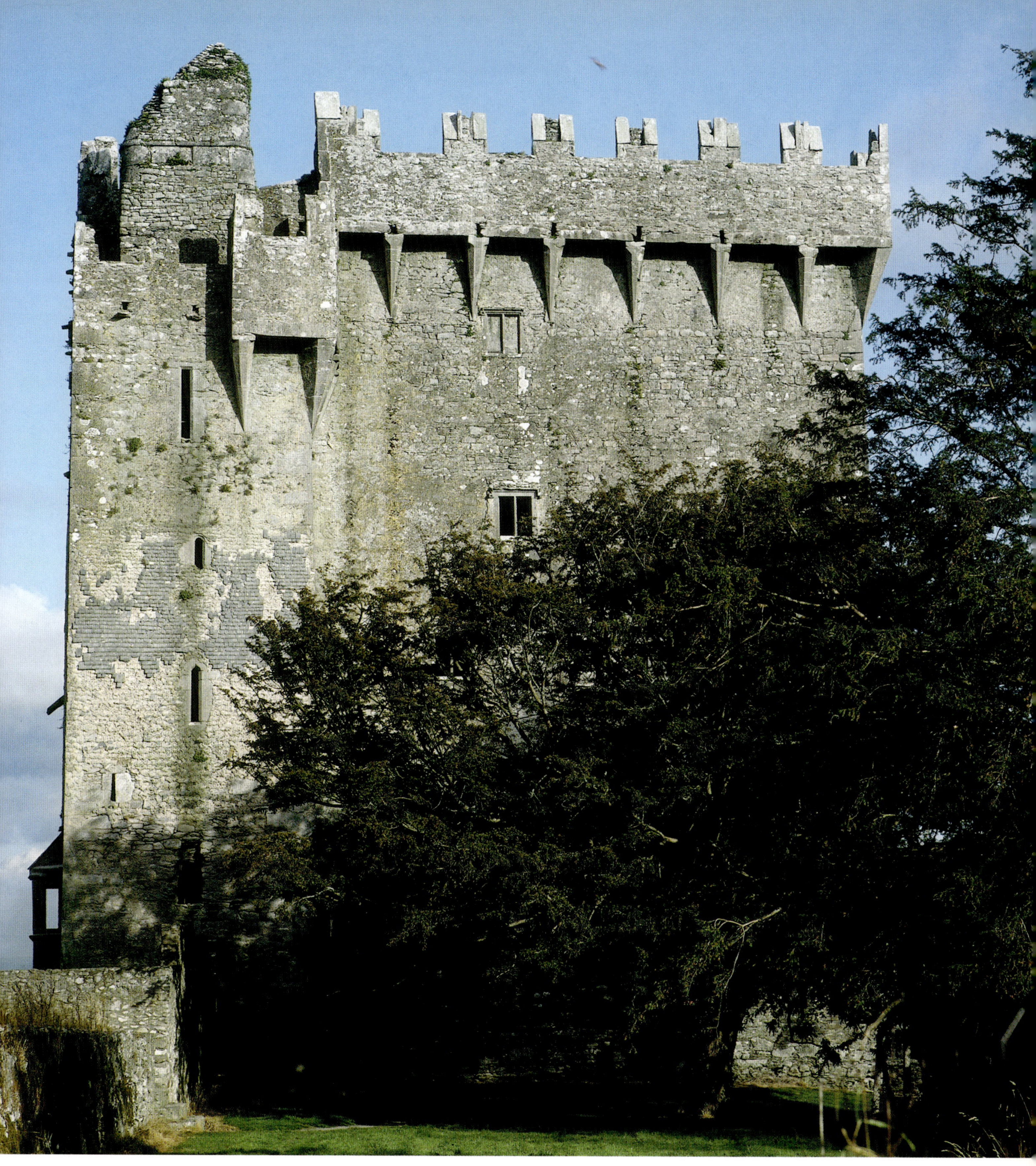

Blarney Castle has gained fame through the Blarney Stone, believed to be half of the Stone of Scone over which Scottish Kings were crowned because it was believed to have special powers.

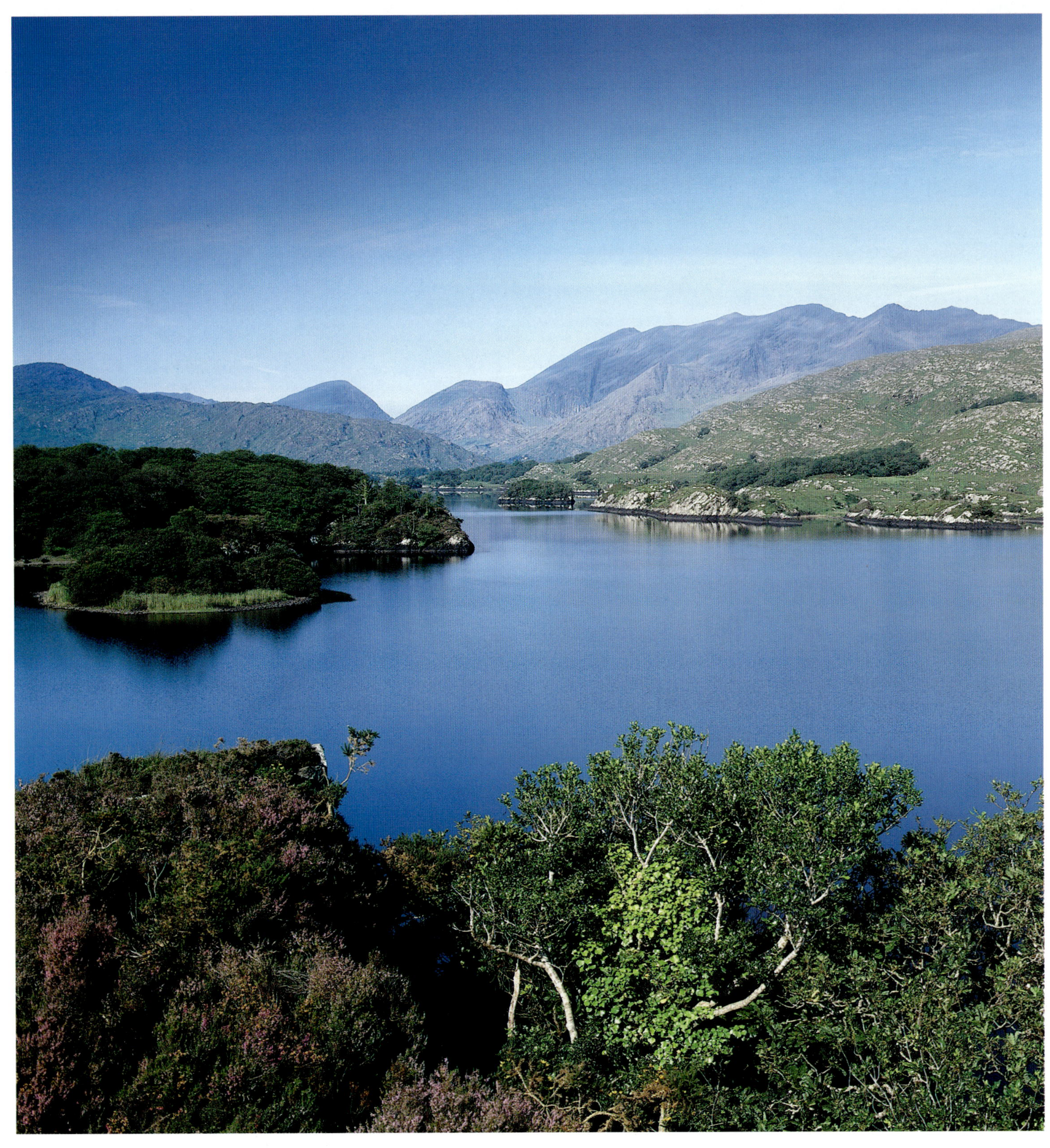

Killarney Lakes (Upper Lakes) with the Macgillycuddy mountain range in the distance.
Opposite: the first lighthouse at Youghal was built in 1190, discontinued in 1542 then taken down in 1848 to make room for the present tower, which was was lit on February 1, 1852. The light was converted to acetylene in 1939 and electric in 1964.

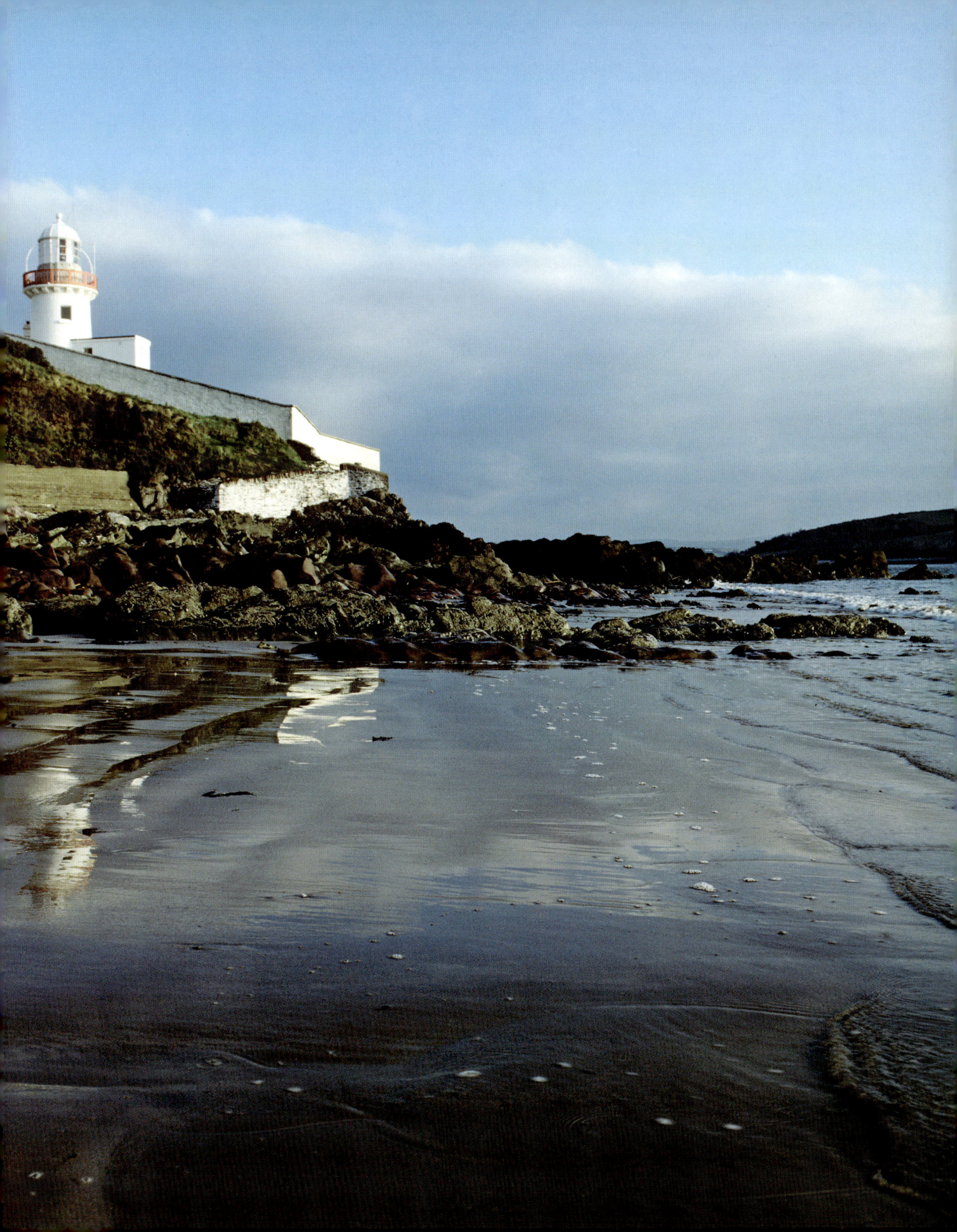

INDEX

ACKNOWLEDGMENTS

The Automobile Association would like to thank the following photographers, companies and picture libraries for their assistance in the preparation of this book.

Abbreviations for the picture credits are as follows: - (t) top; (b) bottom; (l) left; (r) right; (AA) AA World Travel Library.
2t AA/P Zoeller; 2c AA/S Hill; 2b AA/S Day; 3 AA/M Short; 4 AA/J Blandford; 6/7 AA/S Day; 8 AA/M Short; 9 AA/D Forss; 10 AA/J Blandford; 10/11 AA/C Jones; 12 AA/Slidefile; 13 AA/J Blandford; 14/15 AA/J Blandford; 16 AA/S Day; 17 AA/J Blandford; 18t AA/D Forss; 18b AA/J Blandford; 18/19 AA/C Jones; 20 AA/J Blandford; 21 AA/S McBride; 22 AA/S Hill; 22/23 AA/Slidefile; 24/25 AA/S McBride; 26 AA/C Hill; 27 AA/C Jones; 28 AA/S McBride; 29 AA/D Forss; 30/31 AA/S Whitehorne; 32 AA/S McBride; 33 AA/C Jones; 34 AA; 35 AA/S Day; 36/37 AA/C Coe; 38 AA/L Blake; 39 AA/G Munday; 40 AA/L Blake; 41 AA/M Diggin; 42/43 AA/S Day; 43 AA/S Whitehorne; 44/45 AA/C Hill; 46 AA/G Munday; 47 AA/M Short; 48 AA/C Jones; 49 AA/S Whitehorne; 50/51 AA/S McBride; 52 AA/S Hill; 53 AA/D Forss; 54 AA/S Day; 54/55 AA/S McBride; 56/57 AA/C Hill; 58 AA/S McBride; 59 AA/C Coe; 60/61 AA/G Munday; 61 AA; 62 AA/C Jones; 63 AA/G Munday; 64/65 AA/L Blake; 66 AA/S McBride; 67 AA/C Jones; 68/69 AA/C Coe; 70/71 AA/I Dawson; 71 AA/J Blandford; 72 AA/S McBride; 72/73 AA/L Blake; 74 AA/P Zoeller; 75 AA/S McBride; 76/77 AA/G Munday; 78 AA/D Forss; 79 AA/C Jones; 80/81 AA/C Jones; 81t AA/C Jones; 81b AA/C Jones; 82/83 AA/S Hill; 84 AA/C Jones; 85 AA/I Dawson; 86/87 AA/S Hill; 87 AA/M Short; 88 AA/S Day; 89 AA/Slidefile; 90/91 AA/S Hill; 92 AA/C Jones; 93 AA/S Hill; 94 AA/J Blandford; 95 AA/S Hill.

Every effort has been made to trace the copyright holders, and we apologise in advance for any accidental errors. We would be happy to apply the corrections in the following edition of this publication.